THE NEW SONG

The Time For The Dead (Lazarus) To Arise Has Come!
R5:2-5-9; T, p. 74, 3rd p – p. 86, 1st p; NS8: 20c; 14: 3

The Religion of Abraham The True Q2:124-130, 135

"All creatures in the heavens and the Earth have bowed to His Will. A religion
Other than submission to God will not be accepted" Q3:83-85; Intro: 7

As Promised
Lk. 16:22, 31
~ THE BOSOM OF ABRAHAM ~

You have God Quickened,
Who Were Dead In Trespasses and Sins... Ep2:1
The "Lord of The Dawn" Saved Us and Is
Making of Us "A __New People__ Who Do Not
Reject His Truth" Q6:89; 39: 53, 55-60, 63

"The greatest *human struggle*
is that for the conquest of *self."*

"Truth has arrived and falsehood neither creates
anything new nor restores anything (old)" Q34:49

Look and see.

D0167069

Muhammad A. Aziz
The Spirit of the Honorable Elijah Muhammad

M. G. Aziz

10-4-19

ISBN: 1-4392-1922-2
ISBN-13:9781439219225
Library of Congress Control Number: 2008910911

AZRT Publishers
Email: sbi122000@yahoo.com
Third Edition June 2013

Available on Amazon.com and other retailers.

THIS BOOK IS THE KEY TO THE BOTTOMLESS PIT (FOR THE MASSES)

1   The New Song is divided into chapters, verses, numbers, an alphabet making it relatively easy for you to find what you may be looking for yourself, or supporting a group discussion.

2   You may find yourself communicating with people at a distance via email or telephone [a] and telling them exactly what you 're looking at, [b] or exactly at what point in time you are in the book, [c] and how or where you can have them join you in conversation and study.

3   *References to words and ideas* are in smaller letters and abbreviated in the following way: **The Introduction** would be written 'Intro: 5:' **The Prologue** would be 'PL: 5:' The **Epilogue** would be 'EL: 10' and, **The Law of Three** would be 'TLOT: 5.' The Numbered Chapters would of course follow suit, e.g., **The New Song** would be 'NS14:14.' Our **References** would be 'Ref: 3,' **Appendix would be** App I: 7, and **The Concept Index** would be 'CI: I.'

4   **The Bible's Revelations** would be R5: 2-5-9; **The Holy Quran** would be Q3: 83-85; **The Theology of Time** would be T, p. 69, **The True History of Master Fard Muhammad** would be, MFMxxxi; **Our Savior Has Arrived** would be, OSHA105P2-5 and so on (MEMPS Publications). I hope that all the other references not mentioned would be understood by evaluating these examples.

5 **How should you study this Book:** Relate the text to **yourself first**, then back to the text; the world, other people, things and, or issues. Be Clear Here, Holders of *irrational faith* **- when they have the power and the capacity to do otherwise –** allow *and or* inflict pain, suffering and/or death on those who are weaker than they are. Intro: 4

6 If asked: **"What is your religion?"** or **"Are you a ...?"** Your Answers could include:

   A Because Abraham is the Source of faith as I know it, **my** behavior (faith and belief) arises from *understanding* **Abraham's motive** *and* **purpose** which gave rise to Moses, Jesus and Muhammad. NS1: 3

   B What I believe **does not** lift mysticism (tradition, ritual, ideology or culture) above upright, rational, **Conscience - based, Conscious behavior.** My faith *blends its* Truth *and* Values into my *daily living*. Intro: 5

   C Find *your own answers* and *formulation* in The New Song.

   D This is a Message of "hope" and guidance for those **seeking** the "right way," it took us nearly 400 years to find the door.

PREFACE

The New Song - *the essence of the teaching of the Honorable Elijah Muhammad* and *the Prophets*-had its first copyright (unpublished) on July 18, 1995 as "Going to The Root, A Spiritual Study in Essay Form on The Psychology of Man."

It evolved into today's "New Song" for the Original Man in America to raise him up from mental, moral and spiritual death. And, by extension, **_all men_** who are governed by their Conscience and Higher Intellect over dead religious ideas and dead political, cultural and or nationalistic ideology worldwide as evidenced by their behavior and the results of their action. NS12: 69

This Book takes our mind into *the root of "darkness."* Discussing *who* produced "the shadow of death" and the morally "intense darkness" that has spread all over our planet (which we pray about daily). All of which has come upon the world in the last 6000 years. We discuss how we may escape into the Light of Truth and Understanding through personal effort.

Today, all men, people and minds **have an opportunity** to think and live as an **"Original Mind,"** if they choose to, if they can muster up the **inner power** to "overcome" - or **become** "unaffected" by - the negative influences of the world of materialism *and* sin against their own soul or nature.

Having a negative attitude about this Truth - pride, arrogance, envy and jealousy - *will result in personal failure.*

Learn to "overcome" your past (*and* your sicknesses) by **your own inner evolution**.

Identify the "X" Factor in yourself. Find **your own essence.** Stop following the "dead religious ideas and dead political, cultural and or nationalistic ideology," the social and or cultural **programming** of or from our birth - wherever that may have occurred - if that programming *that behavior* does not lead to peace and understanding rather than confusion and war.

That is how we have become *as machines* or **"automated"** people with little or no **"self control"** but, let's begin.

FOREWORD

For those of you who may desire a group discussion on line, this may be possible in the future as Members with this and other expertise arrive in our "New World." I am also available for limited email responses. However, nearly all of your questions are answered in the New Song itself and it is a Self Defender.

Continued reading, evaluation and **living through** the Principles in this Message will help you answer various questions that may arise. Create a new atmosphere and environment in your own mind and in your own home. Invite your family, friends and associates to discuss the New Song and its implications with you. **Action** will go a long way in developing your understanding.

The **more knowledge** one brings to The New Song (or anything else), the **more insight** they can receive from it. I've added references to **The Theology of Time**, M.E.M.P.S., GA, e.g., T, p. 69, as The Messenger's Message in it is the **Essence** of The New Song, unsealing the scripture. See page 2.

Relate this text to **yourself**, back to the text, the world, people, conditions, issues *and* things. Learn to read this Book from the _inside out_, **not** the _outside in_. Become the BOOK, [*eat the scroll*] this requires a _change_ of mind and attitude. Go there, be there, **feel it.** NS17: 15; Ez2: 8; R10: 9, 11

Holders of _**irrational faith**_ – **even when they have the capacity to do otherwise** – allow *and, or* actually inflict pain, suffering and / or death upon those who are weaker than they are than *hide behind their dogma as if they are innocent.* Intro: 4, 5; NS8: 8a

If you are asked: **"What is your religion?"** or **"Are you a ...?"** Your Answers, from our principles, could include: "Because Abraham is the Source of faith as I know it, *my* behavior (manifesting *my unseen* underlying knowledge, faith and belief) arises from understanding **Abraham's motive** *and* **purpose** which gave rise to Moses, Jesus, Muhammad and all of the Prophets." NS1: 3; 8: 19a; 9: 1, 3

The point is: What *I* believe **does not** lift *mysticism* (culture, tradition, ritual or ideology) up **above** upright, rational, **Conscience - based** behavior. My actions and consequently my faith, *blends its* Truth *and* Values into my *daily living* Intro: 5; NS2: 9, 13, Appendix I. "My life is in **submission to God**, not to *mysticism*."

Study this Message, **live** this Message and **find** *your own answers* to the issues of our day and our lives.

Remember: **The greatest human struggle** is that for the conquest of your own "self," your own mental, emotional and cultural life. NS13: 15, 20; TLOT: 3. Are **you** in control of **your own** "self" **right now?** Reflect on this question as you proceed.

If you have no **need** to research the areas that I have made references for in this "Song," than don't. The references are provided for those who would like to **look over my shoulder** *or* **make a scholarly analysis of what I've said.** If, however, the narrative is clear enough for you to **"see"** what I am saying, then read past the references and grasp the whole narrative that we are presenting.

Find or make your own **"Self."** Weigh the prospects of your "own" Heritage as you find it here. The **"Door"** to your "own" future awaits you. NS1: 40; 8: 29, 30

Muhammad A. Aziz,
October 31, 2008 -13

INTRODUCTION TO THE RELIGION OF ABU RAMU (ABRAHAM)

1   I greet you all with the greetings of 'Peace' which comes from 'Paradise,' a "Source" that 'the down trodden' have not known, worldwide, for over 6000 years, although there has been prophetic sparks of **corrective light** during the last 4000 years.

2   The Life that you find in the New Song will be *"new"* *(to your understanding – as it was written to be)*, **for those who do not know** of the Coming of "The Son of Man" to keep God's **"Promise"** Q35:5 and to answer the prayer of **Abraham's 'down trodden' "seed"** in America. NS15: 9 For those who do know, your sight will be clarified as to your role in the world today as *many*, *if not most of you*, have died (in rituals, indifference and or immoral behavior) since 1975, or the **"First Resurrection,"** *leading to 40 years of roaming the spiritual wilderness* seeking a way out, because of not "understanding" the Messenger and the need for *personal inner evolution*. Q34: 49

3   This is the **"Second - and last - Resurrection"** that your scripture and Lessons told you would come. We "found <u>the Door</u>," 1555-2015; 458 years to date. Our work will include **all the people** <u>who want to be included</u>. No one knew how this would come about or what it would look like, including me. The price of admission to the **"New World"** or **"Being Here After"** is the price Abraham paid as *the Author of faith*.

Say as he said: **"I bow my will to God,"** and we say, I Follow "The Way of Abraham the True in Faith," Q6:161 that is the Message and the way. NS1: 40; 8: 32

4 Through The New Song, All of the Prophets have been _brought together_ in the **"Judgment"** Q6:90; NS14: 23a Know that regardless of what you call **your** religion (or where you are on this planet) neither language nor sound is the keystone to "grace." No! **Function, what you strive for** _and_ **what you actually do,** is the only keystone to your future NOT WHAT YOU SAY OR BELIEVE. Q6:164; NS8:5

5 **_Your actions_** arise out of _or_ from "automation" _or_ your "intent." Know that human consciousness will _either_ **have** _or_ **not have - _Conscience_ -** as its **Corner Stone.** NS5: 12 Either way, the presence or absence of conscience **in you** can be seen and understood through your actions **("deeds").** NS1: 40b Thus, _everyone_ can now see **literally,** God and the Devil **_through_** human behavior. There are only two people on Earth, God and the Devil. EL: 9, 11a, b The spirit (function) of a man is the light of "God" within him. _Our Action_ makes manifests our **unseen inner nature,** _by degree_ NS2:6; Prov.: 20: 27; zero thru 100. NS2:7f -10; see Q18: 21; #17 below

6 **_Our individual purpose_** today is to rise up, "grow up," _into_ God (as it was written). Know that the **Upright, "Righteous God"** does not guide to evil or shameful deeds. Q7:28; Prov. 3: 31; Isa.5: 16; see NS2: 8, 13; 5: 16

7 Our **_"Intentions"_** and thus our decisions and behavior **("deeds"** **not** **"beliefs")** is how **The Supreme Being**, God, will judge us. Proceed from here with an **open**

mind, NS8: 29c a closed mind will leave you were you are; believe me, you <u>do not</u> want to stay there.

8 The purpose of our Community, this class, and the New Song is to help you in the process of **mastering** *your* **thought patterns** and consequently *your* **behavior.** This is The Path of Self - mastery it is also <u>the heart</u> of "true" religion (<u>bind back</u> that which <u>is broken</u>). During class, (or study periods) you will write what you *see* and what you *feel* -- both *internally* and *externally* -- this information will be used as <u>your</u> <u>foundation</u> upon which to **build** a greater personality as you evolve. You will also take *mental pictures* of yourself with the method and language that will be shown to you. NS5: 5; 13: 1

9 Accurate notes will be taken at each class they will give material and form, later, to your mental pictures. These notes should be in a solid book from which pages cannot fall out or get lost. Class notes will be *studied* and used as *each weeks* <u>essay outline</u> and for <u>weekly review</u> [**of** how you used what you learned].

   a An essay of **400** or more words will be expected for the first three weeks. Notes, and especially essays, should include *new ideas, your feelings,* and *your thoughts during the class* <u>and</u> *any new understanding that you have achieved.*

   b Make sure that your notes contain the date, time, place, and *anything else* that may be of importance to you later (years from now). Your notes are for future reference. Keep copies of your essays and <u>use them</u> to develop your <u>final</u> **"Orientation"** <u>essay,</u>

which should be one to five thousand words long. Five characters are equal to one word.

10 Each one of you must **verify** *the concepts* that you are being taught, ***within yourself***, <u>in this manner</u> you will have **experiential facts** rather than just written or verbal ideas to build upon. NS5: 4 **Weigh everything, <u>and</u> *ask meaningful questions.***

11 Understanding of the concept of **Intercession** (Shafa'at) should clear the way for our <u>*Class*</u> and <u>*individual undertaking*</u>. Shafa'at (meaning **"intercession"** in Arabic) is derived from the <u>root word shat</u>, which signifies **"the making of a thing, or a person, to be <u>one of a pair</u>."** Footnotes numbered 79 and 607 in the Holy Qur'an, translated by Maulana Muhammad Ali.

12 The <u>*primary significance*</u> of **'intercession'** is two-fold: Q34: 23; 39: 44

- <u>First</u>, it ***enables*** a person to walk in the ways of ***"consciousness"*** or righteousness by **imitating or following his model**,

- <u>Secondly</u>, 'intercession' affords him ***a shelter*** from the evil <u>*consequences*</u> of certain weaknesses, e.g., mysticism, which he is <u>*unable*</u> to overcome by himself.

13 Taking into consideration all of the above, <u>*very soon*</u> after you begin this study, <u>*you will realize*</u> that you are **acquiring** a certain knowledge that opens up **<u>new</u>** *and* **different** possibilities *of understanding.* <u>No one</u> can escape this ***fact if*** they came <u>as a</u> "<u>student</u>" **[to follow guidance or try to be like the teacher]**.

14 <u>After a while</u>, **you will notice changes in yourself that you will not be able to describe**, but which <u>will produce</u> **different attitudes (and later abilities) within you** which others will also be able to see (and generally like, but not necessarily understand). **This is inevitable,** so this <u>evidence</u> will give you <u>a definite sense</u> *that you are moving somewhere and not just standing still.* Rereading your essays and your notes will give you a moving account, a sense of your own <u>living process</u>, if you've written good and clear notes.

15 REMBEMBER: **Breaking of old habits is a must.** <u>Separation</u> from your previous <u>Thoughts and Activities</u> **wherever they interfere with your present goals** <u>*is*</u> **the basis of all your work on your "self."** <u>Unless this idea is understood fully</u>, nothing can be attained. In everything that we do, we must **begin from the idea of "separation" from past negative habits** and <u>*living in the present;*</u> *forming new and beneficial habits.*

16 Coming to grips with this idea - **agreeing to struggle for self - mastery (taking us out of our comfort zone)** - this <u>is the</u> real **difference** <u>*between us and those who are not among us.*</u> **We know** that we are not what we could or should be, **they do not.**

17 "Surely, We have created man into toil and struggle," Q90:4 on the other hand, **"Man can have nothing** <u>except</u> what he strives for, and the result of his striving will soon come in sight."** Q53:39; see #5 above

18 These are the teachings from a message **worthy** of listening to, now let's get busy, <u>*work*</u>, and **find the**

PROLOGUE:
WHAT IS THE "NEW SONG"?

1 The **"New Song"** is the manifestation **- the realization** - of God's Promise. NS8: 14a, b-20a,b; 12: 26, 27; 14: 2, 3; EL: 13 **This "Truth"** will set your mind <u>first</u> and <u>in time</u> your body "free" by removing from you "<u>the mark of the beast</u>**:" *fear, guilt, greed and anxiety*; thus removing the former dead 'slave' from <u>the world of moral darkness and mental illusion</u> built by the former slave master. NS12: 15; 14: 25

    a Your time has come you **_are_** the "Inheritor" of the promise. Q35:5 The New Song is *"the Master Grip"* on the <u>*144,000 dead*</u> NS8:25a, 26a **- who will become the stars of "heaven"** - *it is "the most trustworthy [moral] hand hold that never breaks."* Q2:256; NS8: 19: a, b; 14:2; EL: 2-7a, e;T, p.32, 2ⁿᵈ p

2 **_The Essence_ of the power to control Existence is available to you right now.** <u>In your life</u>, choose **upright behavior** NS8:14a; 15:8; AP: 9 <u>over rituals</u> or <u>external show;</u> **conscience** and **values** over **methods** and **mysticism.** *Internal Peace will arrive.* Don't pray and dress to be *seen* and *heard* of men while disregarding the truth, justice and right in your behavior.

3 *The "New Song" destroys "mysticism"* - <u>the 'root' of Satan</u> - it wipes out ignorance, sickness, darkness and finally death; producing instead <u>idea creators</u> rather than consumers of Satan's ideas and his way of life. Q4:120-123; 14:22; NS8: 8b; 15: 6c

4 *Mysticism consists of* **unchanging beliefs,** *traditions, rituals and ideology,* this is *the* **crippler** of the conscious mind blocking it from *considering* or *evaluating* the new or different. **Only** the *"new"* and *"different"* can change or improve the former slave's condition NS4:21 in America. In His Day: **"God makes all things new."** NS14:14 -19-28

5 The cure for mysticism is immediate, Allah has instructed us: **"Accept your own mind and be yourself."** NS1: 25a; 12: 8 Doing this we *will* gain total control over our **emotional** *and* **our material life.** We will escape from the **suffocating grip, "the yoke,"** of mysticism that has millions *bound* and *chained,* as it were, **to the past** and or **an illusion.** This mental and emotional condition is **"Hell"** NS8: 10, while living in the present. "Hell" produces, *almost unnoticed,* constant *inner tension leading to all diseases, suffering, and for many, death.* NS1: 27, 29; 8: 10 -14; EL: 11c, e

   a You can escape from Hell in a second if you are *prepared* to hear - or learn - what you do not know *now,* the new *idea* or *new information*; and, you are *"seeking," "asking"* or *"knocking."* You can buy a house with nothing in it and *furnish it later.* Otherwise, you have to live in someone else's house until you can afford your own. Prov. 15:33

6 **"Sit your 'self' in heaven at once,"** the Honorable Elijah Muhammad told us. If we follow that guidance *our command there* – **after** our *culturally automated* **"life"** NS11: 14 has become a conscious life NS5: 2C, D-11, 16 - will be: **"Let there be light" (in my own mind):** is he to whom We have given *no light* the equal of he to whom

We have *given light*? How do you judge? NS8: 30j; EL: 17, 18; Q4:174; 57:28

7   Allah is Existence, which is Endless, Eternal, Self-Created and Self-___Existent___. **Human like Consciousness** is the Eternal axis *and* Controller of all Existence. *Human like Consciousness* is **the greatest value** in *and* from all creations (galaxies) in **all of existence.** Q13:15; 17:44; 23:17-86; 30:26; 42:29; App V; VI

8   In all of Existence: ___the greatest effort___ of human like consciousness ___is to become one___ with *All That Is* - in **"His Presence" - Cosmic Consciousness, Self Consciousness -** and assume unique control (as promised to those who "overcome" the *"automated," "machine - like" existence* **and /or** *mysticism*). Jn10: 30; NS4: 12

9   Human like ___"conscience"___ or ___"soul"___ makes possible our ___new vision___ of: **a-** honest thinking, **b-** objective decision making, **c-** correct social behavior, **d-** objective laws and **e-** true social justice. NS 10: 7a, b, c. What has been ___our___, former slave's, ___experience___ in America - True social justice or machine - like treatment?

10 **The only enemy of Allah** (Eternal, Positive Existence) is *a sick* human like "conscious mind" *with less than 70% active "conscience"* and/or ___one controlled by___ ___mysticism.___ NS2: 4, 5; 5: 11, 16; 8: 8, 9, a; 11: 7d;

11 **Mysticism produces ___all___ social negatives**, including mental and physical death; it is characterized by *passion, envy, greed and deceit.* ___Mysticism___ *is the controller of darkness [through ___the mind___ it controls* NS4: 15, 21

and is called "Devil" and or "Satan" in scripture]. See NS8:18, a; 11:7d

12 **Mysticism, anywhere, <u>is the enemy of peace</u> - freedom, justice and equality - <u>everywhere</u>.** Search throughout the world and see *<u>this mind working</u>*.

13 Let your **study of the New Song** - this ***New Language*** - <u>inform your understanding</u> of **yourself, the devil, God or *"Allah"*** and most of all **<u>your own inheritance</u>.** NS1: 28a, b-37; 12: 20a-32; 14:20; EL: 3, 8 [Review Chapter 6; App II: 10]

1 With this **"New Language"** you may **create the culture** and **support the weight** of *<u>our new civilization</u>*. You then possess <u>the whole world</u> expressed and implied through, and by, it. Using ***our language*** <u>and</u> ***spirit*** NS3: 2 you <u>become</u> a powerful force that not only communicates with words, ideas and concepts you actually ***shape them*** and consequently *the world* that these words produce. […?] "Yes," *<u>if I heard</u>* your question; "The New World" ***is within you***. NS1: 28a, b; 8: 33; 12:9-43

   a Say, with me: "Allah, there is no God but He, the Ever Living, the Self -Subsisting, by Whom all subsist.

   b Slumber overtakes Him not - nor sleep - to Him belongs whatever is in the Heavens and whatever is in the Earth.

   c <u>Who is he</u> that can intercede with Him but by *<u>His Permission</u>*. He **Knows** what is **Before** them and what is **Behind** them and they encompass nothing of His knowledge except what He Pleases and His **Knowledge** extends over the Heavens and the

Earth and the **Preservation** of them both tires Him not and He is **the Most High, the Great.**" NS8:8 By whatever name *you call on Him*, His are the Most Beautiful Names (in *functional meaning*). Intro.: 4, 7

14 The New Song exists by **"His Permission."** Q8:29; 34: 23; 76: 22; Jn10: 38

THE LAW OF THREE: *A BRIEF COMMENT*

1   It takes *__three forces__* - functioning in harmony - **to bring into existence any one thing,** e.g., Carbon, Nitrogen, and Oxygen; Red Blood Cells, White Blood Cells and Platelets; Sun, Moon and Earth. App IV

2   Creation does *__ordain__* **consciousness,** but *__does not ordain__* knowledge or self-mastery to human like minds anywhere in The Universe. These functions must be *__sought after__* by a curious and evolving mind if that mind is <u>not</u> born in freedom (from moral darkness and mysticism). The "knocking," "seeking," "asking" or "curious" mind is received in **the New Song.** Q17:44; 76: 22; NS5: 6, 7; 9: 18

    a   Instruction 14: 19, 20 in, and exercise of, **Divine Wisdom** forms and sustains *the upright human nature. __That is__* the "fear of the Lord." The **"Lord" – Our Innate Power of self control -** *functions from* **our** *__upright__* **human nature.** 12: 48; 14: 54b <u>Not having</u> this *accumulated wisdom* NS15: 5a causes a wobble and **insecurity** within us. Our 400 year long trial made possible space, time and opportunity for **deviation** [devilish ideas to fester] and *now, the time is right* for the corrective influence **of upright, God-like, ideas.** Prov.9: 10; NS3: 14; 5: 21a; 8:19a-30c; 15: 8; MFM36: 1170, 1227

3   **A mind** <u>everywhere</u> **must master** *the* **automated laws** of the world of its birth demonstrating evolved mentation (emotional control and mental evolution). TLOT: 2; NS4: 2; 12: 82

4 The ingredient missed by Einstein in his theory of relativity is **"Human Consciousness."** This _universal triad_ is the Creator of all forms and functions, these forms and functions are governed by _evolved_ **"Human like Consciousness," which is the Master of the Universe.** App VI; T, p.169p. 3, 4

   A {1} E=MCSQD, where E=energy; {2} M=mass; {3} C=the speed of light squared.

   The above, Einstein's theory, shows the Integration of energy and mass with the limiting speed of light.

   B Here is **_the integration_** of **knowledge** with **time** and **the speed of light:**

   {1} K=TCSQD, where K=knowledge; {2} T=time; {3} C=the speed of light squared.

5 There is no limit to the capacity of **_human understanding_** - however, there is a limit to the human minds' capacity to **process** and **store** information. At this point, in our evolution, we are nowhere near our processing or storage limitation. _Do you want to get there?_ NS14: 44. 45

6 The mind, **once _out of_ automation**, or **_'instinctive' knee jerk behavior_**, has the capacity to **_expand exponentially._** A review of the **"made man's,"** NS8:18; Gen.1:26, scholarly, scientific and technical advancement during the last 4000 years of Western history should be evidence enough of what is said here. NS5: 10B-4f; 12: 2

7 We have _identified the force_ that **stops - no blocks - the creation, acquisition and the accumulation of new,** _automation reducing_, ideas among us and consequently

the development of <u>*new schools of knowledge*</u>. <u>That force</u> is **Mysticism.** *The New Song* now provides the former slave with *a new force* and *a new vision* for the *evolutionary advancement* of our <u>*original human mind*</u> and <u>*our original nature*</u> back into the **unlimited conscious dimensions** that built the Universe. This is our **"***<u>ladder</u>***"** to Heaven and our return to *'L Sh'b'zz*, <u>*our Source*</u>. Prov.8:22, 33; NS3: 7a; 9:2-21c; 12:78-84; 15: 8; App I: 7; T, p.170 p.2

8   When mysticism - culture, tradition, rituals and ideology - enters the human mind as <u>**unchanging beliefs**</u> they reduce and eventually stop **- block -** <u>the acquisition</u> and <u>accumulation</u> of *new* knowledge and *new* ideas. NS14:19-28

9   **Mysticism blinds the mind, stops the ears and makes the speech of their "believers" ritualistic or like a <u>tape recorder</u>.** This inner state NS5: 2A, B is described by the Prophets as being *'<u>asleep</u>'* or *'<u>dead</u>;'* **unaware** of the cause of their situation, repeaters of yesterday's ideas that have proven unsuccessful today. NS5: 1

10 Again, **history is a witness** to these facts. Review the history of those on earth to- day - and yesterday - who are or where <u>*most prone to mysticism*</u> and <u>*those who are*</u> or <u>*were not*</u>. What do you see? How was your life when you were a mystic and how is it now, if you've been <u>resurrected</u> from the **"mark"** of the beast? PL: 1; NS8: 26a

11 Again, Truth must be verified <u>*within*</u> your **"self,"** *if you are 'awake.'* 'We know that no **conscious beings** will <u>purposely act</u> to *violate their own nature* and *destroy their own future* <u>unless</u> they are **made 'spiritually**

dead' *through* **mysticism** as were the former slaves - those having the "mark of the beast" - who were brought to America in chains **457** years ago. NS1: 7a; 12:13, 15-39, 57

a We know because **we arose - were redeemed - from that death** and we still <u>see</u> and <u>speak to</u> those who are still suffering from this sickness. <u>**Our sorrow**</u> is that <u>**they can't receive**</u> in the state they are in (**not** 'seeking,' 'asking' or 'knocking' <u>beyond</u> the devil's ideas) NS8:5, 6 their **mental and spiritual curiosity for "self" is dead.**

12 **Conscious civilizations** generate knowledge at <u>increasing speeds</u> as is seen by a review of our history on Earth, under the Caucasians, for the last 4000 years. In our day we now see computers using finer and finer components, circuitry smaller than the eye can see. Soon we will see computers using circuitry made of atomic and subatomic particles, showing the power of mental curiosity.

13 Imagine the Originals Who have been Conscious in the Universe for the last 4000 years - let alone **the previous Trillions** - that it took Caucasians to reach where they presently are in mental and technical development. Remember too that much of their scientist's time <u>was and still is</u> spent fighting through mysticism (<u>today, they don't kill them as quick for their new ideas, but they did</u>).

14 They should be thousands of years beyond where they are, but they wanted to sit in the seat of God <u>without earning it</u> (through inner evolution) so **they made up a religion** that mostly <u>blocked conscious development</u>

(for the masses) and ruled through it *and* scientific development. So today they still have a clash going on between their mysticism and their scientific endeavors. Ref: 3, 8

15 The Original Man in the Universe has long ago reached the stage where knowledge advances so fast that **time relatively stands still** ("a day with God is a 1000 years as you count"). This very brief review shows **the wide awake mind** that *consciousness*, as *the controlling component* over *mass* and *energy*, is *the master of the universe* and **our conscious purpose** today is to *create a body* for this **"Consciousness"** to perform through in our life time.

  a Among His Signs is the creation of the heavens and earth, and **the living creatures** that He has scattered through them: and He has power to gather them together when He wills. **Don't let this present life deceive you. Don't let the Chief Deceiver deceive you about God.** Q42:29; 35: 5; NS12: 19; 14: 1

16 **"God"** NS8: 21, 23a has long been *the substitute for the unexplainable*. What will happen when everything is explained? What will happen to the idea of "God" then? The answer is clear. We've been told to **"Grow up** into Him in all things." "Sanctify My House," Allah said. Q2: 125

  a **"House"** in this metaphor is **your body** and its **upright nature** which has been caused to *"deviate"* from its normal function in this (Devils) world. NS8: 9a; 14:25; Q5: 57. **'Allah will produce'** what we cannot now imagine, consider this New Song in your hand you cannot conceive how it was produced. NS14: 45, 49

17 There are many *factors or functions* that set the **conscious original mind** – the <u>one</u> set aside for Allah's use, or the <u>one</u> who is in the world but not of it - <u>*apart*</u> from those who are <u>*spiritually dead*</u> to the knowledge of 'self' as an <u>original</u>. See #11 above

   a **The conscious mind's overall behavior** is such that one does not need a great education to see it. He or she is the same as everyone - <u>*yet somehow different*</u>. He or she will have many other characteristics that may not be so clear to most people because of their lack of exposure, education or conscience, on the other hand *their apparent youth and vitality* will serve <u>as a marker</u> of recognition along with their <u>*unseen inner functions*</u>. Q7:46, 49; 76:19; NS12: 12; App VI

18 **Self Conscious People** and *only self conscious people* can <u>*potentially* **reverse** *the effects of physical aging*</u>. This, again, is <u>a clear indicator</u> - along with **energetic, purposeful** NS9: 3 **behavior** and **conscience** NS4:13 - that **inner** NS5: 6 **evolution** *has* <u>or</u> *is* occurring and shows that the individual has Discovered or is <u>following</u> **Universal Laws** that make this and everything else possible. Q56:17; NS15: 4

   a *Consciousness is immortal*. Primordial matter, NS12:54, stays in perpetual motion *at its apex* because of consciousness. NS12:23 <u>Clarification, focus of purpose</u>, NS11:6c, d, within spatial, atmospheric, emotional, and or psychological constructs or environments <u>determine</u> the shape, form, function, capacity and weight of material manifestations or expression. NS2: 7a, f; App VI

19 Only **Objective Laws** are valid and apply to every being, everywhere at all times. Objective Laws do not arise from the minds of <u>undeveloped</u> men and women; these Laws have always been and will always exist universally and independent of the human mind and its culturally *automated emotions* for their generation.

   a However, **Objective Laws** do *arise in* or are *attracted to an* <u>integrated</u> <u>consciousness</u> which is *designed* by *human like* minds **wherever they arise (showing that** *their* *inner effort* **overcame** *their automated existence***).** TLOT: 3; NS14: 47

20 **No Objective Law is new;** each is **Eternal only needing rediscovery among the formerly 'dead'** NS8:26 **'Lost' and now 'Found' people of God.**

   a **No law is valid** *unless* **that law is** <u>*naturally*</u> <u>*applicable*</u> <u>*universally*</u> *and* <u>*eternally*</u> **therefore we** *have become part of the worldwide change among the Original People of the Earth.*

   b The devil makes *unnatural laws* and *behavior* which produce sickness, suffering and death worldwide in their role as Dajjal. NS5: 16b; 12: 1 Today, *we can literally see the current world wide change in motion, we are witnesses to the clash of worlds.* Through The New Song, we can now see where before we were blind. NS14: 6-14; 5: 10B-4d, f

    c Allah permits us to understand the change of worlds and save ourselves in America if we choose "Him" as our **Savior.** NS8: 9a-14; 12: 3-83; 17: 8; OSHA202P3

21 Teach this Message to your children and see the results Q13:11

THE NEW SONG
The Process of Guidance and Instruction

Section Five – Opening and Sharing the Book {Flower]

CHAPTER ONE
Going To the Root

1 <u>The idea</u> Q10:109 of **GOING TO THE ROOT**, as a means of acquiring *self knowledge* and *self awareness*, is <u>how I learned</u> to study from the Honorable Elijah Muhammad's "Message" to us. For me this started in September of 1962. T, p.3p.3; p.25p.3

2 <u>What do I think</u> sharing this with you will accomplish? First of all, I think that if you are one of those who are *searching* for the truth about our and your position and condition in the world today you will – at the least – do a great deal of thinking. So, **thought** of a *new* and *deeper* kind is my first goal for every "Student." Q39:33; MFM626, 645; Lk6: 40

3 <u>I hope that</u> "going to the root" of yourself is the **primary** reason why you've been *attracted* to this work. NS13: 3 If so, our work together of mentally **"copying" - blending and refracting - the light** Q5: 112; 6:90 *of Abraham,* T, p.3 <u>through</u> Moses (Judaism), Jesus (Christianity - all Bible based religion) and Muhammad (Islam), will provoke a **very deep** and **powerful** <u>*friction*</u> of ideas within you. Intro: 10, 12

    a The result of your inner work - friction - will, when maintained by <u>study</u> and <u>practice</u>, enable you to deal with yourself as you actually *are* and thus, by Allah's leave, you may be able to move closer to **the true goal** <u>of human life</u> which is the **ascension of man's consciousness (thus his behavior) to God:** his upper or **"Higher Self,"** (having <u>one</u> **"purpose"**) as it is written. Ecc.12:13; Q4:83; 6:89, 90; TLOT: 2

b Elijah's <u>role</u> and <u>purpose</u> is to *"make a new path for his people"* as promised by God; today they are in <u>a crooked path</u>. This **New Song** is designed to reach *the heart* and *mind* of all of those <u>who see</u> the crooked path and are **searching** for the right way or path out. NS14: 14, 20

4 <u>We must keep before us</u> the fact that only by **"going to the root"** of <u>*our own*</u> **being** and *<u>verifying</u>* Intro: 10 what we find there with <u>*the reality of the whole environment*</u> that we are a part of, can we arrive at Truth *<u>for our time</u>*. NS5: 4 External studies alone, regardless of the discipline, will never bring us to the whole Truth, Truth that can **guide** and **enrich** - our - *"human"* life and thus positively affect our social environment. XI: 10; NS5: 4; 11:7a, f; Q13:11

5 <u>I thank Allah</u> as a Student of **The Religion - or the Way of Life - of Abraham** Q2:135 ("bowing my will to God" Q3:67, as does "those who follow **the best meaning in this Message**"Q39:18-55) and as a **"Student"** of the Wisdom Prov4: 7; Ch 15 delivered by the Honorable Elijah Muhammad and the *revelations of the Prophets,* Q5: 112; 12:111, <u>through</u> Prophet Muhammad for opening my mind and heart to understand Allah's Purpose today. I've also benefited from what I have studied *from <u>many</u> <u>writers</u>* in various disciplines *over the years.*

a I am also thankful to them for some of the language that helped me to put some of my thoughts into digestible written form. I am especially indebted to G.I. Gurdjieff, P.D. Ouspensky, F. Wallace, M. Hamilton, and W. D. Wattles whose terms for some things I have found to be descriptive and very helpful for *what I am trying to describe.*

6   This work of **collecting, _focusing_** and **sharing** *Divine Wisdom* is analogous to the work of the **"Bee."** And yes, *we **can** fly.* You remember the skeptic's tale: "The poor thing ("Bee"), it can't fly. Its wings are too short. Its body is too heavy, and it's not aerodynamic enough." Sound familiar? This "God Given Work," in your hands, says *"**We can fly**."* It is for *you* to determine how high or how far. Q6:91

   a   A **worker egg** develops into a **Queen** after being fed large quantities of "Royal Jelly." In like manner, the **former slave** develops into the *Original Upright Nature* of "man" NS8:30d; 12:44; 25a below by consuming large quantities of "The New Song." NS14: 23a; 15: 8; 17: 15-21; Review Chapter 9

7   Someone may ask about *my warrant* for doing what I do. NS5:: 20 My warrant came from the teaching of the Honorable Elijah Muhammad and the Prophets before him Mat.13:17; NS8:4 In the **Problem Book that Allah brought us, # 32**, one of the Prophets said that those who believed would number 144, 000 and the rest, he said, "Are **poison** and **rusty**, and will not take the knowledge **on their own (without being punished first** NS8: 8b**)."** OSHA207P7

   a   The Messenger thinks that this knowledge - **the Message** that God revealed to him - would *enable* him to remove all poison and rust from those who would at least *open* their ears, their eyes and their hearts to reflection. NS13: 5, 6-30 32 b The Messenger "desires for <u>every one of you</u>, 'Students,' to ***help solve this Problem*** since you have learned the time14: C-4 - 41; 17:2 - 8, the Master's accomplishment (25,000) and the old Prophet's Number (144,000)." NS1:1 Their prediction is that *"only a few will hear and believe,"* <u>that</u> is what <u>*we are working to overcome*</u> with our effort. Q11:40 "Get out there," the Messenger said, "get after them yourself." We heard and we've made it our mission. T, p.121, 3rd p; NS14: 56

8 Being a "Student" I could describe this work, ***"The New Song,"*** R14: 3 as a ***Dissertation of "Human (Re) Development." Our <u>Blending</u>*** or ***<u>Refracting</u>*** of *the Prophet's Light,* R11: 15, 19 *with Allah's Direct Input* T, 65, 1st p. 74, 3rd p – p. 86, 1st p, is designed to ***reproduce*** <u>the Original (Mind) Man</u> (*not a believer*) and thereby ***restore*** our <u>lost inner powers</u> see #25 below thus create a <u>New Circle of Light</u> (Scientists) **evolved** from the *resurrected* "man" in America. Q3:110; NS5: 19; 8: 26a - 30d; T, p. 182, 2nd p; Ch 9

a "Allah did not come here to show us Who He is, He came to teach us ***who we are*** and then to make us rulers" **-** "<u>inheritors</u>" with Him as it is *written throughout scripture.* This is ***your invitation*** to accept and *<u>reclaim</u>* your own and be yourself. Q25:33; 7:137; NS15: 8-12 <u>Elijah said</u>: **"After Me is God."** The *<u>substance</u>* and *<u>weight</u>* of our effort here, for Allah, on your behalf, <u>speaks for itself</u>. NS14: 48

b "Allah ***gave me a little book,***" Elijah said, "and He is preparing ***another little book***, He is waiting for <u>a certain time</u> to give it to me. If we are to

4

know **the right way**, it cannot be taught by a **wrong way** teacher. Believe it or not." Only **upright behavior** or **self mastery** can get you into the world "here-after." Intro: 8-16; NS15: 6g; T, p. 32: 2nd Paragraph, M.E.M.P.S. See PL: 1

9　I have been one of the Messenger's Students for over 49 years. Now, as for **you** *following Our* guidance <u>through</u> **His Spirit in** <u>this</u> *'little book'*, consider this, your *"<u>ills</u> will be removed - after a real test - and <u>your life</u> improved"* NS15: 2, 6a; Q47:2 **or** <u>no change</u> will occur at all. NS12: 74 I say: let **your life** be <u>the proof of this work</u> and let **your faith** guide your feet here – <u>after</u> testing Our guidance in your life. NS15: 2, 7 Some of you <u>will say</u>: "We don't **understand** much of what you are saying! Nor do we see you as having any strength or authority among us" Q11:91 and, "Where is your Proof?"

　　a　If Allah had sent an "Angel" (to teach you) He still would have sent Him as **a** "man," thus your confusion is compounded though your own ignorance of "self," God and the devil. Q: 6: 7, 9; 14:53C; Ref: 3; App II: 10

10　There is only me and those with me, NS 14: 20 and **Allah** "<u>through</u>" the **"New Song"** we teach along with **our lives.** Q6: 7; 11:40-91 There are no words from the devil or in a library or elsewhere that we look to for *validation* of what we teach (actually, upon reflection, **this Truth** <u>can be seen</u> everywhere it is lived Jn7: 32).

　　a　True Validation is <u>in us</u> and will be <u>in you</u> as you 'grow up into Him.' The real Proof **is** "The New Song" Itself! T, p.257p1, 2 The New Song **answers questions** you've had for years and many you never even imagined or dreamed of or does the devil still have your mind *locked with the fear* of having a thought other than what he taught you. Q5:104; Jn.7: 16; NS12:74; 14:14 -19, 20 - 48, 49; EL: 18g; T, p219p1, 3

11 <u>Coming through</u> the Nation of Islam between 1962 and the passing of The Honorable Elijah Muhammad certainly *affected my life and my thinking.* The **core** of <u>my thinking</u> *and* <u>development</u> is and has been **the Message** to the "lost" NS8: 20 and fallen Original Man in America delivered by Messenger Elijah Muhammad. NS3: 7a

12 <u>In my study</u> of the Holy Qur'an, I see "Muhammad" as **two figures.** I also see, as Allah says, Jesus and his mother as **a sign**; also Moses and his work is a sign NS3: 12 of ***what we should look for*** in our day, **the Day of Resurrection.** This is the time that the Original Scientist called, ***"The Days of Allah,"*** in the Qur'an 45:14 and ***"The Day of Visitation,"*** in Isaiah 10:3; Lk17: 26, 37.

13 I won't go into too much detail here but I added many references in the Book to point the way for those who wish to do some research: reflect upon the **three types of revelation** that are outlined in the Qur'an 42:51. After your reading, answer these questions: What type of revelation did Prophet Muhammad receive? And what kind did Messenger Elijah Muhammad receive?

14 <u>The Honorable Elijah Muhammad's Message</u> *explains* the connection between the Qur'an and the Bible; *the prophecies* relative to white and black, East and West, the **nature of revelation; God or Allah** *and* what it

means; **how to** *"grow up into Him in all things;"* the Universe and its origin; the making and destruction of the devil, and much more. **Review Chapters 2, 4 - 6, 8 - 11, 12 - 14**

15 <u>Reflect here</u> that before The Honorable Elijah Muhammad began to teach, even with all the revelations of the Bible and the Qur'an <u>in our hand</u>, and the various commentaries of the scholars and scientist on religion, we could not understand what was going on *in the world* **at its root,** and we had no way to see **ourselves** in the Scriptures (we did not yet exist as a people nor did "America," hence the name "Mystery Babylon" became a place holder for it. NS7:B; Review in America). **Chapters 8-12-14, 15; Ref: 3**

16 <u>We thank Allah</u> for revealing this **root knowledge**, or **"Word,"** to the "despised" and the "rejected" of men, as it is written of us, so that we may become the *"headstone of the corner"* by *His Authority.* Elijah Muhammad, completing only **the 3rd grade**, could not have designed this message himself if no God had brought it to Him.

17 <u>In discussing the former slave's attitude</u>, **"The Scientist"** argued this way, **"**They (the so-called Negro, now called African American) regard the Jinn (the emotional center **made** *negative,* as devil NS15: 5a) to be partners with Allah, and *He created them* ...**"** Q6:101; 55: 15; 34:41 For those of us who have suffered under 457+ years of **"slavery, suffering and death"** this message should be seen as *"**Good News**"* Q39: 17 as the Prophets declare in both the Bible and the Qur'an T, 182/3

18 But most of the former slaves ***want to be accepted*** by their former slave master's off-spring instead of The God Who searched the globe, coming **9,000 miles** to "find" and "save" them from their suffering. Isaiah, describing this situation, says that <u>this Message</u> - the New Song Q21:2 – ***"... is a vexation..."*** 28:19 for most of the former slaves to even think about because ***they don't believe*** in "<u>the coming of Allah</u>, <u>the coming of The Spirit of Truth</u>, EL: 10 <u>the coming of The Son of Man</u>, or <u>the coming of The Holy One</u>." They believe in the mysticism PL: 11 taught to them by their open enemy. They, the dead, say: "Is (the Messenger) *more than* a man like your selves?" NS 14:53C; EL: 18g; Ref: 3

19 **The dead** <u>***rather believe***</u> **what** the former slave master and their children, *the **murderers** of our people, teach us <u>about God</u>* rather than listen to one of our own who was taught by God. Q32:3 Again, <u>*as it was written* to *happen*</u> in Malachi: "Behold, I will send you **Elijah,** The Prophet, ***before*** the coming of the <u>great</u> and <u>dreadful</u> *Day of the Lord* ..." If the Christians believe that we are anywhere near the Last Day, how do **they** *account for* **Elijah?** Mal. 4:5, 6; Q30:29, 30; 34:44 NS12:36, 38; EL: 18 g; MFM4144 "Conclusion"

20 Mind you, I am quoting scriptures here. NS12:36 If you cannot understand what I am saying ("word"), then how could you possibly understand **the Scientist,** *discussing* <u>*the future*</u>, Who said in Revelations: "<u>I saw a new heaven and a new earth</u>;" *the lead in for these* <u>years of work</u>: organizing, teaching and separating the people Q8:37, Ex21: 16 are described as coming "In **the days** of *the Voice* of <u>the Seventh Angel</u>, when he begins to **sound** (*teach*),

then **the mystery of God** *should be finished."* R10: 7;
consider, Gen32: 30; Ex33: 11;Num12:8: study Chapters 8 and 14

21 *THEN [in that time]* "they shall see "God's" Face and
His name (True knowledge) shall be in their foreheads
(minds)." About this *"Word:"* Moses "called them gods
unto whom **the Word of God** came because that
"Word" NS2: 11 *reproduces* the Original Nature - *Mind*
and **Consciousness** - [*not a believer*] thereby *restoring*
our lost **inner power**, and *self-control*; and the scripture
cannot be broken (or changed as to the intent and purpose
of God)" St. Jn.10:35; NS9: 2a, 3, 4; review Chapters 11; 15

22 The former slaves should be jumping for joy over this
"Good News," however, as Mr. Muhammad said, "They
love the devil because the devil gives them nothing (but
a promise through mysticism)." Allah says, **"The devil
promises** only to deceive." Q4:120-123; "Behold, I set before
you *this day* - presented in this Message - a blessing and a curse..." Deut
11: 26, 28; MFM2618

23 Today we see the Caucasians and those of us NS16: 10 with
their mentality (**educated** *and* **uneducated home
born slaves,** Jer.2: 11-14) constantly degrading the original
people by their attitude or behavior. For our own sanity
we should turn to the Scientist's explanation NS15: 6f for
the *Caucasians presence on the earth* and what Allah will
do with them according to the Prophets:

a "Allah raised you (Caucasians) up from *the seed* of
other (original) people" Q6:134; NS14: 12 to rule for six
days, but at last, because of Elijah, Mal. 4:5, 6, there is *"a
falling away first (separation before their destruction
Q8:37)* and the man of sin (the Caucasian) has been

9

revealed, as **the son of perdition"** (watch his attitude and behavior around the world R16:13, 16).
NS8:18; Prov.16:4; Hab1: 12; IIThes.2:3, 4; Ref.:3

b *"Soon We will visit him with a mountain of calamities..."* Q9: 85; 74:17; 63:1; Ez: 21: 7; OSHA105: P2-5

24 This Truth represents *mental freedom* for the former slaves, now ***he knows*** *what happened to him and why; who his enemy is* and *who he is.* Q8:29

25 The "Truth knocks out falsehood's brain." "No one in the heavens and the earth knows *the unseen* but Allah, and they (so-called Negro / African American) know not when they will be raised (from mental death)." Q27: 65 Just look at how we cry for justice all over America yet we won't look to what would set us free: the true knowledge of **the made-man** and **the nature and history of the original man**.

a **What is an Original Mind?** 12: 9 – 15 An "original mind" is one that has **not been morally** diluted, mixed or tampered with and is thus **"holy;"** *and or* the mind that has **been *restored*** to this "original" state by accepting God's Truth when "He" 14: 2, 6 - 46 comes for you with it. NS5: 14, 15-25; 8: 8, 16 - 30i

b The "Lost" and now "Found" mentally "dead" people who have chosen God have had their minds *renewed* NS 14: 28–39 and their moral strength and mental power ***restored*** they are thus counted among the Inner Circle of Humanity. NS **14:14, 17; 17: 5-17, 18**

26 According to the Quran, some may say I don't know what I'm talking about and call me a liar. Q7:66; 162: 49

However, "Those who listen to **the Word** and *follow the best* meaning *in it:* Those are the ones whom Allah has guided and those are the ones endued with understanding." Q10:39; 34:49; 39:18; Prov4: 7

27 Turning to Prophet Muhammad, did he shed some light on this subject? I say, "Yes he did." Prophet Muhammad told us that what Allah revealed through him (Islam) would retain its purity for only *three centuries* (as was the case with what both Moses and Jesus taught). If that is accurate then *why would we,* who were made **morally and spiritually dead** in "the (north) west" by our captors, look to that which has **lost its life,** *its moral and social effectiveness,* **for our life and future?** Reading the headlines daily (and for some of us, looking in the mirror) should be enough of a witness to this truth.

28 Reading the **Hadith,** we learn that Islam, as revealed through Prophet Muhammad, would retain its purity for only **three centuries** after the death of the historic "Muhammad," then it would be *resurrected* by the prophetic "Muhammad" as a *light giving Sun* in the West to **resurrect (the "body"** Lk17:37) **and restore the 400 year captives** Gen. 15:13 of the Caucasians - **the "eagles"-** in America ("the barrier between the two seas") re-forming them into **'L Sh'b'zz.** See Chapters 9 and 15

   a **The New Song** arrives as the **Sun Light of Truth** (a Pure Language) for the dead in the West with the *power to heal* and *renew* the total life. Q21:2, 3; PL: 13; NS4: 20, 24; 8: 33; 9: 21b; 12: 16

   b Our vocabulary, our language, *shapes our thoughts* and determines what we see; *why* and *how* we

11

"understand" <u>as we do</u>. PL: 13-1; EL: 5, 6; App V: 9, 11 Our <u>Volitional</u> change of vocabulary will **change the elements** our mind is <u>working</u> and <u>building</u> new cells with. NS4:14b Those new "elements" will, over time, produce **neurological changes** in our brain and our body which will then change our body's configuration and thus our behavior, and in time the world around us. NS1: 6a-24, 25-28a; 4:13, 15; 8:30a-32, 33; 11:8-17; 12:9-11a-20a-39, 41-43a-47, 49-52, 56-60-74; 13:1-12-16, 20-26, 32, 33c; 14:6a-13-19a, b, 20-47; 15:1-8; EL: 1-18, a, l, 19; App:1, 7; T, p. 65, p.1-74, p.3 Review Chapters 2- 4 and 9

29   The historic "Muhammad" NS 8: 19b is reported to have stated, "The best of the generations is my generation, then those who follow them, then *after them* will come people who will pride themselves in abundance of wealth and love plumpness." Tr. 31:39. He also said, "There will come a people in whom there is no good." KUVI, 2068, and **finally** "<u>A crooked way</u> - **they are not of me nor I of them.**" KUVI, 2073 **Yet they still call themselves "Muslim" today.** Intro: 4, 7 These sites may also be found in **footnote #1959** (or 32: <u>5a</u> in newer editions) of Maulana Muhammad Ali's translation of the Holy Qur'an, 7th revised edition

30   <u>The Scientist said</u> that "Allah orders the affair from the heaven to the earth; then it will ascend to Him in a day *the measure of which* is a thousand years as you count" Q32:5. This verse was revealed through Prophet Muhammad in 614. Three hundred years of pure Islam added to the time it was revealed plus the one thousand years to go back into Allah's Judgment brings us up to 1914.

31 **Fard Muhammad Ibin Alfonso, "The Holy One, *the Great Mahdi,* Isa5:16; 52:6, 7** revealed to us that Q22: 52, 57 that year ended their **"6 days"** or **6,000 year rule**; and that now the gate to all things Q6:44 would be **open** to them. Today we see the tremendous *material advancement* of western civilization, NS12: 28a which is called a **"beast"** by our Scientists *because of* **its** *effect* on the people who are weak; NS12: 28 that same advancement is leading to their final fall. "The day when the trumpet is blown We shall gather **the guilty, blue-eyed,** on that day." Q20:102; 74:17; 68:44

   a "**By degrees, We shall punish them from directions (and in ways) they perceive not.**" Q68: 44

32 We should note here that the opening of **the gate to all things** for them will and has enabled *some of them* to "*learn* and *do* like the original man" 25a above in less than **"35 to 50 years"** and ***requires us*** to evaluate all people by their *behavior* and *deeds* and not their lineage. Intro: 5, 7; NS8: 18 Because of this we are authorized by the Messenger to **"take a page out of the book [work] of cavy because he is successful."** We have followed that guidance and found that he can - *indirectly* - help us **collapse time** *in our personal development*.

   a They can study what we cannot reach and what we would otherwise know nothing about. TLOT: 12, 15; NS8: 18; see References

33 Note: Please review Maulana Muhammad Ali's translation of the following verses keeping in mind that **Moses was opposed by a government that held his people in**

bondage and that He spoke with Allah. He asked: "O my people! *Why do you vex and insult me?"* Quran 61:5. Elijah had the same complaint among us: 57:16; #2451A, #24548, 528, 21:104; #1665; 41:44; 5:54; 62:2, 3; #2503; Review the time: #1602 and 1603 M.A.A. *2:253; #289 from Maulana Yusuf Ali's Translation. All other verses are also from this translation unless stated otherwise.

34 <u>I realize</u> that some of you may not understand, or even want to accept, certain ideas as I have presented them. I suggest you *"ask questions and learn all about <u>yourself</u>"* NS15:5, 6; Ch16; Q5: 101 however, I would like to remind you of the Scientist's statement, question and admonition in the Holy Quran**: "You are they who dispute about matters of which you have knowledge. *Why do you dispute in matters of which <u>you have no knowledge</u>? It is Allah who knows and you know not!"* Q3:66; NS8:29, 30; 12: 4; OSHA3980

35 Please be patient with me and **the process**. "Be not like those who are divided among themselves and fall into disputations <u>after receiving</u> **clear signs**." Q3:105 Do you *really believe* that **your teacher**, <u>white people</u>, **the murderer of your people**, knows <u>our history</u> better than God Himself? Q3: 60; 7:7-10; NS8:8 Do you think he would teach it to you if he had it? Go back to Malachi 4:5, 6 and reflect.

36 <u>One of The Scientist</u> T, 182/3 Who *saw today's conditions* said, "They (most of the dead and Caucasians) are **disbelievers** <u>in the meeting</u> with their Lord," Q32:10 even though it is written *"The Lord cometh out of His place to punish the inhabitants of the earth for their iniquity."* Allah adds**: "I will proceed to do a**

14

marvelous work among these people..." Isa.29:14 and **"*the remnant* shall return (to Me),** Isa.10:21; Q30:52, 53 from them I will Produce a new people, **'L Sh'b'zz …**" Q5:57; NS1: 8; 14: 55, a; 15: 8, 10

37 <u>The focus</u> of this **School,** this New Circle of Light, Ch 2, is <u>to produce</u> **"the stars" [or Scientist]** who <u>demonstrate</u> in today's life the ***Presence of the Divine Supreme Being. My role, housing the Spirit of Elijah,*** is to present, by ***His Authority***, <u>the ways of ascent</u> to "the power of an endless life," Heb. 7:16 that we may "<u>grow up</u> into Allah in all things." Ep.4:15 <u>That</u> is **the *purpose*** of our lives ***now***, and ***the reason*** Allah Came 9000 miles to save us, to make of us: "the Corner Stone" or "the Ruler," "the Inheritor" of "the <u>New</u> Heaven" and "the <u>New</u> Earth." Hab.3:13; Ch15 "Believe it or not, this book is the Key to <u>the whole world of 'Man</u>." T. p.182p.1; p.183p.3; p.218 p.3

38 *We were* **"the Lost Sheep;" "a prey"** to **"the eagle:"** now, **for the wide awake mind,** <u>that time</u> is no more. **"*Take*" NS1: 7 *your place*** among those whom He has **"Found."** He is *re-forming - <u>with us</u> -* The Ancient God Tribe of Shabazz. **NS9: 1, 4; 14: 3 - 5, 8 - 14, 24 - 41; 17: 17, 18; Ch15**; review #7 above

39 Every student <u>*must*</u> *capture* **the spirit of <u>this</u> Truth** *for themselves*. NS8: 32 Each one of you must <u>acquire</u> *the superior wisdom, new knowledge* and *the **new** <u>self identity</u> - the new world and the new cosmic understanding -* that this study will provide:

a This is done by ***giving yourself to it*** *through <u>study</u>, <u>reflection</u>* and <u>*using*</u> *– or **practicing - what you learn.*** NS2:12 -18, 19; 4:7a; 5: 4; #28a - 37 above

b Don't allow yourself to be (mentally and emotionally) **"tossed about** *by every"* **new idea,** *("wind of* ***Doctrine")*** *or thing*, that "Satan" comes up with. NS11:7d

c Satan's desire is to *capture our mind* and *divert our attention* **away from** *morale* **reality** NS8: 9a, **thus** *changing, causing a* **deviation,** *in "the true nature"* **God Made us in,** Ep.4:14; Q4: 119; 30:30; #25a above leaving us with little or no **self control,** **emotionally** **reactive** *and* **living** **in** **fear** of one kind or another. NS8: 10; EL: 6

40 Allah has said to me: "I have set before you an **Open Door** (through M#4 NS5: 11, 15) and *no man* can shut it…" Rev.3:8; Intro: 12 This "NEW SONG" is *very near correct*; each student should read it, study its verses and practice its principles until your **inner peace**, your **Original Nature, is restored. See #25 above** *Then* you will be living naturally and being yourself Chapter 15 This is your Door to Heaven *while you live.* NS8: 29a; 10: 7A; 14: 2; PL: 1, 2; Lk6: 43, 44; Jn10: 37, 38

a **"Through knowledge** *shall* the just *be delivered."* Prov11:9 This Book has *your KEY* to Wisdom *and* Understanding Prov4: 7; P83: 34a; 172: 6f

b Allah Q37: 171, 182 also said, "Those whom I love, I Am **his hearing** with which he hears, **his seeing** with which he sees, and **his hand** through which he functions and **his foot** with which he walks. Were he to ask of Me, I would surely give it to him." Al-Bukhari; NS2: 4, 5; 4: 12; 8:21, 23; 11: 8-13; Expand your mind in Chapter 2; App VI c I say **to you - "students" -** <u>*I am*</u> *alive in The Day of Elijah* Iks 18:21 and I am anxious to work in The Cause of Allah. Which of you will be my helpers? Q61:14; NS14: 38a- 49

d Again: I am instructed ... to **"speak to 'you'** *a* **word to reach 'your' very souls"** *"with a Spirit from Allah Himself"* Q4:65; 16: 101; 9: 43; 21: 2, 10; 58:22; NS14: 2 and so, for some,

e Your **"vexation"** *may have* begun. For others your study has begun, it will be mentally and emotionally moving. This may take <u>*a few years*</u> [smile] NS12: 53

f During this time you are <u>compelled</u> to be *"fast moving, quick thinking and functioning right down to the modern time in order to be successful."* NS8: 33

This Message began in 1973 and continues today...

CHAPTER TWO
A Key to Understanding

1   Chapter Two is the **'key'** to what you <u>should know</u>, what you <u>need to know</u>, to **form your own mind** and **'create a body'** for your *new existence*. NS 4: 13 That may seem like a strange thought right now TLOT: 3, however, you will soon come to 'understand' it. Are you ready for some *deep water* <u>now</u>? If you are, **study:** NS11:6,7;12:40,41; 13: 16, 20; 15: 6f, h, if not, read on, your **"understanding"** will grow.

2   Once you **realize** that you are living in a **spiritual wilderness** and in a **moral wasteland** 1: 23a, b <u>these ideas</u> – tools – will constitute **the light** and **the building materials** <u>out of which</u>, and <u>through which</u>, you will manifest who and what you really are - **with** *and* **through** <u>*your new body*</u> of concepts, principles and ideas. Q3:10-139; NS1: 28-b; 4: 20, 23

3   You may have heard or know several names for God. We will give you an overall name and definition here, again, *in time*, this will all become clear. We will also broadly outline **how** you - and everyone - *were made* and how you may mentally and spiritually **remake** *yourself* while adding years to your life. Ch15

4   **"ALLAH"** is <u>the title</u> *held by* the **"**<u>Divine Supreme Being</u>;**"** meaning and representing **"*ABOVE ALL* and *IN ALL* and *THROUGH ALL.*"** Ep.4:6; Isa. 5: 16; NS8:17; T, p.178p.3; p.194p.1

5 "ALLAH" is **"the title"** _composed of_ (or housing) 99 NAMES – called Attributes – **describing** *God's Capacity, 'His' Ability* and *'His' Function* which is <u>best manifested</u> **"in," "through"** and *'from the human'* **"form:"** "a body had to be prepared for Him" to "work," _perform_ and "function" "through." PL: 7; App.VI: 4, 5; OSHA101: P5

6 **Developmentally:** all capacity, ability and functionality **evolves** through levels, grades or stages **- in time -** _from zero through 100 in degree_. Knowledge, strength, power, creativity and so on, are seen as **"Light"** _from the human form_.

7 **Understand:** <u>Existence</u>, "Allah," Q21:30 having no beginning nor ending **manifests human like Consciousness** **_in_ forms** and thereby **- through human like inner evolution and functionality - "He"** NS5: 4 controls mass and energy thus creating or maintaining nature's array of types in cyclical repetition, from galaxies to sub-atomic particles and energy waves. NS11: 7; Chapter 12; Q3:1, 3; 51:47

  a Darkness *is* Space, Earth, Mind and Womb out of which Light emerges / Forms take shape and are, **then**, _Manifested_ in Capacity, Ability and Function.

  b The **"Spirit"** or **"Word"** is **_The_** *Possessor* of Power and Force. **Existence:** Consciousness, Space and Time are **Eternal** and **Ever Present** for **your wish** <u>and</u> **desire to be expressed and or manifested through.** NS12:21, 24-42, 43; 14: 2-6a; MFM3333

  c Words are, or spirit is, *Created* or *Formed* from <u>elements</u> or <u>creation</u> (vibration or primordial matter in perpetual motion). NS1: 28b; Jn6: 63

d *"Thoughts"* are **Material** (unseen elements or) **Forms** <u>in a conscious human like mind</u> formulated from <u>intentionally</u> *connected vowels and consonants* – words, spirit or fuel - **to produce specific results, activation or creation.**

e **"Desire,"** produced from <u>Need</u> (internal and external causation) or from "<u>Identification,</u>" generally external in nature, **produces internal fuel or energy (*words or spirit*) for behavior or action.** See Chapters 9 and 13

f The *Manifestation* of thought (form or materialization) is <u>produced</u> from [unseen] "internal movement:" energy, desire, feeling and need. Thoughts or Forms *then* occupy or Reconfigure Space and <u>thus</u> **Produce** Time and *Provide* Operational Capacity and or Functionality in that which is **the new, changed or active.** Consider Chapter 16 around this concept

8 **How** do we *"Grow up...,"* or develop, as the Scripture says we must? Let's look at Identity and the <u>Formation</u> of *"Man."* ["Who are you?" they asked Jesus. "Who do *you* *say* I am?" was his reply, *measuring by my work*] Study Chapter 5; NS12: 44, 48; MFM36: 1170, 1227

9 **How** is <u>identity</u> formed in a "man" [**mind**]? App V One of the better ways to determine this is for the individual to ask himself a question: "<u>Who</u> / <u>What am I?</u>" and **evaluate** this answer. Since **all** *<u>things</u>* – the shaping and forming of all matter – **are the product of words (spoken or unspoken),** *your answer is*, "I am a product,

I am an expression, I am the result; I am the very <u>fruit</u> <u>of</u> **the ideas** that my mind is <u>attracted to</u> or <u>identifies</u> <u>with</u>." NS4: 20, 21; 12:9; 15: 6f

10 You should now *see* and *be thinking:* "The thoughts that **affect my feelings** <u>the most</u> begin to *manifest themselves* - **in time** NS8:22 - *through the agency of my flesh body* and that is <u>how</u> *I am identified or seen* as one kind of mind [person/consciousness] or another."

   a The Scriptures agree: <u>First</u> there is the "Word" – and "the Word *is* God," <u>meaning</u> the **controller of *your* mind and *your* flesh for <u>good</u> *or for* <u>ill</u>.** Q19:76

   b The "Word" **you *accept* or *act-upon*** is <u>the</u> <u>possessor</u> of positive, neutral *or* negative *power* and *force* over the intellectual, emotional and moving centers *in your body.* That "Word" if it is positive, also influences your instinctive and sex centers fostering your inner evolution. Intro: 4, 7; NS4: 20, 24; 11: 1, 9

11 That "Word," *any* "Word" [or set of ideas], that enters your mind, if it sits there – **finds a home there,** *and* <u>is</u> <u>fed</u> - it will, in time, **energize** your emotional center **through identification** NS13: 3 and you will <u>become</u> *a product, an executor, a living reflection* of those "words," ideas and or principles according to your focus, your intellectual development and your purposeful action. This ***straight path*** led Jesus to say, "I and my Father are One." TLOT and PL; NS1: 28-b; 8:21; 10: 7c; 11: 7d; 13: 15, 20; see # 1 above

12 Know here that <u>ideas that are</u> **fueled** by <u>emotion,</u> <u>feeling</u> or <u>desire</u> **shape** or **reshape** <u>our mind</u> **- our consciousness** NSI: 28-b **-** to **conform** to their dictate or nature. As long as we <u>identify</u> *with* **that thought**, <u>we</u> <u>will</u> **project** and **reflect** the <u>attitude</u> **and/or** <u>behavior</u> *in that thought.* See Intro: 11; NS8:22, 23a; review 10 and 11 above again

13 <u>Ask yourself</u> another question: **"Whose thoughts** have *I* identified with, God's or the devils?"** I ask you: *"<u>Do you know the difference</u>?"* If you answer, "Yes I do." Then I ask you: **"By** <u>what means</u> or <u>standard</u> T, p. 57, 2nd p do you know the difference? Did God give you a standard? If so, what is it? When, where and how did He give it to you? Have you identified **God** and **the devil's Voices ["Words"]** in Scripture <u>or</u> in your life?" If so, give us your insights. See XI: 11, 13; Ch 17; OSHA: 56P2

14 The Scripture teaches us that **"He (God)** <u>stood</u> **and** *measured* **the earth,"** NSI4: 46 <u>why did He do that</u>**;** what did He tell you were the results? Do **you** know who **you** <u>are</u>? Do you know **where** <u>you are</u>? What is **your real name**? What is **your language**? Did you receive a name of God or a **Holy Name** <u>from God</u>? NSI: 26a; 14: 6a If you did, <u>what is it? What is its meaning? Are you living it?</u> OSHA57P4

15 As you may see by now, there are many more questions that could be asked of you. These points, statements, comments, questions and Scripture are <u>the basis</u> for your future understanding of yourself, of God, the devil, time, place and much more. *Studying verses 7e and 10 through 12 can make you very wise.* App II: 10

16 I suggest that you consume **Chapter Two** regularly *as you would* ***food.*** Reflect within yourself here. How do you feel right now?

17 You may want to write out some of your thoughts, questions or ideas now. However, <u>most</u> *or* <u>all of your questions</u> will be answered by the time you finish reading, studying, discussing, living <u>*through*</u> and <u>*thinking about*</u> The New Song. NS1: 9, 10

18 Consider, as you read on, that this is - *in **effect*** - a conversation between **you** and ***your "Lord,"*** for the most part. **Soon you will become conscious of an <u>internal dialogue</u>.** Whatever you do <u>*after*</u> reading, studying, or discussion will constitute your response to **"Him"** and <u>*your answer*</u> to **"His"** Call, Guidance and Teaching. *Review the footnote to* TLOT: 2; NS9: 2a, 3

19 **Develop a good habit:** reading, study and reflection around <u>*your*</u> **"essence"** desire NS9: 1, 3, a minimum of an hour each day. Don't be afraid of something you didn't ***do*** or ***think*** yesterday, <u>open your mind to the new</u>. That is where you will find the **"God, Who <u>*makes all things new*</u>.** He leads the blind <u>*in*</u> and<u>*_by*</u> **a way** that <u>*they did not know*</u>.**"** NS14: 14 -19

 a *"**God**" is or means* **"The Possessor of Power and Force," or the "Truth of the Originator that *affects change* in the 'spiritually or mentally dead'"** *or* a **"Possessor of this Truth" or knowledge.** NS1: 21; 8: 22, 23a; 11: 12; 14: 31; 13: 19; Ps106: 36 (this is measurable by functional degree) Allah's **Throne** (Power and Authority) is *manifested* on, over and through water Q11: 7; 21: 11, App VI

20 *Rational Disciplined Conscious behavior* is the important point here. Consider #8, go back and reflect upon TLOT: 11. Devils *and* holders of **irrational** - ***morally powerless*** - **"faith," even when they have the capacity to do otherwise,** <u>allow</u> *and / or* <u>inflict</u> pain, suffering and / or death upon the weak, Intro: 4, 7; NS12:8; Prov3: 27 <u>including themselves</u>, e.g., through uncontrolled emotion, mental laziness, various controlling intoxicants, inappropriate eating, gambling, cunning, deceit and more. NSI: 27 All or most of them touting their faith or belief in God as they *unconsciously* or *mechanically* destroy themselves and others with the mistaken belief that God is still on their side.

21 If asked, **"What is your religion?"** or **"Are you a ...?"** Your Answer could include: "<u>What I believe</u> ***does not*** <u>left mysticism</u> (or *my* traditions, rituals, ideology or culture) above ***upright, rational, Conscience based, behavior.***" PL: 11, 13; TLOT: 11; NS4: 2; 8: 25

22 ***Say:*** "My faith *blends its* <u>Truth</u> and <u>Values</u> into my <u>*daily living*</u>, Intro: 5; NS12: 60 I am of those who submit" to Truth when it is presented to me. Intro: 10; NSI: 4; 5: 4-12; 12: 41

23 This "New Song" provides us with a developmental frame work for our personal evolution. Let's use it. Study it until you are ***motivated from within*** to build a "Self" that you and God can honor and be proud of.

CHAPTER THREE
Who Are We?

Rev. 7: 13, 17;App II: 10

---

1   We Are Among **The First** of The 144,000,Who Slept For Over 400 Years.

2   We are among *The First Fruits* UNTO GOD AND THE LAMB having God's KNOWLEDGE **FUNCTIONING** in our minds. "We sing, *AS IT WERE*, A **NEW SONG** before the Throne Q11:7, and before THE FOUR BEASTS, and THE ELDERS: and **NO MAN - MIND - COULD LEARN THIS SONG** but those of the 144,000 whom **WE ARE REDEEMING** from the Earth"Rev.14:3 through the POWER of GOD *IN* the WORDS, or "Language," of this "NEW SONG."NS11: 8; 15: 6, a

3   Our sickle has been thrust into the Earth NS14: 53c; 15:4 loosing the SEVEN ANGELS Q6:9 with **the last PLAGUES** for THE MODERN WORLD MADE OF STEEL, CONCRETE and GLASS - fueled by OIL.

4   'We the first of the formally dead, 144,000, *DO NOT* know the **HOUR of FINAL JUDGMENT.** We just continue to sing-**TEACH - the SONG OF MOSES THE SERVANT OF GOD and THE SONG OF THE LAMB.** We **DO KNOW** how great and marvelous the HOLY ONE'S WORKS ARE, we are products of His Thoughts. HE IS OUR KING. *HE IS* **THE ONLY HOLY ONE.**' Which of you will lend "Him" a beautiful loan?
R14: 3; 15:1, 4; IIThes.2; 8, 9; Q74:17; NS2: 11, 12

5   The Day approaches that **EVERYONE** will desire to hide from the **FACE OF THE MOST HIGH** Who Sits on the THRONE OF UNIVERSAL POWER and from the WRATH OF THE LAMB. Woe to those upon whom this STONE falls. Who will be able to stand in **HIS TIME**?
R6:16; Lk19: 27

6   We have worked day and night to remain **"THE APPLE OF HIS EYE"** Zec.2: 8 We work in and under THE POWER of HIS WISDOM. We continue to raise the dead with **THE "NEW SONG"** revealed to us, **DEMONSTRATING** that "GOD is with us;" and that Elijah came and his Wisdom is restoring our original nature. NS8: 23a; 15: 8; Mat17:11; Q9: 105

7   *We have seen HIS FACE and we are working day and night to remain Awake* Prov6: 9 *and thus* MANIFEST HIS LIKENESS while growing up into *HIM* in all things. Ep4:15; 16:8 The Honorable Elijah Muhammad said: "You are the righteous, the best and the most powerful." Q3:110-113 Looking at his future, Jacob or rather…

8   Yakub (Jacob) saw a "Ladder" that *did* **not** *belong to him* - The New Song – reaching out *from* Heaven *to* the Earth and he saw the Angels descending and ascending on and through it. These Angels are **our people** connecting **through the language and understanding of The New Song** up the Ladder of Time and Divine Teaching and returning to share their new capacity with our people.

9   Above, Yakub is describing the *reconnecting, "binding back"* or *"ascending" of you and me* with **the God of**

righteous people who are called Angels in scriptures.
T, p.159; Please review the Appendix, all of them. **Yakub** *means* "trickster" or "deceiver" see, NS12: 1, 4

10 Yakub saw us **connecting through this pure language** with our original righteous <u>reformulated</u> **inner** "self" and later with like-minded people, Angels, on the Earth. He saw himself <u>internally defeated</u> within our mind and spirit **through our willing inner evolution back to Original.** Q8: 30 The Angels of the Earth and his enemies will determine the quality of Yakub's physical existence after this.

11 About Heaven: **"**<u>*The Bridegroom*</u> is here,**"** the parable says, **"come out and meet him,** don't be like the foolish virgins who, because the Judgment tarried, didn't have any <u>*oil*</u> and **let** their lamps die out**"** or like those who <u>*would not leave*</u> Babylon when Elijah declared her to be **the home of devils.** T, p. 163; Mt. 25: 6; R18: 4; NS1: 7-10; 5: 20

12 About "Elijah" [meaning 'God is with us T, p.183p.1'], **Allah said to Moses**: **"**I will raise them NS8: 19, a, b up a Prophet from among their brothers like unto Thee and I will put *My Words in His mouth; and He shall speak unto them all that I shall Command Him.* And *it shall come to pass,* that whosoever will <u>not listen</u> to Him <u>or hear</u> My Words which **He shall speak in My name**, I shall require **it** (submission) of him, if he wants to live Deut. 18:18, 19. This message, idea and understanding, flows **throughout** "the volume of (all) the (Scriptural) Book(s)."

13 This New Song is MFM3919 the **Foundation Stone** of our **new "self," our new mind, <u>our new life</u>,** treat it as such.

NS14: 47 **Elijah said: "Misunderstanding is the hell of man."** T, p.167, 4th p, NS8: 10; 12: 9 Ask *all of your questions* about "self" **NS13: 15, 20** development so that you *do not misunderstand* your potential. Know that this book is the **Key to the Bottomless Pit:** *unfulfilled hopes, dreams* and *aspirations. Everything starts with you.* Go back and Re-read the **Introduction** carefully. NS 5: 21, 23 Understand here:

14 Allah did not *physically stay* among us since July 4, 1930 NS1: 31; 12: 26, 2714: 2, 3, He **proves His Truth** by raising up *from among us* One like Himself, Q84: 6 **One having the same ideas** and **speaking in the same Voice.** T, 216/2; 225/3; NS14: 6-31-39; 15: 1-11 The Originator that Created the Heavens and the Earth did not live forever. However, the Flame which was ignited then *exists in us today* enabling us to ignite creation anew when **"Our Flame" is focused** and *pure.* NS5: 18, 22; 8: 21, 23; 15: 12; App VI "Let there be light." PL: 13-1; NS10: 7, A, B, C; T, p. 199/1

15 The Sun is *a symbol* of the Work of God. Today we Calculate Time from the Work of the Sun, it is a Divine Life Force for us we extract our life from it. The Sun is so powerful that it makes everything in its Circle of Influence Move. T, p.27p.3

16 Allah said we are descendents of The Tribe of *Shabazz* - **'L Sh'b'zz - "A Mighty and Glorious People!"** The New Song is our *"Way"* back to our *"Source,"* as the Original People Who came with this part of the planet Earth over 66 Trillion years ago. See NS Chapter 9 – 15 and 17

17 We who follow **Elijah** out of mental, emotional and spiritual darkness must *know* our *"self"* as an *Original*

NS1: 8; 17: 5, 10 or we will not escape the Fire of Hell. NS8: 10 We must also learn the *nature of* – *that is* **the law of** - *life* to become Masters in the new world that is being built. OSHA: 44P2; NS17: 8

18 Like **the evolution** of the caterpillar into a butterfly and the worker bee into a queen, **the inner evolution of our people** through **three distinct phases** of inner evolution and development is characterized by the expansion of inner Power, Force and Will as manifested by their enhanced knowledge, influence and authority within the Universal Order NS4: 12 **producing within them** the New *"Man:"* Quranically - on the heights, Levels: **5, 6** and **7.** NS5: 2D; Q7: 46, 49; 58: 11

19 Know that you cannot develop a solution to or for something you know nothing about Q34: 49 *nor* can you change what you cannot measure - For example, "Lend Allah a beautiful loan," #4 above, meaning **give up** your capacity (given to you by God) to choose a negative course or action in life, consequently accepting Truth, Right conduct and a proper attitude in your daily affairs. Let go and gain Paradise. NS8: 32

20 Save *your life* before the destruction is to widespread to think through the change of worlds. **"God is making all things new."** NS2: 19; 5: 2D; 14: 19; T, p.27.p3

[THE TABERNACLE OF GOD IS WITH MEN. REV. 21:3]
"HE THAT OVERCOMES SHALL INHERIT ALL THINGS. I WILL BE HIS GOD AND HE SHALL BE MY SON." R21:7; **STUDY 21 AND 22 See St. Lk. 16th Chapter on the role of the "Steward."**
T, p27p2, 3

CHAPTER FOUR
Inner Evolution

1   **Knowledge begins** with the *Universal Order of things* and <u>our relationship to it</u>. This knowledge includes *The Eternal which is* **Existence:** Consciousness, Space, Time; including all elements, sound and your present *position* and *condition* in life. Review PL: 7, 8; EL: 16 and Chapter 2; T, p25p3 Here are <u>the roots of everything</u>.

2   *The first requirement to learn* is a <u>willingness</u> to *escape the effects*, get out, of **"the Law of Accident,"** NS5:5a; 11:7a e.g., where you were born, the negative side of your culture, social norms or peer pressure, and unchanging religious ideas (when conditions have changed. **The manifestation** of *"Essence"* <u>depends on</u> **conditions**: consider the different states of *"water."*)

   a   So than the *ability to "hear"* and "a *desire to escape"* is <u>the basis for learning</u> *and* "<u>understanding</u>" on *this plane.* Note here that a person doesn't desire to escape from a place where they see no danger, or they are frozen in fear. Nor can they navigate if they are blind, deaf or dumb, without a guide.

   b   **<u>The force</u>** that <u>*stops*</u> or <u>*diverts*</u> your capacity to **'reason'** and <u>*stops*</u> or <u>*diverts*</u> clear **'emotional behavior'** also stops your happiness; stops your 'peace of mind and your emotional contentment'. PL: 1; NS7: E

3   **"The New Song,"** our study of Scriptures, principles, diagrams, laws, and what **Elijah** taught us, will give us <u>a new world view</u>, new reference points, and a new mind; <u>actually</u> *a "new life" and a "new Consciousness" with new ideas.*

> a   In this world there are <u>no concepts </u>or <u>ideas</u> of a negative nature: 'political,' 'social' or 'personal' (fear, grief, anxiety, anger, etc.). <u>Recognition</u> and <u>submission</u> to **Truth** <u>produces</u> Peace of mind and emotional contentment! Q3:60

> b   Number #3 above is **the Standard Way, Method or Path** to <u>bind back</u> that *upright nature* which has been broken *in us* by Satan. Q30:29, 30; Ecc7:29; NS8: 9a-13; 10: 7a; 14:2

4   Our model of the universe is not only theoretical, it is *very practical*. It will help your **understanding** to grow and *it will create within you* a <u>firm</u> **basis** for your personal growth and **conscious evolution.**

> *a*   <u>Truth</u> will always mirror <u>reality,</u> moral *and* material **reality,** or you have an <u>illusion.</u>

5   Our "Ray of Creation" is **a system of elimination,** <u>of simplification</u> – it does away with all knowledge that is <u>not</u> or has no relation to you and can't be understood <u>practically</u> by you. ***Illusions*** PL: 1; 5:2A-4B always produces <u>harmful</u> <u>end results.</u> (Starting out sweet to the lips then turning bitter in function) Q7:179; 25:43, 44; NS11: 14d

6   Learning the **fundamental laws of the universe** is necessary, without It *we cannot* **know God, higher Mind** *or any* **"Objective" thing.** PL: 8 **We cannot know ourselves**. Q21: 30; 25:61, 62 *This knowledge will keep our thoughts in the right channels and help us to get results from our* **efforts** *thus helping us in our practice of* **"self-remembering"** *and* **actually being** *who we say we are, or want to be.* Chapter 2; PL: 13

7   **"The New Song"** will <u>**enable**</u> you to love and **"<u>accept</u> your own original people and <u>be</u> yourself,"** *rather than an imitation Caucasian - <u>serving idols</u> and <u>sacrificing your children</u> to* Devils Ps.106: 36, 37; EL: 6, *as well as provide you with the spiritual power to* **"<u>sit yourself</u> in heaven at once."** NS2: 20; 8:32; Q7: 46, 48

    a   **Heaven is <u>not</u> <u>a place</u>, heaven is an <u>inner</u> <u>state</u> <u>of being</u>** NS5: 4; EL: 7; T. p.214p. 1 **– "existence as"** NS5: 4a – a **condition** <u>promised</u> to those who accept Allah [as <u>demonstrated</u> by the power of your *function* and *deeds*]. This is what **"the Son of Man"** traveled <u>9000 miles</u> to accomplish among His 'elect.' See, 1 and 2 above; NS9: 21

8   Reviewing this period - **after** 400 years NS12: 15 *and* "joining ourselves to a citizen of this country" Lk15: 15 *while* in <u>spiritual</u>, <u>mental</u>, and <u>physical</u> *captivity* **- Isaiah** said that some of the former ('*home grown*') slaves would **see this message**, *The New Song*, as a mental and emotional **"vexation"** *because today they see themselves as free.* Q2:78 However, **'Jesus'** and '**Allah**' see this Message as **"Good News."** We will know what you think – or believe - shortly. Q6:48; Intro: 17; NS8: 9, 210; EL: 6

9 **Understand here:** "Allah does not love those given to perfidy and crime." *Satan has made* <u>criminal behavior,</u> following him, *credible* in some of our minds. Q4:104-37; 5:65; Ref: 5, 7

10 Know too that **Satan's plan** is to <u>excite</u> enmity, envy and greed among us through intoxicants, gambling and our **unchecked appetites** for what he, also known as **Magog**, has or the things he has made. Q5:94; 6:119; NS8: 13; 12: 15; 14: 25; EL: 6; Hab.2: 5, 8

  a **Avoid their trick,** when they use terms like <u>mankind,</u> <u>human,</u> <u>we,</u> <u>us</u> and <u>our,</u> *translate it to mean* **"Teutons"** and **"Anglo-Saxons,"** historically **"Gog** and **Magog."** *<u>Originals are not that.</u>* If some how you are not sure, review how they and their cousins have treated originals around the world in the last **4000** years and the former slave for the last **458** years.

  b If you say, **"Things are changing today."** Ask yourself, **"Why? What do they know that I don't know?"** See NS14: 4a

  c **Gog and Magog** are the traditional guardians of Guildhall in the City of London to this day.

11 "We have sent Messengers too many nations before you **– the former slaves,** NS9: 14 **to whom <u>no Warner</u> has come** <u>before</u> **Elijah,** Q32:3 **-** We afflicted those nations with *suffering* and *adversity*, that they may learn *humility*; and <u>some We destroyed.</u>" Q6:42; NS8: 20a; 12:15; 14:25

12 *For those who* NS17: 13 *"meet" and "grow up into Him:"* He has **subjected to you** - <u>as from Himself</u> -

all that is in the heavens and on earth. Behold, *in that are Signs indeed for those who reflect.* Tell those who believe, to forgive those who do not look forward to **the Days of Allah (God)**: He will reward everyone according to what they have <u>earned</u> (good or ill). Q45:13, 14; see, Intro: 5, 7; NS14: 2-55; Ps110:1; App VI **We "sit at His right hand."**

13 Knowing NS14:14-18, c, and living **through our nature** will allow **"<u>us</u>"** (our consciousness and energy) to shape a **"self'** or a **"person"** within <u>our flesh</u> that *reflects the image we have in our mind, positive or negative.* NS2: 1; 5: 2; 13: 10, 23; 14: 26; EL: 13

14 In the bigger picture, NS8:21, 23a **We may produce as a father, a mother, a family or <u>as a School</u>:** a "<u>Student</u>," an "<u>Heir</u>," or a "<u>Son</u>;" A Person who is "Able" **to overcome** *a future problem,* **realize** a plan or a written goal or to **materialize** <u>prophesy</u> as it was written NS5: 8; 8:23a

    a "A body had to be prepared for him," Heb 10:5, NS12: 26 is how the Scripture describes **the making** of "The Son of Man:" **a body of** NS2:10, **knowledge** taught, <u>in our case</u>, to *a conscious <u>upright mind</u> born to resurrect the mentally "dead"* in America. NS12: 26, 27a

    b **This process** describes <u>the making of both</u> the righteous and the wicked. The <u>quality of the body</u> or <u>the materials</u> *out of which* or <u>*in which*</u> or <u>*through which*</u> a thing is made **determines its nature and functionality.** NS8:26, a; 12: 20a; Prov20: 11

c Notice **"*The Sons* of God"** NS8:16-22, mentioned in Job 1 and elsewhere, I won't belabor that point here. NS1: 28, a, b; 14: 23-39-43, 47

15 To make or remake our "self," or begin, *we must be aware of our origin, our nature,* <u>and</u> *its significance;* **the quality** of our communication; **the nature of our behavior** which demonstrates <u>the level</u> of **our inner culture;** all of this will be expressive of **our judgment** *which can be* <u>seen</u> *and* <u>objectively measured</u> Intro: 4, 7

16 Our behavioral characteristics NS15:7, 12, will tell any <u>wise person</u> who we are **by nature (negative, neutral or positive [-- 0 +]** 14b) however, know that <u>the world we know</u> – made by Satan, NS8: 14, 15; 14: 25 - <u>is not</u> populated with spiritually wise or righteous and upright people NS5: 16; 13: 28, 32 that is the reason for the **"*making*"** and <u>coming</u> of The Son of Man to save His "lost" people who don't know that they are His people nor that they are "lost" from Him. NS2: 20; 12: 4, 5-9

17 Our **Foundation** NS3: 13; MFM4102 and **Framework** for <u>building</u> <u>a new world</u> and <u>maintaining</u> <u>Freedom</u> is "The New Song." Our Judges and Scientists will be involved in all aspects of our life while helping everyone to maximize their **inner potential** for growth. Our **organic nature** is there for us to **evolve** or "grow-up" <u>through</u>, and **into** "Him," see #12 above, the powers of Allah: Hearing, Seeing, kinetic-energy; and power over gravity, water, winds and other universal forces that are not easily described Ps 92; T, p.68, 69, <u>when</u> and <u>as</u> "He" Pleases. See Chapter 2 and 5; MFM4100

18 REFLECT ON DEVELOPING OUR HUMAN POTENTIAL App V

1 "By *the evidence* of our Time,

2 Surely *automated man* NS Chapter 5 *is* internally at **"loss,"** *the fact* of not having or *'being able'* to use *personal inner power* NS2: 20; 8: 9a -14; 15: 8.

3 Except, those who **evolve *and* DO...."** NS14:55c1, 3

19 Below are *the results of Time* as we meet *it* or *them*. NS5:10; 8: 22 **[CNO]**

1 TIME	MIND	BRAIN	EFFECT	NO EFFECT
3 CREATION	GOD	TARGET	PERSONALITY	BEING
2 Everything	ALL	Builds according to input	Seen	Source of Time
Activity	UNSEEN	Habits	Influence	Original
Input	-- 0 +	Senses	Results	Knowledge
----------	CREATOR	Conscience	Power	Will
Conscious		Self– remembering		Individual
Habitual		Mechanical		
Emotional		Neurological **inner construction** that Shapes **the**		
- 0 +		**brain, the body** and **the world** To its ability		
		capacity through words, Feelings and experiences. You		
		become **a reflection** of your input. [see 22 below]		

20 **Our vocabulary**, *our language*, **shapes our thoughts** and **determines** *what we see*; EL: 18e, language and vocabulary clarify **why** and **how** we "understand" *the way* we do. NS2: 10b; 13: 23-27; 15: 4, 5; Mt15: 8-13-24; OSHA124: P 2, 3

21 **Volitionally Changing Our Vocabulary - Words -** NS 13: 23; 14: 18 *changes the "Essence," the vibrations, the elements* or *the fuel* that our mind [The Thrown of Power, AppVI: 2] is using and processing to **build new neurons** in our brain and spinal cord. MFM3380

22 Our **new thoughts** and **needs** change our internal environment Ch 16, while changing our neurological brain and other cellular structures and *then* (over time) change our body's configuration via **new** and **higher quality** inner vibrations which arise from our new spiritual, mental, and emotional concepts, our new words and ideas. XVIII: 1; 8: 33

23 The New Song's concepts are the food of the 'God', NS1: 6; these concepts *change our behavior* and produce **Internal construction** through internally structured water - including *sperm* or *ovum*, NS2: 7; 17: 21. **Through** this **internal building process**, which takes years, our individual capacity to function is enhanced. App VI: 4; review 1: 6

24 In time, **the ripple effect** of **our overall change** touches the world around us and, depending on *the purity and the quality of our inner light*, spreads afar. NS1:28-a, b; 8: 21, 23a; 10: 7A; 12: 17-58; 14: 18c-35

CHAPTER FIVE
The Developmental Function of "Man"

The Function of 'Man' Jer31:33

1   Ordinary - undeveloped - 'Man' functions as **a machine**, his **"work,"** or purpose, NS9: 3 is to **"wake up"** and _learn how to_ **"stay awake"** (One of the Scientists asked, concerning us: "How long will you sleep, O sluggard? When will you arise?" Prov6:9; NS9: 9, 11; OSHA81: P 3

2   The human mind has four states of consciousness:

   A - Sleep State – subjective dream state [Illusions, automated, affected] NS11: 8, 9-14d
   B - Waking state – objective dream state ['yes' and 'no' through education] NS5: 10B4b, d-14; 11: 14
   C - Self Consciousness [inner freedom through inner evolution, Man #4; #5]
   D - Higher Consciousness [unaffected, on the Heights Q7:46, 49; 58:11; NS4:19 -1]

Knowledge and Being

3   **Knowledge:** Analytical (or any other) knowledge is not necessarily cosmically _effective_ knowledge. Knowledge is often like an _appendage_, like a donkey _carrying books_. When your knowledge does not agree with your **"being"** (when it is higher or lower than what you **internally exist as**) it does not produce _personal action from you_;

41

often that knowledge (or idea) **blocks** personal action. You know but cannot do, or you can do but don't know what to do. NS4: 6-13, 14b; 15: 5

4 **"Being,"** NS12: 42b _the Presence of it_ PL 8, is seen or experienced mentally, emotionally and / or physically **by the action or functionality** of its possessor. This state, or **inner reality**, is arrived at through _self discovery_ and _verifying truth_ and _ideas - outer reality - with your inner experience and capacity_.

   a **"Being"** or **"Consciousness"** is **"_Existence As_"** Intro: 11 _or **"Being One" with**_ the _idea_ or _personality_ NS1: 40; 12:22-43a; 14: 2-6 that you are **identified with,** or **attracted to even before being fully able to materialize its capacity or functionality within your "flesh-self," or being certified as "it."**

   b The unbalanced idea or personality leads to _illusion_ and _perversion:_ internal split. see #2A above

   c Inner Balance leads to Health, Beauty and Beneficial decisions or one purpose, thus producing more than is received (as in the fusion process of the sun). Chapters 2; 13

Personality and Power

5 **Personality (acquired from your _knowledge_ and _experience_) is equal to your Power:** What we see from ordinary people is Personality or Power, the two _measurable_ sides of that person. Power is the **external ramifications** _of their personality. Personality_

42

*is **their inner side, or their mask.*** This side contains **the spirituality** or **the psychological basis** <u>of that</u> <u>person's mind.</u> NS4:20; App V. **How** they grew up, **where** they were educated, trained and so on. **What** they have an affinity for. Weigh them here.

    a <u>Personality</u> is the **temporary, made**, or a person's **current 'self'** formed from ***desire*** and ***accumulated cultural input, <u>their</u> <u>use</u> <u>of</u> <u>knowledge</u>*** - what they were '<u>attracted</u>' to - which <u>produces their world of</u> <u>objects and or 'illusions.'</u> NS12: 15; 17: 14; App V Here *they become victims* of the "<u>Law of Accident</u>" NS4: 2 if they don't volitionally evolve. Each person must destroy the ***blockage*** to their own 'Individuality' or their "True Self" otherwise **that person will not become conscious of a made "self"** within their flesh. Intro: 10, 16; 4: 12, 16; Chapter 2

6   The 'mask' of personality is **the target** for ***"Self" Development or Inner Evolution.* However, the personality or 'inner made self'** must <u>*want*</u> or <u>*seek*</u> 'intercession' or *change it cannot be imposed on them.* NS2:9, 12; 14: 19a, b; 13: 15, 23; TLOT: 3; See # 5 above

7   **"Self"** - development <u>cannot</u> be achieved or acquired by, or through, ***"automation"*** nor through nature. Change must at least <u>*start out*</u> consciously, <u>but</u> if and <u>*when*</u> mysticism, tradition and or rituals enter the mind those ideas <u>reduce</u> and <u>eventually</u> **stop the accumulation** of <u>*new knowledge*</u>. **Those beliefs** and **practices** eventually ***destroy*** the human <u>innate capacity</u> to create or accept new ideas, process and accumulate new knowledge and put us to – or, back to - sleep or into machine like

automation (some machines are "smarter" than others). NS12: 9

8   **Individuality** is *the infinite conscious property of "Being."* "True Self" is *Able* to *think* or *imagine* a thing **into existence**. NS12: 41 **"His"** PL: 8 Action is expressed as *"Will,"* not desire. Individuality, Consciousness, Will, Being and True Self are all synonymous properties of "Allah" <u>not</u> of undeveloped "man." NS12: 41-10; T, p184, 3rd p; 186, 3rd p

9   **Discuss what A-B- & C Influences are.**

10 **Discuss how A- B- & C Influences Develop** *Personality & Being*

A   **BEING (Cosmically oriented functionality: "In the (devil's) world but not of it".)** see #15 below

---

3% +/- of the people have **outstanding success!**

5 Accept responsibility

4 Compounded effect over time **.01**

3 No noticeable difference immediately

2 Uncomfortable

1 Simple Disciplines

---

* LIFE LINE → *Being*

---

* LIFE LINE → *Personality*

---

1 Simple error in Judgment

2 Comfortable

3 No noticeable difference immediately

4 Compounded effect over time .01

5 Not teachable

97% +/- of the people "fit in", "blame others" *and are not successful! #7 above*

B PERSONALITY (National, Societal, Tribal, or Group oriented mentality and functionality)

1. The **example,** or <u>measuring standard,</u> given is the use of '**.01,**' **a penny,** which Represents **the compounded effect of a person's [1] knowledge, [2] over-all development and [3] 'behavior,'** as seen through <u>the growth</u> of **a penny - doubled daily -** over 30 days for the penny (or a life time for a developing mind).

2. Follow this <u>*same process*</u> over 30 years (or a life time) for **a person's growth, evolution** or **development,** [1] spiritually, [2] mentally, [3] emotionally and or [4] physically.

3. **Measure the effect** <u>they have</u> on their society, their group, their tribe or nation for '**good** or **for ill.'**

4. Now <u>you may provide</u> and *extrapolate* the **metaphorical meaning** for these numbers as you **evaluate meaning** <u>*looking at yourself*</u>, than meaning

for other individuals, groups and nations. You may be surprised at what you "see."

a *The cold reptilian nature* and *the hot animal nature* are all _conscienceless_ and NS11: 7d, Ref: 3, 5, Satanic; Devilish when found in *a "_human_" _form_.* The mental and emotional characteristics in those animal forms were intended to be manifested <u>in</u> and <u>through</u> *those animal forms, not a "human" form.*

b When a "human" form _does not_ develop its **upright potential** "above" and "below" Jn. 8: 23 with balance, e.g., [1] Evolve through education and or training into a "human" - <u>conscience</u> <u>possessing</u> - "being;" and [2] "Grow up into God" as outlined in this "NEW SONG," they become "<u>opposite to</u>" or "<u>anti</u>," *in practice*, NS2: 20 what the Upright God is.

c Having consciousness, they become **an opponent**, a disbeliever, a misbeliever, or a hypocrite to their professed faith. Their personal "power" is then manifested through their desires, education, or level of development causing distress in the environment.

d They are then *disguised as "human" "beings"* however **they are reptilian, animal, Devil or Satanic "beings"** _in nature_. Especially their educated ones, they are capable of *great deceit, hate and violence.* Review their _historical behavior_ since Moses _released them_ from the caves 4000 years ago.

e Caucasians as a group, with a few exceptions, exemplify the **"Anti-Christ" or people whose behavior is opposite of morally upright.** NS12: 1, 2a-34-42, 46-51, 56; 14:6-26, 28; Chapter 6. **Evaluate how they react to this insight.**

f Through their laws, governing practices and greed, they "make mischief and shed blood" worldwide; and through their politics they produce fraud, deceit and war while playing the peace maker with clean hands. NS12: 19

1 .01 Idea, Attraction, ID	16 327.68
	17 655.36
2 .02	18 1,310.72
3 .04	19 2,621.44
4 .08	20 5,242.88
5 .16	21 10,485.76
6 .32	22 20,971.52
7 .64	23 41,943.04
8 1.28	24 83,886.08
9 2.56	25 167,772.16
10 5.12	26 335,544.32
11 10.24	27 671,088.64
12 20.48	28 1,342,177.28

13 40.96	29 2, 684, 354.56
14 81.92	30 5, 368, 709.12
15 163.84	Final maturity

11 Evaluate Human Inner Evolution Ch 4 as seen from **Man Number Seven** *through* **Man Number One** in the form of a **numerical metaphor** of Self Development, School Work, or the "Making of a Body [through "Self NS13:16, 19 –30 Remembering"]" to perform the work a person has designed for themselves, or Parents and or Schools have designed for their Students. NS4: 13-14b; 14: 43, 44, 45; 16: 17; TLOT: 2

12 An **Internal Body of Conscience** ["B influences"] must be developed in Man Numbers One, Two and Three. NS12; 41 This "Body" will serve as the foundation for that mind's growth. This "Body" must grow a predictive behavioral capacity **past 60** % or Man Number Four will not be able to develop within and from him.

   a Inner Development **past 70%** must take place NS14: 34 in Man Number Four, processing H24, or Man Number Five *cannot begin* to attract or crystallize Hydrogen 12. NS 12: 44 All of this activity takes place *in*, *on* and *through* water. App VI

13 Man Numbers One, Two and Three, ["The Carriage" NS12: 13], may have anywhere between **0 and 50%,** *or more*, predictive behavioral capacity, or Conscience NS12:55, however **50%** is **not enough** to be a part of the **Inner Circle or World.** PL: 10; NS9: 17, 19 **50%** is not enough

to cause a *positive "Spiritual" ripple effect* NS15:6h *or to radiate "Spiritual" behavioral or environmental change.* NS12: 34

   a On the other hand, **concentrated feeling or conscience** from them in some **moment of crisis** or an **inordinate situation** may enable them to unconsciously be the conduit for the "Spirit" from Man **"4 or 5,"** if they know one, to be displayed through them in a given situation. See NS2:7e; 11: 12; if 50% does produce change, it will be rooted in need, fear, desire or "identification" with an intercessor.

14 **"C Influences"** represent the Inner Circle of Humanity. Their "Highest" or **"Causal Body"** functions through Cosmic Consciousness, Will, Permanent **"I"** [Unaffected]; Higher Consciousness; and Self Consciousness. NS5: 8; 8: 21, 24; 9: 9, 10; 11: 13; 14: 2-38a-55 **"I am (My Mind is) not of** this **(Devil made) world"** Jn.8: 23, Jesus said.

15 Man Number 7, 6, 5 and 4 are the "Over Comers" *They are in this world, but They are "not of this world."* NS8: 32; 9: 7abc; 11: 15; 14:2-55; PL: 8; App VI; Ch 6; Q8: 4; Jesus would say, "You are from below, but I am from above."

1 2 3 4 5 6 **7#7Causal Body [Unaffected-Inside out] NS12: 11-16-53, 54**
  1 2 3 4 5 6 7**#6 Higher Mental Body**
    1 2 3 4 5 6 7**#5 Higher Emotional Body NS12: 55**
      1 2 3 4 5 6 7**#4 Submissive Body (or fake "Man" #4: Dajjal)**
        1 2 3 4 5 6 7**#3 Mental Body**
          1 2 3 4 5 6 7**#2 Emotional Body**
            1 2 3 4 5 6 7**#1 Physical Body [Outside in] NS14: 50; 15: 6b-f**

16 An open mind is needed here **reflect** on The New Song and your own life. Do not remain _spiritually_ where you are. Intro: 7; PL: 4; NS12: 42ab, 43a; 16: 2, 3

  a Seeing Through the spiritual metaphor: **_"The right eye of this world_** - which would represent The Inner Circle of Humanity or Man Numbers **4** through **7**, or "Heaven" in our world – **_is blind."_** NS12:39a, 48; EL: 11c

  b **_The Caucasian world has blurred vision_**, see 13 above, they function essentially with one eye, **"the left eye,"** representing man numbers 1 through their fake "man" #4, called **"Dajjal," by Prophet Muhammad,** meaning one given to "fraud" and "deceit," Al-Bukhari 77: 68, 93: 27; NS12:2a. Their civilization, historically, is called **Gog** and **Magog** in both the Bible and Quran; his left eye is **"bright like a shining star"** [representing **their mastery of the physical world** NS1: 23-32; 8: 17, 18; 12: 3; 14: 1].

  c **"The Caucasians left eye"** represents their world of materialism in _all_ of its _ramifications_. In their world **_morality and right conduct takes second place to profit or personal gain and advancement_**. This can easily be seen today.

17 God and morality, for most Caucasians, is something to talk about, deceive others about NS12: 2, 3, not something for them to actually **live by** or **do.** For most Caucasians God and morality has very little practical effect when dealing with original people. NS14: 47 **With no knowledge of our own, we generally follow in their footsteps.** NS8: 8b; 12: 15-39a; 17: 14

18 **"God,"** NS2: 10; 8: 21, 23 like any *doctor* or *lawyer*, is *a "title"* representing **our** mental, emotional and **or** moral *inner evolution* and or *social accomplishment*, arrived at by **our** specific actions in time. See #7 above

    a <u>We have calculated</u> from the number "One," as Elijah taught us, MFM3360 The Original Upright Nature and Mind of Allah NS14: 19, a, b "Himself" NS2: 4, 5 <u>as our starting point</u> T, p.121 **in the making of "a new mind"** NS12: 9 thereby we have *awakened from the dead.* NS3: 19

19 Through our *new mind* and *consciousness* NS9: 4 we have developed **a new method** an alignment of Divine concepts and principles through an instrument, this '<u>little book</u>,' to foster "the resurrection" or make the dead PL: 3, 5 wake up <u>in our upright path</u>. NS 12: 74; 13: 8 "A class of (new) rulers must be *prepared,* Elijah said, to rule the people." "We are the ones." T, p. 27p2, 3; p65p4;NS2: 19; PL: 13,

20 The New Song is <u>our</u> <u>evidence</u>, NS1: 7-10 our *"proof of life,"* it is a product evolved by specific actions over my 50 years of work (added to our trillions of years; NS15:4, 5, 6c; Prov8: 22, 36)**:** weigh it, evaluate it, measure it, *live by it* and <u>experience</u> *the natural life* of The Number "One," the <u>first consciousness</u> in existence **T, p. 56, 1ˢᵗ p** – The One that formed the "Original Nature of Man" – experience it as it arises *in, through* and *from* <u>your own</u> biological *"self"* NS13: 16, 20 <u>in our life time</u>. App VI; NS14: 48, 49; Q16: 101

21 The Original Spark of Life Created Its' "Self" out of an atom of water in the total triple darkness of space, how long it took that Original Spark of Life to produce a

form, or make one atom for Its' "Self," we cannot know precisely. NS3: 13, 15

   a However, Elijah said: <u>That</u> **Original "Mind"** or **"Consciousness"** laid a base for a wise "God" - They didn't use that term - to arise NS3: 19 and produce a platform out of the **"First One's"** <u>Work</u> of **"Self-Creating,"** Q4: 1; 39: 6; NS7: L for "His" and Our future. This <u>innate process</u> has been in use for over **66 trillion years** among the Wise Originals. T, p. 60, 1st p; p. 96, 2nd p; R14: 3; App V; VI; NS8: 14a-23; TLOT: 18a; review Chapter 15

22 With this "New Song" we have produced such "a *platform,*" PL: 1 <u>through it</u> *we can strive hard* - <u>with a method</u> - *to become a "God"* **over** *our own "self."* T, p74, 3rd p; p. 80, 2nd p; NS2: 8, 12; 3: 19; 8: 21, 23; 13: 16, 21; 15: 8; EL: 16; Q2: 129; 32: 3; PL: 13

23 Can you <u>master the mission</u> – "the conquest of (your) self" - outlined in this New Song NS1: 7b that I give you from The Originator? T, p. 68, 70; NS9: 1, 2

   b Do you want to remain **the slave of a smart man** rather than **be the smart man yourself?** T, p.71, 3rd p Talk to me, I'm your brother and I'm listening, I can hear you. Intro: 15, 18

24 The Spirit of Elijah, "will need scientists, builders and wreckers" just as He did, and much more.

   c All that is needed to wake-up the dead is <u>guidance</u> and <u>direction</u> you have it in this New Song. T, 222/2 **This Wisdom was kept as a secret among**

our people before the making of "The Son of Man" and His raising of Elijah. NS3:12; 12:6; 14:43,47; 15:8; OSHA: Ch19; MFM4038

25 For this Second Resurrection, you will need to <u>become</u> a "God" over your own "self," as outlined in this "Song," *this is a requirement.* Intro: 3; NS1: 28-39; 8: 30; 12: 6; MFM: 3353, 3388

    a My "Degree" in this Work is the making – or formulation - of **"man,"** or as we call it, the **"Self"** **NS1: 8 - 25; #22 above;** Our work is <u>not built</u> on yesterday's dogma or yesterdays ideas T, p. 151; Intro: 4, 7 we are building a New Foundation, PL: 13-1 **a New Mind** for <u>the New World</u>. NS8: 14a; 14: 18, 20-28-44, 45; OSHA25: P2; 113: P4

    b Elijah directs us from his spirit to God *in our life time* and *in our reality.* T, 222/2; OSHA: 25P3

    c This New Song is **a Light** and *<u>a Path</u>* to freedom, justice and equality for *<u>all who seek it</u>* **and** *<u>are willing to work and sacrifice for it.</u>* NS14: 35

CHAPTER SIX
Sealed Talking Points for Review and Discussion

1   This is what others don't, and can't, know about. It is **"sealed"** to them. R5: 2-5-9 **"My Design is to _keep it Hidden_** for every soul to receive Its reward by <u>measure of its own endeavor."</u> Q20:15; NS14: 15; Ref: 3; Isa29: 11

2   By focusing the minds of their followers on "Jesus," <u>the mystery,</u> the devil obscures the guidance and instruction Jesus <u>received</u> from the previous Prophets that helped him to **evolve** to the level of "Christ," meaning, <u>developed</u> or <u>Divine Mind</u>**: "MAN."**

3   Jesus told us that He came to **"Fulfill"** Mat.5: 17 the Prophet's Teaching and manifest what **The Prophets** had **taught Him (in school).** We are told by Jesus, **"The works that I do shall _you do_ also; and _greater works_ than these shall _you_ do."** Jn.14: 12 It is clear that we need a new understanding of "Jesus." Q5: 111, 120

4   Clearly this makes Jesus and <u>us</u> a product, Student, or as Jesus would say, a **"Son,"** meaning a result <u>of the Word of God</u> or "Christ" **controlling our "body."** NS1: 18, 22; 2: 8, 14; 4:14; 8: 19, 23; 12: 78; Jn5: 30; OSHA184P1

5   We need to know Jesus <u>the reality</u> Jn6: 42, 46-57-63; 3: 6 and **The Word of God** <u>in Him</u> (and us) that is **Fostering** <u>a new reality</u> upon us and the world in our life time.

6   We need to **understand** the **Reality** that rises to our consciousness *from* answering the questions below, *then* seeing **our role and place** in the world today and acting upon it.

7   This knowledge will enable us to **"bring four devils"** - destroying passion, envy, greed *and* deceit within ourselves - and *thereby* **"accept our own mind and be our self"** rather than imitating the Caucasian way of life. NS8: 8b; 14: 42; 15: 8; 17; 8

8   Today it is **our role** to "reform" our Consciousness; thus opening the door to Heaven ("peace of mind and emotional contentment"). Q81:11, 29; review Chapters 2; 15

9   Are you ready for Heaven while you live? Let's start by answering these questions?

> 1   "Let us make man…" Who are these people and what are they talking about?
>
> 2   Abraham, Elijah, and Lazarus, what is their relationship? Ex21: 16; 12: 40; Mat3: 3
>
> 3   Abraham's seed, who are they and how are they described? Gen15: 13, 14
>
> 4   Who are "the Lost Sheep," where are they now? Lk15: 24; 19: 10
>
> 5   Who are the blind, deaf and dumb? Isa.29: 18

6 **"THEY** are created now and **not** from the beginning," who are **"_they_"**? Isa.48:7, 8; Prov8: 22, 36; NS5: 20

7 Who is the God from Teman?

8 Who is The Holy One from Mt. Paran? R21: 3

9 The House of Israel, Rome, Egypt, Babylon, Sodom and Gomorrah, what is their relationship; what/who do they represent today?

10 Who is "The Son of Man"? "As lightning strikes from the East…"

11 "Who is this that cometh from Edom …?" Isa63: 1; 26: 21; Hab3: 3; Deut33: 2; Ez34:16; Mat24: 27; II Sam 7:23 **"I** that speak in righteousness…"? Lk4: 25 Who is that?

12 I will send **My Messenger** before **thy face**…" Who, Who and Who are these people?

13 "Elijah must come first…" When and Where - before what?

14 "Where ever the carcass is the eagles will be gathered together." Where and Who is being talked about? Lk17: 30, 37

15 When He, "The Spirit of Truth" comes He will guide you into all Truth. Who? Jn.16: 13, who is the "Comforter?" Jn14: 16; Mk. 9: 12; NS14: 42

16 Who is the Seventh Angel that removes the mystery of God? R: 10: 7

17 Who are the Devil, Satan, Lucifer, and Beelzebub? LK.11: 15

18 Whose world do we live in right now, God's or the Devil's? Who is God and Who is Devil? See Page PLXV: 3, 4; App II: 10

19 What and where is "the Stone the builders rejected?"

20 What is the relationship between Job, God, the Devil and You? NS15: 8, 10

21 What is the difference between the first and the last Adam? NS14: 33

10 The answer to all of the above questions can be found in this New Song. Clearly, ***any answer*** that you may have offered came from those whose great grandparents brought us into slavery or through the books written by them, or theirs, to show **their story**, not ours. **This is our story** revealed to us by God Himself, **believe it or not.** NS8: 8; 12: 27; 14: 43-46-52; 17: 2-18; reflect on 10, 11 above. We must get out of our 400 *and* Caucasian 6000 year frame of intellectual and spiritual reference *both will leave us in our present condition*: injustice inequality; begging. NS4:1-15; 12: 36

11 Many of our captors and their families - worldwide, to this day - owe their social, financial and or political position in the world that they built to our captivity

and our free labor. _You cannot forget that, if you want to_ _"escape"!_ **God won't!** NS14: 4; 15: 6f

12 **Our first task** is to "accept our own people and _be our selves._" This book will help you to do that. It will also help you to _make_ a "self" that we _and_ "God" can respect while living in the midst of the scriptural "hell." NS8: 8-14; EL: 1

13 Let's **psychologically** step out of 'the world,' **'our world,'** and attempt to look back at it, its values, and look around in it at its behavior, and practices and look again at our own lives; what we've done with it and what our environment has done with it. What do you see, how do you feel, how do you evaluate what you've experienced in your life? TLOT: 3

14 Let's actually see what we've been a part of, measure its impact on the rest of the originals on the earth, and how we can change it and ourselves, _if we choose to._ The "seals" are off. What will you do now? NS8: 8b; 12: 83

15 God's hope is that _our hope_ is in Him NS14: 4 not in our and His **open enemy** NS12:15; 8: 8-10-16

CHAPTER SEVEN
"Accept Your Own And Be Yourself"

Mahdi; Isa45: 15-20

A **"*UNSEALING*"** THE SIGNS AND SYMBOLS OF <u>THE DEAD</u>. Q20:15; 81: 10, 11 Who Are The Dead? From What Are - Where Are - The Dead Resurrected? NS17: 11 The Bible does not explain <u>in plain language</u> the issue of the "captives" brought to America <u>starting in 1555</u>; over <u>453 years</u> ago Allah taught us, and what is to be done about <u>that crime</u> and <u>our captors</u>. See Rev13:10; NS 8: 14, 16; 14: 4a; 15: 9, 10; study Ch 8, 12 and 15; see Hab3: 2 and the Appendix

B **That story is *still alive* in the Bible**. However, <u>who</u> the captives are, <u>where</u> this would take place and <u>when</u>, were all **hidden** under <u>signs</u> and <u>symbols</u> by Europeans (also known as **Dajjal, 'a group of liars')** when they **crafted** the Bible at the Council of Nice, beginning in 325 AD, (Nicene Creed) to be their *instrument* - to suit their purposes - of world domination ("sitting themselves in the seat of God as if they are God") with a <u>made</u> scripture as the god of this, *their* world.

C They were instructed by **their maker** to "Be fruitful and multiply, fill the earth with your kind (of thoughts and beliefs) and subdue it... (Along with) every living thing that moves upon the earth" (Europeans have done exactly **that** in the last **6691+ years**) Gen. 1: 26

D   Caucasians, especially America (a **"Pale Horse"** R6:8), are styled in scripture as **"the Prince of Darkness"** (among many other names). The vision of Constantine, in 312, has been followed for nearly 1700 years now, **"in hoc signo vinces"** (with this sign Job1:7 - *the cross* - you shall conquer).

E   The Prophets gave **us** various *characteristics* <u>through</u> *Their teachings,* <u>in</u> *Their names* and <u>in</u> *Their behavior* that tell us *the story* NS15:9 of the "Lost" <u>African</u> Blacks in America (the Seed of Abram). We learn of their 400 years of captivity and what *their future* is according to what the Prophets received from God, and Taught. NS8: 19, 23; 12: 36, 38; 15: 19; 17: 5

F   We, **"The Lost Sheep,"** had been unable to <u>find ourselves</u> in the scripture so <u>*we accepted the view*</u> of God and religion that our <u>captors</u> and <u>tormentors</u> provided us (being spiritually inclined by nature), just **to live.** We became – as the Prophets saw it, **"home grown slaves,"** today we can be called victims of the **Stockholm syndrome**, study it carefully. NS12: 15; 17: 18; EL: 5, 6

G   About this God told us: "Your *covenant with death* shall be disannulled, and your *agreement with hell* shall not stand." Isa.28: 18; EL: 12. Out of *fear* and *ignorance*, we made **"an agreement with hell (America) and death (their religion and way of life)"** <u>**that**</u> God said *He will not let stand in His Time.* This is **the reason** for The Judgment, coming *after* <u>their time</u> of 6,000 years of world domination which expired in 1914. Calculate from <u>*then*</u> **the diminishing of Caucasian**

world dominance, Rev.14:11: Isa.14:12, 17; NS12:26, 27 even though they *appear to have* immense political, economic and military power. NS3: 19

H Recognizing *who* the "Lost Sheep" *are* will **enable us** to see and understand what God's *purpose* is in our (His) time and what *our role* is today as **the world political and financial order** we knew *falls before our eyes.* NS 1: 31; 8: 14b-20b; 14: 7- 55b

I What do you see of the *"African" [our] experience* in America through these Biblical characteristics? Q7:127 (making of the slave through mental and spiritual death) NS8: 8b; 12: 15

1. The Captives	15. Deaf	29 Doers
2. The Dead	16. Dumb	30 Jesus
3. The Slaves	18. Servants	31 The Chosen
5. The Afflicted	19. Lost Sheep	32 The Chained
6. The Raped	20. Abraham's Seed	33 Dry Bones Ez37: 2
7. The Robbed	21. The Original Man	34 Prodigal Son
8. The Spoiled	22. Poisoned and Rusty	Lk15:11, 32
9. The Prey	23. The Stone Dan2:	35 Stiff Necked 32: 9
10. The Snared	24. The Temple	36 Found 34-45
11. Prisoners	25. The Regenerated	37 The Faithful
12. Lazarus	26. The Purified	38 Immoral
13. Corruptible	27. The Sons of God	39 Redeemed
14. Blind	28. Job	

J The Lord of the Worlds said: **"Accept Your Own and Be Yourself"** PL:5; NS12:66a; 15:8; 17:9, 10 what is the meaning, the effect, of that statement or command - obedience to it will put us into the "Pursuit of Happiness!"

What is Happiness?

1. Happiness is accepting (*living through*) our own NS15:6, 8 (*nature or values* NS8: 30) and being (or *"existing as"* NS5: 4a) our own - *self* - **our *internally evolved* "self"** PL: 7; NS4: 7a; 13: 15, 20-23-28 (*not* the externally derived "self" produced from the devil's culture, vocation and language NS5: 3, 8; 8: 8b-14; 15: 8). TLOT: 2; NS8: 21, 23; 13: 6, 7; IV: 1, 3

2. HAPPINESS IS **THE POSITIVE SENSE OF OUR "SELF"** DERIVED FROM OUR AWARENESS OF SOME "VALUE" - INTERNALLY OR EXTERNALLY PERCIEVED NS11:5,6 –AND OR OUR APPRECIATION AND GRADITUDE THAT OTHERS HAVE SHOWN OR EXPRESSED FOR OUR "CREATION," "ACHIEVEMENT" OR "PRODUCTION," WHICH EVOLVED FROM HAVING A **FOCUSED** AND MEANINGFUL **PURPOSE** FOR OUR ACTION(S). NS2: 9, 12; 4: 2- 9; 5: 7; 13: 6

What is Love?

3 Mental and Emotional Excitement, NS2: 6, 7e OUR "LOVE" FOR A PERSON OR A THING *SHOULD BE* ROOTED IN THE VALUE, QUALITY, BENEFITS, RESULTS AND OR ACHIEVEMENTS - *THE WHY* OR *THE PURPOSE* - OF THE PERSON or THE THING WE LOVE. NS14: 38a Otherwise our "love" is "blind" and will *in time* manifest a perverse result.

K SELF LOVE, AND OR OUR LOVE FOR OTHERS, ARISES FROM OUR OR THEIR **VALUE CREATION, PRODUCTION,** AND OR **ACHIEVEMENTS** WHICH

THEMSELVES *ARISE FROM* OR *ARE ROOTED IN A VALUED* OR *MEANINGFUL* PURPOSE; THIS CREATES A TRUE - OR **FUNCTIONAL** - "IDENTITY" and "INDIVIDUALITY." NS5: 8; 12: 54, 56; 13: 1, 6

> I "People <u>build</u> *who they really* are <u>into the world</u> around them" - Positively or negatively, according to their mental and other assets. Intro: 5; NS4: 21; 9: 20a; 12; 64, 65; 16: 1-11-15-17, 18

L The faster we **learn** *and* **use** <u>the knowledge</u> in The New Song, *the slower our biological time cloak will pass* NS15: 2, 8 allowing a *new force* and a *new vision* to evolve within us. NS4: 1, 7a-15-20, 21; 9: 1, 3, This "new force" and "new vision" will advance us — *through our children* [if we can't stay alive long enough] - into the unlimited dimensions that built our present Universe. TLOT: 6, 7-19, 21; NS5: 21a; 12: 9; 15: 15, 17

> I Our **new behavior** and **ability** will not only give us - *personally* - a longer and a healthier life, it will give us a happy life marked by Creative Wisdom. NS11: 15, 17; 15: 6f, h, 7; OSHA: 51P2

2 In fact, all of what we have been looking for and hoping for our whole life - **"peace of mind *and* emotional contentment"** - while <u>practicing the illusions of life</u> in America, *will now become a reality for* us as we progress through our own inner evolution. NS8:30a, j; 15: 6d, e; EL: 18g; Q21: 2, 3

M **"Your agreement with hell shall not stand."** NS12:66a, b, 67a, b; EL: 13 *"Before our 'New Song,'* most minds are dead (not 'self'- conscious NS5:2a, b) in trespasses and sins..."Ep2:1 The New Song will <u>focus</u> the "quickening" process EL: 16, 19, **from zero through 100** *in our inner evolution*. NS2: 6; 8: 30d; 11: 9; 14f: 33

1   <u>Note here</u>, "The only enemy NS5: 10B of Eternal, Positive Existence is a **sick** *human like* "conscious mind" – called the "Devil" and "Satan" - which has less than a 60% developed "conscience" and or a mind controlled by mysticism NS14:38a and **bound by the consequences of bad habits**, NS10: 7A; 12:39a; PL: 10; EL: 5

N   IT TAKES **"UNDERSTANDING"** OR **THREE FORCES**, *WORKING IN HARMONY*, TO *BRING INTO EXISTANCE* <u>ANY</u> <u>ONE</u> <u>THING</u>! (e.g., to **defeat the internal "Devil"** NS11: 7d) NS1: 37; 4: 13, 14; 8:30i; 11: 15 Review TLOT; App IV; Mt15:15, 16

O   CONSCIOUSLY *INVITE* THESE <u>FORCES</u> TO *FUNCTION IN YOUR MIND.* NS4: 21; 5: 2c,d-8 Interact with **your world** of people and events, **OBSERVE** WHAT YOU COME UP WITH BY EVALUATING *Your people and events* <u>through</u> the WORDS, IDEAS AND CONCEPTS IN THE NEW SONG NS4: 15, 21 affixing (+), (0) or (-) to each and affixing a value to each from zero through 100. Consider Intro: 4, 7

1   E.g., if the characteristics listed under "Passive (-)" were changed to "Active (+)" what would then be the new "Neutralizing" and "Passive" forces? You would have to produce them from what is **now** the *"Unseen" category of forces* and they would **then** be manifested – **take a shape or form** - through **the new** "Neutralizing (0)" and "Passive (-)" Force as *"man" (-).* NS2: 6; 4:14b

("100" is a measure <u>not</u> a verbal or numerical limit.) Describe, write out, the "neutralizing" and "active" characteristics of "man" (-). NS5: 11, 13; Review App: IV

PASSIVE (-)   NEUTRALIZING   ACTIVE (+)
(-0-)   NS13: 16, 20

Illusion	Unseen	Reality
Negative	**Stimulation**	Positive
Hell NS8: 8, 10	Consciousness	Heaven
Outer Control	Crystallization	Inner Control
Perversion	Neutral	Love
Force	Hope	Peace
Automated	Awake	Self Consciousness
Bored man	**"Man" (+)**	Creative
	NS4: 14a	

P   Next year at this time show us *your accomplishment.* Bring **them** with you to our next annual meeting. NS1: 6, 8; 8: 30j; 9: 17-20a; Intro: 17

CHAPTER EIGHT
The Basis of "Religion"

1   Let's start with a clarification for our **study** and **research**. We want to make sure we are on <u>the same page</u> regarding our understanding of <u>words</u> and <u>concepts</u>. Let this also be your criterion Q8:29 as you go throughout <u>your future</u> research, studies and conversations, in <u>all</u> areas. In some areas I will tell you **what I mean** in the use of a word, if you don't understand refer to a dictionary: better still, ask a question. Chapter 14 is actually the heart of this Work and can stand alone. Chapter One is The Root of our new beginning. Eight and other Chapters show how things happened **and** how <u>we can change them</u>. NS3: 19

2   "Religion" is the word we are looking at as we begin. The word **"Religare"** is its *Latin* <u>root</u> meaning **"to reconnect, to bind together, or to bind back that which is broken,"** NS4:3: 7: H this is the origin of the English word "religion." Now, what if anything does that suggest to your mind? *Who was <u>disconnected</u>?* See # 9, below, who needs to be reconnected? Does **"The Holy One"** ("God") have a Religion? Q30: 30

The Devil's Point Of View:

3   That he could deceive the people of the world into believing in him and in his way of life called *Christianity* - or **all Bible based religions** - and *democracy* after thousands of years of living a savage life in the caves of Europe. About 2,000 years into the 6,000 years of time allotted to him it became apparent that he could not

get out of the caves of West Asia, which they now call Europe, on their own, without God's help. Q18th Chapter God sent Ozar Sef, or **Osarsiph**, of Heliopolis, Egypt, **Musa**, (Moses) to bring him out and set him on the path to world ruler-ship, as it was written, Moses functioned as their god. Q18: 18-84; NS12: 36, 37

4   Previously, God had chosen Abram (who inadvertently became the devils help) to be the basis for His return and rule **after** the devil's time is up. He told Abram who became Abraham, (**Abu Ramu** - Exalted Father) **"I will make you an Imam to the Nations."**Q2:124 **That warrant** enabled Abraham to lay the foundation for what we today call religion and all of "the prophets" R11: 18 of God used that basis for their revelations from God so that God would have a warrant upon which to return for the ancestors of those who lived and died in His Name. MFM40: 1302, 1335; NS12: 36

5   Less than 2,000 years ago Satan saw a way to use God's method for his own rule with **lies spliced into God's Truth.** Q3:24-71The devil developed his own religion (way of life) R16: 13, 16 calling it **Christianity - which is not Abraham's, nor the Prophet's religion,** and **Jesus never heard of it** - Intro4; Q3:67; 7:71; MFM2887; OSHA93P6 using God's basis. Mt15: 8 Up until Abraham's time there was no such thing as "religion" in **our** world, just Truth (Measurable Reality) and the **upright nature** and **behavior** of "man" which has been called the **right way** or **path** containing access to the **"All-in-All."** App VI, This is the "Garden" or "Paradise" the Devil was thrown out of and marched 2200 miles into the caves.

a In his religion, Satan made <u>everything</u> *mysterious* and *other worldly*. It's philosophical under pinning is Plato, St. Augustine; and the writer of Hebrews. He 'put himself *in the seat of God* <u>as if</u> he were God through the use of **imagery, signs, statues** <u>and</u> **color –** all the things that God said **not to do** while *not actually saying* he was **"God"** <u>**out loud.**</u> One need only watch his ***attitude*** <u>and</u> ***behavior*** around the world to see the truth of *what he thinks of his role in the world.* Intro: 5; NS14:1; 17: 19

6 With religion, *the ideas* and *accreditation process*, **in his control** he finally won control *over his people's minds* without having to fight wars for control over <u>their behavior</u> as he had for the previous 4,000 years, although they've had many wars among themselves to see which *tribe* or *family* would rule over us and our world. Today it is the Anglo-Americans (the "five brothers" Lk16: 27) and *their system of rule*, refuted by Gog.

a His **missionary training** and **conversion work** for our mind continues today - **world wide -** through **("Traders," "missionaries"** and**)** those who have <u>his</u> **'mark.'** PL: 1; Q25:55 The **Upright God** Isa. 5:16 <u>**never**</u> sends an army of 'preachers or traders.' T, P.127, 1st p He only sends **one** Prophet or Messenger ***at a time*** with <u>One Message, One Faith</u>**: "Bow your will to Me."** Q2:131-135; Ecc12:11, 14

b There are *two primary voices* in the scripture, can you tell the difference between them? NS2: 13; See #'s 17 and 18a below; App II: 10

c **Supernatural events** don't all originate with the God of right. The **"Three foul spirits"** of the Devil are **Education and Politics; the Capitalist Financial System**; and **Bible** NS7: B **based Religion:** Representing "The Dragon, the Beast and the False Prophet" **or** "The spirits of devils *with power to work miracles* **(of deception)**" R16:13, 16 among those *ignorant of the nature of "God"* and those **locked into ritual behavior** learned from Caucasians. PL: 4; NS12:15; EL: 18g

d Among their other scriptural names, titles and descriptions are Gog, Magog and Dajjal. **Gog,** Russia, *has sway over* Eastern and Southern states and **Magog**, the U.S. and Britain - leading the nations of Europe - *have sway* over the Western and Northern states, with some contention for states on both sides of the equation. Their false religion and deceit is represented by **Dajjal, Satan** and the **Anti-Christ** among other titles.

7 With the people who believed in his teaching **mystified,** and generally quiet, at first only Caucasians, he then had enough social and political "peace" to build a world to rival God. Using conquered **original people**, deceit, rape, robbery, murder, war and what he found and or stole from among us, *he has* constructed **his heaven (through mysticism)** on earth and *he is* **the ruler of it** NS12: 1a - politically, economically, financially, scientifically, militarily and spiritually – functioning as god of it, otherwise known as the **Prince of Darkness** among other names or titles. IICor.4:34; Jn.14:30; Today his military budget is greater than the rest of the world *combined*, why?

a However, "they" NS6: 9-6 **"have <u>no power</u> to deny the Grace of God"** to the Over Comers of their falsehood. Q57:29; Intro: 4; NS5: 15

8 **Review the devil's conversation with God in the Holy Qur'an, Allah says: "We shall recount their whole story** <u>with knowledge</u> NS14: 52 [We *show* and *explain* in this *"<u>New</u> Song"* *(or Message)* what brought us to these Days Isa43:9, 11] for We PL; 7, 8 were never absent (at any time or place)."** Q7:7; 27: 75; EL: 18g

a The guilty always put incense and roses **around their filth** to cover it while attacking others for perceived wrongs. **<u>Attacking this Song about the explanation presented will be in vain</u>.** EL: 18g *Time is <u>the Best Judge</u> of all affairs and will verify its truth!* NS1:23b

b We have been warned **not to** *<u>envy our oppressor</u>,* **nor** *<u>practice his way of life</u>.* Prov3:31 **To the Devil, I council:** Consider taking the path of Nineveh, <u>Jonah taught that Nineveh was an evil city</u>. God sent Jonah to preach to Nineveh, **they submitted and lived, for a while.** Prov14: 34; NS15: 6; Jonah's 40 days is <u>our</u> 40 years

9 The Devil said: **"Because You have** *<u>thrown me out</u>* **of The Way** ("God's Upright Nature" #18; 30b below), I will *<u>lie in wait</u>* for them (the **"lost and found"** former slaves and others) *<u>on</u>* **Your Straight Way** (he *<u>substituted</u>* his *<u>made</u>* **"religion,"** or **way of life**):

a <u>Then</u> **I will assault them** from *before* them and *behind* them, from their *right* and their *left* [Mentally,

73

Emotionally, Physically and Spiritually]. **You will not find** *in most of them* **thankfulness** [or **gratitude** for **Your** Mercies, or the fact that **You came** for them with Truth, to 'resurrect' and 'save' them]." Q2:204, 206; 4:119; 7:16.17; see # 13 below

10 Allah replies: **"If any of them (original people) follow you, I will fill hell with you all."** Hell's life is filled with *fear, guilt, greed,* and *anxiety* along with joy, tears, and sorrow. PL: 1 Hell is a psychological and an emotional condition likened to a roller-coaster and or a physical torture: the Prophets called it (an emotional) **"Fire"** *(change your inner state and cool your inner "Fire")*. EL: 5 **Heaven**, by contrast, is *peace of mind* and *emotional contentment,* also called a **"Garden"** or a **"Paradise,"** *a state of internal 'peace' or 'rest.'* NS14: 55b-7; OSHA199P2

11 "The devil's religious scholars and scientist tried to make themselves *equals with God* by saying that "mankind," using *their* name for all people, were created at the same time, 6000 years ago, and therefore everyone is equal. The Truth is that God, *The Original Man,* is **not part of** "man-kind." Review PL; TLOT; Q51:47 In fact, just so you won't be deceived, whenever their scholars talk of "mankind," "human" anything, "we" and so forth, understand, they are speaking of themselves in **code language.** The "freedom" they talk about is their freedom to continue to exploit and kill original people around the world. See #7 above If you continue to use *their terms for yourself,* you will find yourself lost as to what is actually transmitted or what is happening. How people are taking what you say. Your own communications will become confused. Test it and see. Ask questions if you don't understand. NS12: 2

74

12 God **"made"** the Caucasians and they falsely – <u>without knowledge</u> – attribute to Him sons and daughters. The Original Man *Produced* <u>all life</u> from a single Person, Himself. To Allah - **The Original Consciousness** - is due the Primal Origin of the Heavens and the Earth: How could He have a son when **He had no consort** (in the beginning NS5:21)? No, He created all things and has full knowledge of all things.Q6:98-101 Elijah said: "He wanted a different human being than Himself, so *He studied Himself.* He made a woman by studying Himself genetically; finding the X and Y Chromosomes, this solved His problem of a search, or making of another man." MFM3333, 88

13 "The devil replies: Give me respite till the Day <u>they</u> (my "home grown slaves," **"the dead"** R11:18) <u>are raised</u>? As you have put me in the wrong, <u>I will make</u> <u>wrong</u> *fair seeming* to them <u>on the earth</u>, I will put them *all* in the wrong *by changing their nature* or **inclinations** Q30:30; Ecc7:29 <u>except your servants</u> from among them, the *purified* and **complete** <u>because of</u> *Your coming."* NS14: 2-5-8; Q15: 36, 40; OSHA184P1

   a Those who were "dead" and now *accept Him* will <u>become</u> *"unaffected"* by the negative emotional attractions in their environment. NS15: 11; Ch 5

14 "So, *by deceit* Q4:120-123 Satan brought about their fall… proving his idea to be true, Q34:20, 21 that the disbelievers would *give him authority* <u>over</u> them. NS1: 27; Note 20c below The Devil and his civilization **see you** from a [mental and spiritual] position *where you cannot see them* See NS 12:1; 14: 17 [because *they* have **not** <u>taught</u> you

to <u>see</u> or <u>hear</u> **their secrets. We unseal them here.**
NS1:26b]**"** Q7:22 - 27; Intro: 4, 7; Ref: 3, 7

    a **This New Song (or Message) is God's Promise to us**, PL: 1; NS14:2: (the devil knows of it) "This (<u>Way of My sincere servants</u>) is *indeed* <u>a Way</u> that *leads straight to Me (The Upright Original Nature)."*Q 14: 22; 15: 41

    b God said: **"I will destroy them that destroy the earth!"** R11:18; Prov.:16:4 No people *destroyed* **the earth** before Caucasians. Consider Global warming and poisoned air, poisoned water, wasted forests, whole species of animals; wasted people, war and more. *"Allah is pushing them all together (financially?), so that He can destroy them all at once."*T, 239, 2nd p

15 The devil Q7:13 believed he could *change* our "Standard or Original way of living, *through* <u>Conscience</u>," Q30:30; Ecc7:29 by teaching us his <u>false</u> **ideology** and **beliefs** <u>through</u> *"mysticism,"* PL: 3. thereby <u>mastering</u> God's creation including a majority of the original people - if *given enough time* and <u>the freedom</u> to act totally without restraint - <u>except</u> he couldn't destroy us **"<u>root</u> and <u>branch</u>"**NS14:14, 19, Review Chapter 9.

    a This time and "freedom" was <u>given</u> to him. R17:17; NS12: 1a We **"<u>let them have</u> dominion"** over the <u>physical creation</u> for **6000** years. Q7:7-10; 37:28, 33; NS14:1; Dan7: 25, 26

16 Though it can be found in other places, the best **'essence'** of this story - in the Bible - is found in the conversations

between **God, The Sons of God,** and **the Devil.** Job
1:6, 12; IPet.5: 8; IIPet.2: 10-12 **["Job,"** a metaphor for the
"Original Man," said: **"I** knew of Thee <u>then</u> [for 452
years] <u>only by</u> (the slave masters) <u>report</u> [or teaching to
me, *I knew nothing else*], but now I see *'You'* with my
own eyes [through The New Song], NS14:3, and I bow to
Thy Will" [Job 42:5, 6] NS12: 28;14: 23; EL: 18g; MFM: 3398

a Know that we **are** *living in "the latter days"* Dan2:
28; 10:14-21 and that **"the Book of Life"** Dan2; 1; R20:12
that *our name* should be **written in** is <u>our own</u> **true
and *upright nature*:** "the Book of Wisdom" which
was written *within us from the beginning.* NS5: 21a

b If *our "name"* – or <u>true essence</u> NS9: 1, 3 - is not
manifested <u>through</u> **our behavior** we will perish.
See Intro: 7; Chapters 2 - 4 and 15; NS8: 22; 9: 12a; 12: 15 - 43a – 54
- 67a;14: 2

The Supreme Human Beings' Point of View:

17 Why did God make the devil? To show forth His Power,
meaning "The Wisdom that was *locked up* inside the
Original Man." T, p.145] Here, Satan had challenged God
saying that He would lose His Power to *an opposite*
NS15:5a of Himself, *His Nature,* if He took away His
protection, His **"hedge,"** from around His people, hence
<u>the story of</u> an *Original Mind,* **"Job"** NS14: 15; Ch 17

a The Original People had searched for a
"mystery God" for trillions of years TLOT: 13
and They were unable to find a "mystery God;"
They have <u>agreed</u> R17:17 that *the only 'God'* is

77

'the Son of a Man.' He, _The Most Evolved of Them_, is The R11:17, 18 **Supreme Human Being, even over the Biblical 24 Elders.** He is All-Wise and Righteous, His Essence, by degree, is **_All-in-All- That-Is_**. Isa5:1; PL: 2; NS1: 40; 2: 4, 5; 5: 21a; 9: 2a; App VI; OSHA12P3

18 They decided as _the last test_ Q5:51 of the proposition: "_the only 'God'_ is **'the Son of a Man,'**" that They would make a Devil – in other words, let evil out on the Earth _with_ - or in - _the form of_ 'an original man'- but he would be a **_recessive_** "unalike" man T, p 60: **"opposite"** _in nature_ and **_devoid of color_**. NS12: 1 This made 'man' would be "(morally) **_weak_**" and "(mentally) **_wicked_**" by nature. NS12: 18; OSHA: 34P3

a Study the history **they** - the 'made' man Q50: 16; Dan4:16 - **have written about themselves** for the last **4000** years. Q54: 52 Even now with their advanced knowledge watch how they **_conduct themselves_** in the world. Their **_daily life_** is a testament as to who they are NS14: 25. Although **_some of them can learn to live our life as they have taught us to live theirs_** (regrettably, this **is the cause of our confusion** TLOT: 2a). EL: 5 **_However know that "God has made the wicked for a day of disaster."_** Prov.:16:4; Q2: 276; NS1: 23; 12: 15; 14:11- 40; Intro: 3, 7; Ref: 8

b He would be _given_ power to rule the entire earth for 6,000 years and **then** Allah would return NS14:41-46, 47 and destroy the Devil in **one day** without falling as "_a victim_" to the Devil's "_unalike_" civilization. NS14: 40, 41-55b, c Otherwise, to **show** and **prove** that Allah, **_The Original Upright Human Nature_**, is **"GOD"**

78

always has been and always will be: The First and The Last in creation. Chs.2 and 9; PL: 10, 13; NS5: 21a; 11:7d; 17: 1, 6; Prov.8: 21, 33

19 The Most High outlines His overall Plan *in the lives* and *teaching* of His Prophets NS15:9; 14: 2, 3-5, 9: What life will be like under the devil's rule before, during and after God's Return. Q34:49 He also discussed His *time line* for return as outlined in His **conversation with Abram**, Gen.15: 13, 14 which takes us directly to the End of the Forth Beast of Yakub's Revelations. NS14: 1 Surely Allah has cast the mantle of Truth over this Message. Q34: 48

   a **Listen to Abraham's prayer for us:** "Our Lord! Send among them, the spiritually dead NS 12: 36, a Messenger *of their own*, who shall rehearse Thy Signs to them and *instruct them in Scripture and Wisdom, and purify them: For Thou art Exalted-in-Might, the Wise.*" Q2:129; 32:3; NS15:8

   b The description above does not outline **the work** of Jesus or Muhammad, Q3:67; Ex. 21: 16; Joel 3:7 it does describe **the work of Elijah (exemplified by Moses)** which we continue in The New Song. See Q32: 3; NS3: 12 "It is the Truth from thy Lord so that you may warn a people to whom **no Warner has come before thee, Elijah,** in order that they may receive guidance." This verse refers to the "mentally dead" in America more than one 1000 years **after** the "historic Muhammad." See, NS1: 29, 31; Q20:15 **Arabia had many Prophets *before* the "historic" Muhammad, including Abu Ramu. Islamic scholars overlook this fact! "Muhammad"**

was raised among a people who *never had a* **Warner"** Q32: 3 and is therefore like Moses.?

20 The Most High has the Prophets tell us **how** He will *Return* to choose a "Messenger" (**Elijah,** Mt17: 11) for us whose responsibility will be to turn the hearts *of the fathers* (non-Caucasians in the East) back to *the children* brought into slavery over 400 years ago, and the hearts of those **"the Lost Found mentally 'dead'"** children back to their fathers (Originals in the East) less He (God), the Prophets say, *smites the earth with a curse.*

a This work among us has been going on over the last 78 years by Allah, His Messenger and His Followers. We have gone through **the First** and we are now in **the Second Creation or Resurrection** of Elijah's work. Hab3: 2; Q53:47; Intro: 2, 3 **"Know that when** *the mountains* (those **great business** and **financial institutions that controlled and supported their quality of life)** *crumble to earth* as **heaps of sand let loose**, we are in '<u>the Days</u>, *The Time,* <u>of</u> **Allah.'"** Q81:3; NS1: 12

b "We will <u>destroy</u> or <u>punish</u> with *a dreadful punishment* <u>every population before</u> the Day of Judgment," says Allah. Q17:58; PS110: 6; NS4:11 **Pay attention today** to the <u>unusual</u> <u>occurrences</u> that are going on in the world around you, e.g., cyclones, typhoons, hurricanes, tornados, floods, sever cold and melting snow, heat, drought, lightening and hail storms, earthquakes, volcanic eruptions; deceit, confusion, disease, hunger, murder, debauchery, and war. Don't argue *reflect upon what you are seeing*

80

and feeling. Or is it that you are <u>not</u> watching? Thess2: 9; OSHA169P4

c **Abu Ramu** and his teaching point to **the spiritually "dead" captives** in America and is the key to ***root understanding*** for today's world. The Work of <u>all Prophets</u> flowed from his Work, as does the New Song. Q2:135; 3:71; 42:13; 57: 26; NS12:2 **Return to Abraham** through this New Song. Acceptance of - and living through - this message will solve your problems and bring in a reign of peace. PL: 10, 12; NS10: 6, 7

d Do you consider me <u>weak</u> and <u>poor</u> and thus you despise what <u>Allah has caused me to see</u> and <u>say</u>? You should know that **Wisdom** Prov4: 7 **is better than strength.** Ecc9:16; NS15:8 "This is an *instructive warning* for those who fear God" Q79: 26-34, 46 Most people know only <u>the outer things</u> in the life of this world <u>created by Satan</u>: but of the **end of things** they are heedless, thus they are easily led in the wrong direction and very hard to lead into the right direction. Q30: 7-10; Mt15: 13, 14; Lk16: 19, 31

21 <u>Elijah told us</u>: "God sent me to make **Gods** (<u>Doers</u> NS5: 18) out of you, **not believers (or fearful people)."** "<u>Allah</u>" is ***The Title*** of The Supreme Human Being Who is called God "He" has 99 attributes *each* **name** (or *Description*) shows something of "His" **essence, ability, power, and wisdom.** Review Chapter 2 All Originals have a role from 1% to 100% in His Essence. *Our inner evolution* will determine our role in the New World. Review 17a above; NS12: 81, 83; Chapter 4

22 **"God** (a "Possessor of Power and Force" reached through conscious *inner evolution*) is ***a product of time***." "God makes us *like Himself,* NS1: 18" the Honorable Elijah said, "in order to *prove His Truth*, if we did not look like Him, He could deny making us and we could deny being made by Him." Consider your *Inner Evolution* here and through Chapters 2 - 4 - 5 -9 -11, 12 and 15 The Revelator has God saying, *"I will write on them* **My Own *New* Name***"* (just as Yakub did with his people in his time). R3:12; NS1: 15, 16; 2:10

23 When we have God's Name *through inner evolution* it signifies *'our growth'* **[by degree, 1% to 100%]** into one or more of His Attributes. "Our word **"Be,"** Elijah revealed to us, over the creation of **The First God** Who said, *"Be,"* will come to pass." *"Our word must be that now* (over our own flesh). NS5: 21, 25 God is giving us 'the Kingdom,'" - through *a method* to command our own mind and body NS3: 13, 14; 14a above - this is the *functional* meaning of *the resurrection of "Christ"* (**the mind and spirit** *of Truth in the Word* NS2:7d, f-10, 12) in our time. NS11:7C; 12: 42, 46 "Words come from your heart" Mt15:15, 20 they may be positive or negative in nature.

    a So: how do we **see** "God"? Intro: 4, 7; Ps73:17-20-22; 74: 22; 78:65; 82:8 Today, the *"upright* God*"* NS14:2-5-14 *rises* up Ps68:1 through minds "grafted," "quickened" or "changed" NS14:38 from *the evil nature* or *inclination* - words - of Satan. NS8:18; 14:1-4a These minds have *evolved* - regenerated – *back* NS4: 21 into the original form, *nature* and *in_clination* - words - of The Originator, saying: **"Look, I come. In the volume of the book, it is written of me."** Ps40:

6, 7 Or **we notice** *The All Hearing* and *All Knowing Consciousness* working <u>through</u> the **arisen minds** NS13: 19 of those "Found" by <u>The Originator's Truth</u> from among the "mentally and spiritually dead" NS14:6-46 in America. NS1:17, 21-37; Ch 2; 4:12; 8:26a-30d; 11:15; 12:25, 27-33-76; 14:7, 8-14, 18a, c-23a-25-28-31-39-50

24 We have <u>identified the force</u> that **stops the accumulation** of <u>new knowledge</u> and therefore the **evolutionary advance** of the human mind, or *'our own growth'* - it **is Mysticism** Q7:148. *When* mysticism, tradition and rituals enter the human mind as **<u>unchanging beliefs</u>** those beliefs reduce and eventually stop - **block** - the <u>accumulation</u> of new knowledge or new ideas. NS14: 19a, b-28-42

   a **Mysticism <u>blinds</u> the mind, <u>stops</u> the ears and makes the <u>speech</u> of its "believers" ritualistic or like a tape recorder,** while Satan maintains his grip on their behavior. See #'s 13, 15 above; NS10: 7a

   b Moses' people said, "We found our fathers doing <u>this</u>, *who are you* to tell us to <u>change our beliefs</u> and <u>practices</u>?" and *so it is today* with the former slaves among us in America. Q5:70; 17: 53; 58:14, 22; 11th **Chapter:** e.g., 40-53-62-89-91, review the treatment of the prophets by their people.

25 The Messenger, in **doing this work** of *identifying* <u>the Original Man</u> and <u>the devil</u> [by their nature], *contends* with the Beast by *unraveling* <u>his deceitful</u> way of life, see 9a -17, 18 above, causing a (spiritual or "religious" #2 above and thus mental and emotional) *"separation"* of <u>his followers</u> *from* Satan and *fostering* their <u>mental</u>

and <u>spiritual</u> <u>resurrection from hell</u> – or our **"grave of ignorance"** – and **changing our way of life back to our Original Nature.** Ecc7:29 This releases **("Frees")** *our inner nature to be 'our' morally* **strong** *and mentally* **powerful** *"self"* in contrast to the "weak and wicked" Caucasian devil thus we **identify** <u>ourselves</u> with the Originator and His Warrant NS8: 4 for our return. NS2: 8, 12; 13: 3; 14: 39; #6c -14, 15 above

    a However, we are still **"here"** in his world *but* <u>not of it</u> – we are not followers of his *emotion laden directions, using "God,"* Q38:82; therefore, we <u>function</u> **as examples** for **the seekers** <u>of truth</u> in his world *"after"* <u>having been</u> **corrupted** morally, spiritually, and 'found' mentally dead ourselves by Allah. Ep2:1; NS14: 4, 5 - 17a - 25; Chapter 7; Intro: 4; Q15: 70

26 This is the declaration of the Most High to Abram that *identifies* <u>who He has come for</u> (Abram's Seed, numbering 144000), His Messenger **("His Anointed")** and His *resurrected* (from the dead) *"chosen and faithful"* Rev.17:14 *followers* <u>having</u> **the Spirit Of** <u>the</u> **Living God** <u>and</u> *His* **Name.** They are all *renewed* <u>in the spirit of their minds</u> from 'the devil's grave of ignorance.' Q16: 90, 91-101; NS9: 6a, b

    a *'You have God Quickened, Who* R7: 13, 17 *Were Dead In Trespasses and Sins...'* Ep2: 1; NS12: 11a -15 *He* <u>changed the evil</u> *of these people to good* Q25:70 – **they and we** <u>do not</u> *carry the 'mark' (behavior) of 'the beast'.* PL: 1; Q25:63; 55: 41; Dan 4:17

27 Notice how God describes **His Presence** <u>within us</u> in Q8:17, metaphorically as *All Hearing* and *All Knowing*

Consciousness working through our *formally automated minds.* PL: 8 It is not possible for the unconscious mind to see more than the All Knowing Consciousness, We are taught what should be expected before and after <u>His Coming</u> (Return) to save us and close out the Book on Satan and his world; and…

a   **We ask:** "Grant me from **Thy Presence** <u>*an authority*</u> to aid me." Q17:80; PL: 14; 1: 7b; 5: 20

28 *Throughout the Prophet's teaching:* They discuss, "<u>through</u>" Their Work, what would be happening to Abrahams' people and They <u>point the way</u> for us to **save our spirit** and **our lives** <u>in the Last Days</u> of Satan's rule. NS15: 9 We follow in Their footsteps and travel Their Path entering **"Paradise"** through The Gate of Truth. NS15:9 **The Great Mahdi,** NS1:31; T, p. 80, 1ˢᵗ p, came in <u>***Our Days***</u> using the name "Jesus," **among other titles, to "save the Lost Sheep" (Original People here in America)…** Mt15: 24; NS12: 26, 28; 14: 3

29 For us, Abraham is ***The Key*** to understanding scripture Q2: 135; 50: 29 **not** the Jesus of 2000 years ago, Isa Ibn Yusuf. He came to ***"fulfill"*** NS6: 3 ***(reform) what was revealed to the Jews before Him, and like the Others, He was unsuccessful in reforming the Devil. They killed Him and reshaped His Message;*** <u>He did</u> <u>not</u> <u>start</u> <u>something</u> <u>new</u> "under the Sun **("I am God and I change not"** is God's reaction). That is **an example** of **Satan's tricks.** See #5 above

a   Christianity is <u>based on</u> **their, Caucasians, <u>*murder*</u> of Jesus 2000 years ago** and <u>the sign</u> Job1: 7; NS7: D; #16 above that they use to represent this murder is <u>*not*</u> in accord with the universal order of things. They *trick the ignorant* about Jesus' life and death – *saying that He died for* <u>their</u> *sins (yet neither the slave nor his master have* <u>stopped</u> sinning) – teaching them also that they will come back *from a* <u>physical death</u>. *However, the scripture says,* **He is a "God of the - *spiritually* - living,"** the physically dead <u>do not</u> return. ***Our work here*** <u>*exemplifies*</u> the resurrection of the *mentally* and the *spiritually* dead. Mat. 22:32; Ecc9: 4, 5, 6-10; IISam12:22, 23; Ps.78:39; EL: 13

1 **The devil assumes that we would not read the scripture for ourselves, but if we did we wouldn't understand it.** *That was the case* **until the coming of "God" in Person to raise Elijah.** NS1: 31; 12: 27

    b Abraham is *the Father of Faith* as we know it, ***then*** and ***now***. Q2: 124-135; OSHA148P5; Lk16: 19, 31; NS15: 9

    c Christians, (and most others) *not being taught about* <u>*the creation*</u> **and** <u>*their relation to it*</u> don't and can't **"<u>understand</u>"** Prov. 4: 7 what they are taught to believe in. That which has been **"<u>broken</u>"** - *in us* - is our **upright nature** fixing it requires a **change of behavior** and **attitude** <u>*not*</u> ideological, religious or any other kind of argument. See Chapter 6; #30, c, d below; Intro: 5; review Chapter 4.

    d ***The doubters say:*** **"This is fake, never have we heard teaching like yours among our fathers."** Q28:36 <u>So said</u> all of the people of the past who **didn't want to change** or, *through* <u>*fear*</u>, loved their enemies more than their own people. Q2:268; PL: 1; NS2:19; 14: 14-19, review #'s 8, 10 above

30 <u>Say</u>: *I know from Allah that which you know not.*
NS12:44,45 This is my Way: I invite you to Allah on **evidence**
as clear as the <u>seeing with your own eyes</u> and the reasoning
of your own mind. Q33:8

    a In *The New Song* there is **Instruction** for minds
seeking, or endued with, "understanding." Prov4:7 It
is *a confirmation* of what is before it and *a detailed
exposition* on the development of "man." Q2: 272; 12:
86 -108 -111; Ecc7: 29; NS Ch 6; 5: 25; EL: 18g

    b To this <u>the disbelievers say</u>, "If you obey a man **like
yourselves**, you will surely be lost." Q23:34 Say: "Do
you not ponder over The Word (of God), or has
anything come to **you** that did not come to **your**
fathers of old (like this **The New Song**)?"Q23:68
Disbelievers and **misbelievers** will be <u>vexed</u> or in
<u>agitation</u>. Q79: 8

    c Allah's Way of Life is found in **the Universal Order
of things**, He built the universe according to **the
pattern** on which He made His Own Nature. See
#17above; NS5: 21; 8: 22, 24; Prov8: 22, 36

    d Allah created **the Original Nature** by Creating
Himself First, <u>He is Self Created</u>; <u>our human nature</u>
(when uncorrupted by Satan or **resurrected by
Allah's Truth**) <u>reflects His Own</u>. Q30:30; NS4: 17; 12:55, 57;
T, p. 59, 61. Study Chapter 2

    e Unless our <u>upright nature</u> **builds our future,**
whoever works on <u>the future</u> is only working in vain
(especially if they are using Satan's ideas Ps5:9). Ps.127:1;

TLOT: 2 **"We made a people,"** Allah said, **"considered weak** (and of no account), *inheritors* of lands in both the East and the West" Q7: 137 The Messenger taught me that **"Only the principles [original essence or nature, not dogma]** of the present Islam will remain the same." **Their rituals will not be carried into the future.** OSHA111: P3; NS14: 41

f We, **'L Sh'b'zz**, are *created an animated from* the Spirit of God's Word in The New Song. Ps104:30; NS4: 21; 14:2-6 It is Allah Who is bringing us together, (growing - up in) to Him is our final goal before achieving *crystallized* peace of mind and inner contentment. Q42:15; NS14: 35

g The *"original* - **Upright** - *nature"* is opposite to the devil's nature, #'s17, 18 therefore Satan wants to **subvert** the original nature with *his mark*. Satan wants our peoples "appetites (or behavior, to be) *unchecked* by **("SELF")** knowledge" Q6:119; 25:43 thereby enabling him to maintain control over *the world he has built* #5, 7 above while we sit and / or complain about *how* he rules (while trying to get a little piece of his world wherever we can). Q15:39; PL: 1; NS12: 63; 14: 25; #7-17 above; Ps5: 9

h Allah, however, through this Message NS13: 1; Q76: 22; PL: 14, has provided us with the means to rule over our own spirit *through Him* by giving it back NS3: 4-19 to Him Prov.25: 2-28; #26a above and inherit the ruler-ship of the Heavens and the Earth. Intro: 5, 6-18; App VI

i **Understand here,** *the originality* of the **Original Man,** Chap.9 *His Unseen Essence,* is **not** bound up in his *original physical material* – "black earth or mud fashioned into shape" NS11: 4a nor is it found in his *physical appearance* – NS15:6c *"Originality" is found in the purity, the focus, the temperament, the quality of thinking, the behavior, capacity* and *functionality of the "Being" Possessing "Originality."* See 23 above; NS12:20-a; 13: 19

j **The intent** and **motivation** of *the Original Mind* is **upright**, as exemplified by the half originals (in body) **"Fard,"** and **"Musa"** or **Moses**. Then there is **Adam**, the "reddish" *Caucasian made man* exemplified by **"Muhammad"** [said to have black hair and eyes, if he did he was half original], who overcame his "Jinn." "Dear holy Apostle, he was asked, do you have a 'Jinn?'" "Yes, but I conquered mine." NS12: 47- 55, 56

k Don't forget *most of us* are "half original" ourselves. This New Song will enable us to conquer our own "Jinn," or *the devil's characteristics in ourselves produced by Hell.* Chapter 6; see #10 above

l The first degree in our inner evolution on the path *back to "God,"* or *"Originality"* NS12: 33-43-49 is seen in **our destruction of the devil:** passion, envy, greed and deceit, or moral death, *in ourselves.* NS1:39c; 2: 6; 5: 25; 12:63; 14: 38-a-50; 15: 5a; review the Epilogue. **The Original man** is morally **strong** and mentally **powerful. Allah has Power over All things.** NS2: 7

31 "After Learning Mathematics - which is submission to, and the use of, Truth or Reality: know that this same

Truth or Reality functions as **a Light** Ps119:105, or as a metaphor for Mathematics, *which is* **this New Song** and – it stands true. You can always prove it in no limit of time by living it. Then *you must learn to use it* and secure *some benefit for yourself* while you are living, Q28:77 such as friendship in all walks of life, a good home, money, and maybe some luxury while still living in hell. See Chapter 2 and 4; Q28: 77

32 *Sit yourself in heaven at once!* NS14:50; T, p.239p1 That is *the greatest Desire* of your Brother and Teachers." We cannot *'Will'* heaven *for you* - you must *want it,* and *live for it,* yourself. The New Song is your Guide MFM4097; NS12:76-80 that shows you The Way, it is surely an answer to **my prayer:**

    a Dear Savior, "Grant me from **Thy Presence** *an authority* to aid me." PL: 7, 8 **The Living** "God" NS3: 7a is feared *only* *among* *His saints* (we should translate "feared" here to mean they *"understood"* Prov4:7 what an illusion, or destroying **our** "upright human nature," would produce: Hell. See 10 above). NS11: 7-d; TLOT: 11; Ps89:7; see 23a -26-a above

33 "Now you must **speak the Language** (*of the New Song*) so that you can use **this Mathematical Theology** in the proper term, otherwise you will not be successful - helping the people, and yourself - unless you do speak (think) well." PL13:1; NS4: 21, 22; 15: 6b

34 **The Light of Abu Ramu,** Q2:135 *articulated* and *shaped* through all of the Prophets; with **Moses, Jesus,**

Muhammad and (our lives through) Elijah takes us up to and through the Judgment.

a   One of our Scientist said: *"Through knowledge* NS1: 40a shall <u>the Just</u> be delivered." Prov.11:9 Apply this Message to every aspect of your life and experience its mercy producing work and concrete results *in your own life.* NS2: 20

b   <u>Abraham</u>, <u>Lazarus</u> and <u>Elijah</u> are *the keys* to <u>understanding the End</u> of western dominance of the original world. Gen.15:13, 14; EX.21: 16; Lk.16: 22, 31; NS12: 1, 3

CHAPTER NINE
Understanding the Unseen Nature, the Essence, of the Original

1 How can we grasp the Alfa and the Omega, the First and the Last; the Original and **the Original _from_ the Original?** The **_"Last"_** and still **_"First!"_ Let's See!** NS15: 6c

2 The Alfa, The First, The Original, **_is_ The Source**, The Cause and **_"The ESSENCE"_** of _All Created_ - firstly constructed, made, or built - things. NS8:15; Pro: 2

   a **_'ESSENCE'_** contains the integrated **_"thinking"_** and actions that make "All Created" and _other_ things possible: 'Essence' **_is_** the internal unseen primordial energy that shapes _purpose_ as **seen** in _responsive_ and _conforming_ material and **Fosters** duplication or replication. NS3: 13, 15; 5: 18, 23; 8: 21, 23-30; 12:11; Chapter 15; App VI: 4, 5

3 What is "Purpose"? Without "purpose" there is no excitement, no reason, spirit, intent or drive to **"fulfill"** _in_ the human form. When a human being _absorbs_ **"Essence Responsibilities"** in the form of words, concepts and ideas, NS2:11; 13:3 those "Responsibilities" drive "Original Purpose" into existence thereby creating building or forming – according to their type. This process continues

to build more and more "responsibilities" *in responsive materials* after their own kind. NS4: 20, 24

4   Mental integration or *fusion* NS14: 45-52 - of the Bible, the Quran, and The Lessons to the "Lost and Found in N. America" and other writing *attracted* by the "Essence" of *The Original Source* - has produced **"The New Mind"** which has *"constructed"* **"The New Song"** from **Original Source Principles and Materials** to benefit and resurrect *The fallen* but yet "Original Man:" "The First and The Last," "The Alfa and the Omega." NS1: 21; 2: 2

5   Let's evaluate a 'branch' **"separated"** from a tree - whose *origin* we don't know - as a metaphor of *our plight* in America. What we do know is that *this particular* 'branch' [*you*] is *not* 'The First or Original' of its type or kind in its *undeveloped state*, as we find it (it's missing six other parts, dry and nearly dead).

    a   Can we **find out** its *'Original Source'* and *'Nature'* with six parts missing? Can we **discover** its 'essence' ("the *internal unseen primordial energy* that shapes *'original' purpose"*)? Can we do that? I think so. NS12: 11; Ecc7: 25

6   Our first requirement is that the **growth of the branch be in *'reverse replication'*** (since it is not in its original form) *absorbing water* - meaning, absorbing through water, **"Essence Responsibilities"** #3 above - so that the 'branch' may **evolve** in *three dimensions* (in the light) and there-by **demonstrate to us its inner' essence.'** NS17: 5

a **That nature** (as seen by the 'functional' **"_response_"** of the branch to 'water') is **driving the Original Unseen Essence** <u>into existence</u> nearly before our eyes <u>from within</u>. See NS2: 11, 12 Look at this idea in Chapter 3: 14, **"The Flame that was ignited in the beginning (still) exists in us today enabling us to ignite creation anew when Our Flame** *(on the same wavelength)* is *focused* and *pure*.**"** Let this idea *light your path* to new opportunities. NS 8: 16a, b

b The 'branch,' now fostering growth from *within itself,* see #16 below **in time**, manifests the **"Seed"** or the **"Unseen Original Essence"** to us from itself, <u>in our time</u>, **AFTER** having <u>evolved</u> **through** <u>six previously unseen stages</u> (which are *realized* and *demonstrated* to us). NS3: 14; 8: 16a-26a

7 The process of guidance and instruction. Pxxvii An analogy of the *'resurrection'* and growth of the **"Lost and Found"** 'Original people' in North America can be seen in these six (seven total, chapter 15) stages, we'll look at the last three as an evolutionary process:

The 'Branch' evolves into a 'new mind:'

[a] "Leaf" - which <u>self creates</u> from '*integration* and *fusion*' eating from *above* and *below* acquiring 'the Essence of the Original Source,' see #1 above, NS8: 30d

[b] "Flower:" A book or writing from the **'new mind'** with a message outlining the nature of *'Essence'* and 'the *purpose*' for fostering 'the Branch or *'Tree'* into *renewed life*. NS1: 10a-28a b-37

[c] "Fruit:" A Living Person purposely' '**replicated**' from this activity clearly being a product of *It*, and showing all the 'marks' of 'the Original Source and Purpose:' see #2 above; and NS4: 20, 21; 8: 22, here is the *Original from* the *Original* with **The Seed of Replication**. **"The Last and still First"** NS5: 18-25

8 **The secret** here is that undeveloped man has a mind that is <u>controlled by nature</u>. NS5: 1 That mind cannot handle growing complexities it breaks down under stress and seeks help and guidance or follows whatever course or person that seems to lead it to **security.** TLOT: 3; NS11: 9; PL: 1; Ref and Chapter 11

   a Satan's knowledge NS2: 20; 12: 19; 14: 25 of man's nature is the *underpinning of their secret societies.* They use this knowledge to create *fear* and *anxiety* among the masses (especially the former slaves EL: 5, 8)

   b They promote and market *ideas* and *things* that cause a *"deviation"* **in the original nature of 'man.'** NS14: 25; Ps5: 9 They raise negative emotions by teaching and spreading fear, guilt, greed and anxiety in schools and through the media. There is always something else to 'want:' producing joy and or sorrow; and always someone else to hate or *focus their political or social rage.* That is how 'they' NS6: 6 rule the mind of undeveloped man, incitement or excitement. NS8:30b, c

9 To survive man had to **"evolve"** from a mind controlled by nature - **"He has produced you from the earth"** - into a far more powerful mind that man *controlled himself.* PL: 13-1 Man has to develop a *conscience*, become

self-conscious and finally *cosmically Conscious;* TLOT: 3 for this, **school work** NS1: 37; 14C **is required** that is how **secret schools** and later **open schools**, with different curriculum, were born. Q7:176; 71:17; NS12:53, 60; Ref: 3, 6; Ch 5

10 The *automated mind* **of nature** had to *become* 'self' and 'cosmically' conscious. The automated mind Instructed but the people were too automated to 'hear' their own inner Voice - **being rooted in socially produced automated mental laziness and later moral decay** Ep4:14, 15; NS2: 20 - "Grow-Up *In-to Him* in All Things" was the "Lord's" inner Command. TLOT: 2a

    a Only a few hearts were inclined to *'hear'* the "Lord" within, TLOT: 2 the rest formed in their secret (and later open) schools to make plans to '*subdue*' and to '*rule*' the unlearned who are **"tossed about"** by every emotionally charged thing presented to them and find themselves powerless living with unjust laws, fear, violence, and death. NS8: 14

11 Secret school graduates never, themselves, reach the highest levels of '*human* growth (**conscience**) and development' they practice rituals and traditions without **Cosmic Understanding. They do however become the 'gods,' masters or 'gate keepers' of their own world.** NS8:7; 14:11; Q30:29, 30

12 Reflect here: If **the original of a type** were not available, if *the Founder* was not Present, NS3: 14, the one who would occupy that position (e.g.**: a 'branch'**) must go through a process we describe as **'reverse replication' (having *no seed* to begin).** NS4: 14, 17

   a That person must get <u>deeply</u> **'engrossed'** [Q10: 61] with *'the energy'* that "the Original" interacted <u>with</u> - or <u>through</u> – and anoint, as it were, his head with 'oil' (knowledge) and **"Do the First - *internal*** R2:5 *and later **external** -* **Work"** required R2: 5; NS Ch 5 and thereby demonstrate the <u>*'Essence of the Original'*</u> *as* **"Present."** NS5: 4a-20, 21; Chapter 15 **Did you see how?** See #1 *above*

13 **Analogy** continued: 'The Branch' <u>is not</u> and <u>was not</u> '**the First' of its type.** For the 'branch' to gain the Power and the Insight of 'the Original' it must, and <u>had to</u>, *do the work,* namely, driving the **'Essence Responsibilities of the Original'** into <u>existence from within itself</u> and then *Foster them* into unlimited potential for growth and assure *it* or *them* of <u>the capacity</u> for *replication* (if they evolve). Chapter 2; 7c above

14 This <u>function</u> and ***inner*** <u>evolution</u>, ***becoming*** <u>Root</u> and <u>Seed</u>, turns the 'Branch' *into the* <u>*Living*</u> *Original* of the type. NS4:12 This is the 'Good News' to the <u>'four hundred'</u> year old **"dead,"** Ep2:1 we <u>*can*</u> live with peace of mind and emotional contentment. NS1: 6: 17: 21

15 To ensure that the **Last** <u>are</u> *First*, we must clearly come to **"understand"** and <u>accept</u> **our 'responsibilities'** as the *Living Original* of Man by **re-creating** the 'seed' of the future: **'L Sh'b'zz,** out of 'Allah's Word;' that is our work, and that is our mission. PL: 13 -1; NS2: 7-11; 3:7a; 8:22, 23a-30d

16 Notice that the branch found itself doing <u>its first work</u> in water NS8: 12 *revealing its nature to itself* as it grew roots in the soil and went down and back <u>into the dark past.</u> The branch

(stem) rose higher with time, in the light, <u>weak at first</u>, but it started demonstrating what it would look like and *the nature of the work* it would do in its mature stage. Ecc12:13

a **Time** <u>produced</u> strength, power and recognition for the branch (trunk),

b *Its fruit* and *internal seed* for replication NS14: 38a was the **Final Product** of its growth and *the manifesting of its inner - unseen - power:* the original seed (God) is possessor of the power and force to reproduce the original tree which occupies space and produces time.. NS15:1

17 In <u>our Circle</u>, our 'responsibilities' are **"Essence Responsibilities,"** see #3 above, **our personal 'responsibility integration' (fully** *'integrated'* **thinking and honesty) will push and drive** <u>our</u> **'Essence' to its final manifestation.** NS5:8

18 **Again, remember, "Essence Responsibilities"** <u>drive</u> <u>"Original Universal Purpose"</u> <u>into existence</u> thereby *Creating* - *building* or *forming* - according to their type or need. Reflect on your inner essence, NS4:12 what is <u>your</u> natural inclination? PL: 7, 8; TLOT: 2, 3-18a; NS8:13 This may take some time or school work NS1:37 to determine, we have not been living **the upright conscious life.** We must *learn how to disconnect* from the social world of our upbringing or training, *with balance.*

19 *The New World* arrives from the development and the manifestation of a *"**New Mind**"* within *you.* Ecc7: 29; Ps44: 23; 78: 65; NS12: 43

a Like "The Branch," the **New Mind** is a product produced <u>in time</u> and was **resurrected** like the "Branch" NS8: 15 that finally **became** <u>a Tree</u> it was produced and **'replicated'** from its "<u>Original Source</u>" found within itself. NS14:47; 8:22; 12:33; 11:8-12, 17; 1:20-37 **these references reflect the Spirit of Our NEW Circle of Light - there are many more.** Ps119: 105; NS1: 28a

20 The Cosmic Law is **attracted to** everyone who **"strives"** through <u>conscience</u> and <u>consciousness</u> **with a purpose.** TLOT: 18a, 19a; NS5: 21

a Soon, the results of **<u>your striving</u>** will enter into our world to be seen by everyone with "eyes" that "see" Reality. Intro: 17; TLOT: 19, a; 7: K1

21 *<u>Did you apprehend the answer to question number one above</u>?* The Prophets asked it and answered it below - between them you should have your answer.

a "<u>Who will stand when he appears</u>? He is like a **refiner's fire**, and like **fullers' soap**; he will sit as a <u>refiner</u> and <u>purifier</u> [of minds, turning them back to their "Original Source," nature and inclination NS1: 25]" Mal 3:2, 3; Q2: 84; 30:30; Ecc7:29; #2 above; 3: 5; 12: 5

b For those of you that are blessed to "see" or "hear" this "Message:" "The **Sun** of **Righteousness** (Through The New Song) has arisen (among us) with healing in his wings (**"wings"** <u>represent</u> **functional**

power). Power to "save" the <u>listening</u> ear, the <u>observant</u> mind *and* the <u>seeking</u> *and* <u>open</u> spirit thus <u>*producing*</u> **"New life"** and **"Upright"** *Thoughts* and *Behavior* **- "Righteousness" - in those who, before this, were mentally and or morally dead to the knowledge of 'self'**). See #19a above; 5: 18, 25; 14: 17-20; Q16: 101

c Allah has <u>made the nature of the Lost Found Original man</u> *beautiful* and in *due proportion,* NS8: 30a, c *<u>after</u>* his **resurrection** *from* **mental** and **moral** "death." NS7: A; 12: 34; 14: 17- 32 Now, our conscious inner evolution, NS4: 3b will raise us up, by degree, to Him. Q64: 3; 54: 49; Intro: 4, 5; TLOT: 2, 3 NOTE: "The spirit (function) of a man (mind) demonstrates the **quality +/- of the Lord** (possessor of power and force) *<u>within</u>* **his flesh."** Prov. 20: 27

I **There are only two people on Earth, God and the devil, their qualities range between one and 100 left and right, positive or negative.** Intro: 5 **Do the Math and evaluate what you see or learn.** NS2: 6; 8: 21-23a; Prov25: 28

II **The basic principle** of *thought* and *action* in <u>the new world</u> of mind and spirit is *entire submission* to "Truth" and "Right Action." PL: 5 <u>That is</u> the "right way" of life *for you* to "return" to *your own mind,* NS1: 36; 8: 20c; 12: 78a; 14: 55a or "bind back that which has been broken" in us by our historic and open enemy. OSHA176P3; NS8: 2-9, 10; 11: 6

d   Now it is **your turn** to put on wings. Manifest power and functionality from your own flesh, your own inner developed "self."

e It is now your turn to fly **back to our Source**.
Mal 4:2; NS1: 6, a; 3: 7; App. I: 7, 8; 17: 21; OSHA214P5, 6

CHAPTER TEN
"The Star of Piercing Brightness"

1 This is **the Comer by Night!** And what will help you realize who 'the Comer by Night' is? Q86:1; NS9: 21b **(He has many titles)**

2 He is made from a drop emitted, as are all men, and **he is Able.** His Power arises from The Original Essence - **Cosmically based knowledge**; Chapter 4 **- rooted in a Consciousness _checked_ _by_ Conscience** - to bring back to life those who have died on, or around, the Cross. NS5: 21

3 He arrives in the time of **spiritual darkness,** the time that _all hidden things_ are being _made manifest_ to those _who want or need to know._ NS9: 3 He functions **like** a Star in the Night NS14:14. In that time man has _no moral_ or _spiritual strength_ and **no helper** against the **spiritual darkness** and the **material forces** of Satan or *Society Based Consciousness _without_ conscience (or "self-remembering").*

4 'The Comer by Night' opens up both the heavens and the earth - with Essence insights - to the 'dead' bringing forth to their eye, their ear and their mind, _new life_, _new 'hope'_ and _the capacity_ **to fulfill their own dreams, hopes and aspirations' _with_ "the Key to the Bottomless Pit" (The New Song** Q3: 110; 8: 29**).** Q85: 4, 16; 91: 7, 10; 95: 4, 8

5   This is **'The Word'** that distinguishes <u>Good</u> from <u>evil,</u> review two and three above.

6   This 'Word' is not a thing of amusement. I Am Executing My Plan World Wide; Satan is trying to keep and maintain his world, and the "Unbelievers" have a little more time to reflect within themselves and see who is the best of planners.

7   But! Because of their attitude and arrogance, **The Time for many** <u>will end</u> - <u>*abruptly*</u>. Q7:95; Jn17: 9; Mt10: 34

   A "The Star of Piercing Brightness" lights up "<u>The Straight Path</u>" NS8:9-13 *to* **"The Up-hill Road"** - **during the time of spiritual darkness.** And what will make you realize what the *'Up-hill Road'* is? **The Up-hill Road** is '<u>the work</u>' of **freeing a slave**, or *<u>a mind bound by the consequences of bad habits</u> or <u>social automation</u>.* Dan 12:2, 4-10; NS5: 2a, b-6; 12: 80; MFM4070; OSHA113P2; 184P1; Q90: 12, 13

   B Your 'essence,' when <u>*developed in you*</u>, is the power that lights up **your** path. The growth of <u>*your*</u> *'essence'* determines what *you see,* what *you learn* and *what you will do.* NS4: 21; 9: 2, 3; 15: 6h

   C Plant your 'essence' in **"the New Song"** then use the light of **prudence:** it leads to listening; use the light of **kindness:** it leads to conscience; follow the light of **wisdom:** it leads to self-consciousness; you will then **become the light** of *charity:* which develops from Consciousness; finally this process **demonstrated** your <u>living</u> *faith:* which is **the Work**

of God (Functioning through **The Conscious Human Being**). NS2:21; Mt12: 28; 5: 12-14, 15

D Star Light, Moon Light, Dawn, and our Sun: Use the original creation as your source, your basis, for generating insightful metaphors for living your life and working in your own environment.

CHAPTER ELEVEN
"Kingdom of God/Heaven"

1 The Law - **Requirement** - That Would Unlock the **Essence of God** from our Earth Bound Minds - (minds that are now controlled by Culturally Automated or Socially Mechanical Forces that produce our **behavior: the human - automated - nature that controls us** [and that we were born with]) - is **"Consciousness"** **with** a developed *functioning* **"Conscience."** PL: 10; NS14: 50; MFM4000

2 **"Deliver Thy-self,"** we are instructed, Zec.2:7, <u>and</u> **"Guard your own souls,"** Q5:108; NS5: I These commands cannot be performed while **"asleep"** or **"spiritually dead"** or with **"automated," or "ritual behavior."** There must be internal *volitional* effort or evolution first. TLOT: I I, a; NS4: 21; EL: 11; Q10: 61

3 Consider that *"man is made complete and incomplete"* out of dust, sperm, a clot and a morsel of flesh in order that God may <u>manifest</u> His Power **in – or through - <u>him</u>** Q11:61; 22:5; NS2: 4, 5; 3: 14; OSHA128: P3.

4 Man is produced, or made, **first** by the Earth as a sentient being, I Cor.15:45, 48, <u>not</u> as an intellectual being <u>or</u> a spiritual being. He is a being born possessing the powers of *sense perception,* having **sensation** as *immediate experience* in his youthful stage as distinguished from **thought** which is that aspect in him that is *"incomplete or partly unformed"* at birth, or in his early evolution from

a morsel of flesh or a baby *(requiring his conscious participation to form or complete)* - *which is <u>easily polluted</u> by <u>negative ideas</u> (environments)* NS8:9, 18

   a Note here that *every living thing on earth is a sentient being,* their differences are seen in the degree of complexity that each displays in nature's array of types. The young or undeveloped human mind *is <u>easily polluted</u>* when unguarded. NS9: 8, 10; 16: 5

5 Perception is always external in origin and arises from the excitation of one or more **sense organs.** Perception involves *interpretation* of a stimulus and the *recognition* of the external object that has produced the inner sensation. AppV:10 We call this **"the Highway to the Self,"** where the Universe, starting with our small world, NS4: I enters our biological core and is than environmentally differentiated to maximize our individual development according to our interests. NS4: 21; 9: 12a; 16: 1

6 *Balanced perception* produces **"Conception" of language, calculation, metaphors, analogy, understanding** and so on. NS4: 20; NS12: 78 We refer to idea conception *or* creation as **fully '<u>integrated</u>' thinking** *when it is achieved through* **"Conscience."** This formulation produces social **honesty** and <u>inner</u> **peace** when a sentient being has *evolved past natures' automation* Q11:61 *and or cultural mysticism.* PL: 4-11; NS2: 20; TLOT: 3; App V

7 The point here is that **human life** has two primary sides, Ch5 namely **biological (physical/automated)** and **mental/spiritual (potentially volitional).**

a - *The biological side* contains all of the sense connectors that are **automated, controlled by nature, _nature_ - mind you - has no "self" to control,** PL: 8; NS4: 2, until the being (person) _evolves_ to the higher plane of conscience. NS12: 47, 48-55 This is where _you_ step out of The Law of Accident (**conditioned control through** culture, rituals, and dogma) TLOT: 2-11; NS2: 20; Ch2 and 13 otherwise supervision is required for that person or group since they **have not** made a "self" that **they control.** MFM: 2784

b - *The mental/spiritual side (personality and being)* is where "conscience," "self-consciousness" and "cosmic-consciousness" **may evolve** if a person is _free_ from _automation_ and _mysticism_ (this requires personal effort or re-socialization NS4: 21**).**

c - Within a person, their capacity for **"inner evolution,"** there are *levels of* **potential "existence," "being" or "functionality"** which arise from **zero through 100** degrees in knowledge, ability, strength, power and much more depending on how, where and to what we apply ourselves to and or what we may identify with or become attracted to. NS Chapter 2 and 5; 8: 23

d - Know here that *"Consciousness _without_ conscience"* *will produce a* **"Devil"** *or* **"Satan,"** *a being made in the "image" and "likeness" of the original.* Gen1:26 *These are _titles_ representing Cunning, calculating, savage and or beast like characteristics emanating from the "human" form* NS2: 20 *which was originally* *designed to accumulate, crystallize and manifest Universal Consciousness - Capacity, Ability and Functionality* NS2: 5 *- from the "human" being; a treasure hidden from us today under conscienceless deception.* NS5: 10B4a, e; 8:18, a; PL: 11; Q8:18; IIThess2:3, 4-8, 9; IThess2: 15; Ps5: 9

e - *Biological balance* is seen through the health and strength of the individual; and

f - *Mental or Spiritual balance* is seen through the presence or absence of **"conscience"** on the one hand and the level of <u>developed</u> **"consciousness"** achieved by the **"Individual"** on the other <u>as</u> <u>demonstrated</u> by their activity and or achievements in life. IThess2: 10, 13; NS5: 7, 8 You know a tree by the Fruit that it bears.

8   **The Secret to <u>*Spiritual Life*</u> is "The Word:" "The Possessor of Power and Force in the human form,"** NS2: 7 meaning the analogy, the parable, the metaphoric *"Word" that energizes human action.* That **"WORD"** <u>expands the mind</u> and *enables* a person to <u>extract himself</u> - separate himself - from *the law of nature* and from **stifling *automated, mechanical, animalistic, reptilian, or ritualistic culturally based behavior.*** Review 3 and 4 above;TLOT: 7, 9 **In time, the Student learns, they <u>can</u> "FLY"** or *evolve within their own flesh.* NS1: 6; 17:21

   a Knowing this one may enter <u>the new world</u> of **"Consciousness."** A world where One has *the power of self-control* and <u>the ability</u> *to see the past,* *the present* and *the future* which machines and <u>lower animals</u> cannot do - **and** <u>*there*</u> **"*after*"** make plans and decisions for one's 'self' EL: 18 instead of being lead by someone or something - an authority figure - outside of your **"self."** *This is what Jesus wanted to say, but the people were not ready yet, they could not bear to hear it.* <u>**Are you ready now?**</u> <u>**Can you bear to hear it**</u> *(This 'Good News')?* NS12:9, a

9 **"*Before* <u>this</u> (New Song), most minds are dead (unconscious) in trespasses and sins..."** Ep2:1 The New Song will <u>focus</u> *the* **"quickening"** *process*, from **zero through 100** in **"human" - our -** evolution. The automated mind **makes no <u>decisions</u>** (as opposed to safety choices) it is innocent it is *led* and *shaped by manipulators, and <u>external</u> controllers.* **The hidden Evil One** *is in control of your present life and your future, unless you evolve. All the while you think you are deciding your own life and future.* Review EL: 3-16, 19; NS12: 1a, 4; 17: 17, 18

10 This was Jesus' Message for the people, but the people were unable to understand Him. Because of their **un-conscious - of "self"- minds**, they could not "hear" what He was saying. To "hear the Word" is to "<u>see</u>" - *through the metaphor* - and *function* in a 'new (**mental**) world' while physically remaining right where you are, and being "*here (alive) after*" your automated mind and social spirit evolves. #7d; 1: 6; 17: 21; Q2: 26

a *The difference* for the **"Self Conscious"** mind (what it can do, see, hear and feel) is like coming from a

different galaxy (or world) while living in this one.
NS5: 2c

b We are fully aware of **the price** of our growing Conscience, "when we increase our wisdom we increase our sorrow," since the power to *do* *externally*, or bring about **external** change, does <u>not</u> arrive **automatically** because of our increased wisdom. NS3: 5; 9: 16

11 "He, *the Spirit of Truth,*" *not me* Jesus was saying, "will lead you into **All Truth**." "Blessed are those who *hear these "Words" and understand*, they see and *live with* God in **His Kingdom** (the world of personal *inner control* and *power* through *consciousness* and *conscience*)." NS1: 21; 2: 5, 7; 4: 3a, b; 8: 22; 9: 21b; 12: 43; 14: 31

12 Today "Jesus" is calling the "Lost Sheep" to "*mental* and *spiritual* freedom" Mt10: 5, 8-16 but they are "chained" or "yoked" to automated, mechanical, socially shaped and motivated **behavior.** He is calling them to "**grow up into God**" through this message. NS2:19

a Only **the conscious** among them understood Moses' "Words:" "He to whom the 'Word of God' comes *is* **God: <u>meaning,</u>** a Possessor of Power over ones *'self'* and **not** living under the behavioral laws of nature, nor having Satan's cultural gravity, education and peer pressure controlling ones behavior." Q13; 5; PL: 11; Dan 4: 17; NS15: 5, 8; 16: 7, 10

13 **"Consciousness"** coupled with **'conscience'** is the <u>KEY into "Heaven"</u> ["peace of mind and emotional

contentment"]. Now is the time to **unlock the Universal Power - "the Kingdom of God/Heaven" - in** and **from your "self."** OSHAP2P3L7

   a **"He that overcomes** (the culturally automated life and or mysticism) shall inherit all things (that **they can mentally conceive and emotionally believe**). I (*Consciousness*) will be his God (*Leader or Guide*) and He (*Evolved Inner Function*) will be My Son (*Expressed or Manifested Results of learning*)." R21:7; NS4:7a; Intro: 17; Lk17:20, 21

14 People in "this world" have "consciousness," however many have *no, or limited, 'conscience.'* NS2: 20; 5: 12, 13 They can lie and mislead, they can steal, rape and kill thinking they are okay because of their social position or momentary condition. Yakub's law gave them their sense of **"manifest destiny."** NS5: 16; 12: 1, 6; 14: 1

   a They think *their 'God'* (Yakub) will continue to forgive just about anything they do. **He did for 6000 years.** However, now, **today** we are in a *new* and *different time.* NS15: 12 Caucasians are **not doing** "The Holy God's Work." NS12: 37, 38 No, they are *far from the Spirit of the Upright God* Jn16:2 they are doing the work of **their father** whom Jesus called 'the devil.' NS12: 37, 38

   b *Caucasian leadership continues to manifest and extend* "Hell." NS8: 10; 12: 1a: Consider the world around you. **All negative events** current and for the past 4000 years **lead back to them** and their unjust military, financial, political and spiritual hegemony over the original people of the earth. NS1: 16; 8: 8-12, 15

c   Murder, stealing, slavery, rape, sickness, greed, lying. They are masters of deceit, and of course their god's primary characteristic, **"jealousy,"** has marked their behavior to this day. NS9: 8a, b-11; 12: 1, 6

d   Our *"Consciousness"* does not permit **illusions** to go past us *unnoticed, if or when they do that is a mark of mental or moral death.* EL: 11a, e; 4: 5

15   How does *each person* achieve their "Crown of Life?" **The New Song** will orient you into the knowledge of *your* "self," God and the devil. As a "Conscious morally upright *Individual*" you will be *using* **the Universal Law of Attraction,** that Law will, in time, remove you from **the automated world of the animals, lower life forms and the spiritually dead (whose life is hell).** NS5:10b4a, d In other words, you will have escaped from the Law of Nature *manifesting* #12 above. TLOT: 11

16   Why must we be **"conscious"** of this Universal Law of Attraction? Because **The Law of Attraction is obedient - it _serves_ and _services_ "The Conscious Human Mind." You become and attract - *you attract and become* - what you think about.** AP: 11; Ch 5 What is the quality of *your* thoughts? You should be thinking about your own *inner evolution* and the *"Door"* way out of hell. NS1:40; 8: 30i

17   **_Every thought has a frequency_ and your passion** *speeds up the frequency you are on **enabling you*** to become or attract **to yourself** what you think about *or* focus your mind upon. For those who are negative in their thoughts and feelings *they also attract*

those outcomes to themselves. NS12: 1, 3 Focus, Time and Frequency **determines** outcome. NS Chapter 4; EL: 16; CI: 7; App1: 6;VI

18 You've heard it said that **"God is Love,"** how do you **understand** that? Let's *look at love* from **'our'** <u>perspective</u> of "Conscience *and* Consciousness," **or "self control,"** vs. nature's automated reactions:

[a] **For a "man" [male],** NS2: 4, 6; Ch5 **"love"** for something starts with his or their **"achievement(s)"**, **"production," "creativity,"** and or **"value creation"** all of which *result from having a* **focused purpose**; NS9: 2a, 3 the <u>elements</u> of **"a" (Attribute - "Being" or "Self" - Creation)** *produce the elements of..."b"*

[b] A man's **"happiness"** (self-assurance, and or self esteem). **"Gratitude"** and **"Appreciation"** for <u>each sex</u> is also found on this line fortifying **"Happiness." Exportable Feelings** then *produce "a" and or* **"c"** see NS2: 7a, f

[c] **For a "woman" [female],** Giving **"Honor,"** **"Respect"** and **"Adoration"** to the *possessors* of **"a"** is first. This is the woman's **Thought, "why" and "purpose."** Love is **the result** of happiness. Happiness **energizes** the mind and body for **objective love** ("peace of mind and emotional contentment"). *Automation,* animal passion and carnal desire animate or energize **perverse 'love.' Line A and C outline the male and female**

> **approach to "Love."** <u>Remember</u>: Nature has no "self" **it is automated.**

19 Why does a woman fall in **"love"** with a man? **In our world *"love"* originates with the elements in "18a"** above. If her **"love"** (or relationship) starts out for <u>any other reason</u>, as we see in the outer circle, we would call that **"perverse love"** recognized because it *produces perverse results.*

20 A woman is *"attracted to"* and falls in love with a man's *achievements, creativity and/or values (which represent her security).* She is *"energized"* by his **happiness (self-assurance) at being successful** at whatever his task. If a woman was not attracted *to a man because of* **"18a,"** she could not - and <u>will not</u> - *honor, respect* and *adore* him. If a man does not get that (**"18c"**) from the woman in his life, ***he will not be happy*** **(with her and he may be tempted by another woman or perversion).**

21 A woman has to <u>*innately*</u> respect, honor and love her man for what he *has done* and or *is doing – actually or abstractly -* or the relationship *cannot work or last.* This, of course, requires sharing of concepts or ideas; love and trust. App III

22 **A man's "love"** for a woman (and for some men, <u>*how they see themselves*</u>) is based on <u>*her perception*</u> of his efforts, **"18a,"** and her subsequent emotional and or psychological support of them as his **"help meet"** **18c.** Otherwise, <u>a man's attraction</u> to a woman is from the perverse side of **"love,"** "animal passion and carnal

desire" demonstrated, among other things, by leaving their children, disrespect and or violence.

    a In the outer world people are together, as we can see, for <u>all the wrong reasons</u>. Most people cannot differentiate between "objective" and "perverse" **'love'** and the proper male and female role in life while living in this highly **experimental society**, called 'hell' [NS8:10] by the evolving **"Holy Ones."** NS1: 25a

23 A woman's happiness **may come** as does a man's, 18a. **However,** a woman may also achieve her happiness *from* and *through* her man's success. His success *is also hers* because she talks to him as an 'help meet' and she *encourages and supports* what he does along with teaching and raising their children to love the world <u>they are building</u>, this makes for ideal family fusion. NS16: 13

24 A woman should not **expect** from a man what she gave him in **emotional support,** <u>if she too goes out to work</u>: (what she gave him when she was <u>not</u> <u>*working*</u>). Although she may get it in some cases, <u>most men</u> are **not taught** *that kind of sensitivity* and *don't have a feeling for it*. <u>*By working*</u> she also diminishes what she can and may be willing to give him, especially if she needs emotional support <u>that is not offered</u> or <u>*even noticed*</u>.

25 18b, above, points out that a man's love, gratitude and appreciation for a woman should grow <u>from</u> a woman's adoration, respect and honor <u>for what he does</u> (not her

legs, hips and so on: *if it's only a physical attraction*, that's perversion).

   a Generally, a woman working takes away from a man's self image as well as in some ways her respect and adoration for him because she has to work. She may want to work however her working may take away from what she really gives the relationship, **emotional *and* psychological stability.** When she gets home, she may not be emotionally stable herself this too leaves an opening for perversion.

26 A <u>balanced woman</u> has more ways to be happy than a man, physically, psychologically and emotionally, when she is being her innate "self" rather than a copy of a negative *made* "**man**" in her <u>behavior</u> and <u>attitude</u>. Being a woman does not mean being weak or second best. The question is: What constitutes her strength? We say, Uprightness. NS8:30j, 33; 12: 82; 16: 17, 18. The same basis from which Allah made Himself. PL: 7; NS2: 4, 7

27 Evaluating this Chapter carefully enables us to "see" why and how "God *is* Love." *Love is* the *"Functional **Essence"** - connection -* between the Balanced Biological Life and its resulting Health along with Conscience as **the corner stone** of a person's Consciousness producing familial harmony.

   a *Love is the creative, energizing and productive power (energy* NS2: 11,12*) of happiness*, it demonstrates why we honor God by emulating "His" Love, Honor and Respect *in* and *through* our lives. See 3 above What would our Circle be like other than the Kingdom of

Heaven understanding and following these "Words" of the Wise before us: The Original People of the Earth. NS3:7a; 15:8

b "Blessed are those who hear" these "words" through their heart.

28 If you've "chosen" or "identified" with a word, NS2: 9; 13: 3 a verse, a paragraph, a page or a concept from The New Song you *can change* your psychological and your physical life. NS2: 10, 13 MFM: 3385

29 Through "The New Song" you can open a Door NS1: 40 to a world of influence, power and understanding that is beyond your present conception.

30 Today **the Universal Mind** (or "God") and **the Devil** (or the Caucasian minded world) are both sending to us the vibrations, the forms and the elements that would make up the world tomorrow. Which of these forces is your mind and spirit open to, which vibration will win in your life? For whom have **you made** a sitting or a resting place, a "home" within your mind, your heart, and your body? NS2: 11

31 Which of these **two forces** will win the final battle between "Truth" and "Falsehood" within **your world** of mind and body? Have you made an *operational* **"self"** NS13: 16, 19 within your flesh body through which to engage Satan's world? NS12: 15 Satan has certainly prepared for you. And so has "God," NS8:13-26; EL: 13-18g through this message, which one are **you** inclined to?

119

32 Any Feeling or Emotion that is **not positive**, or mentally life giving and emotionally affirming for you, must be considered negative if it finds a home in "your mind" or affects your "emotional center" and thus your behavior *downward* or *negatively*. NS2: 10, 12; TLOT: 11

33 If you **identify** with a Negative Force <u>it can</u> deny you peace of mind; this feeling can be internally sickening for **"the self"** *you are making* <u>and</u> "your" physical body. Real "fear" arises when **"false evidence appears as real."** EL: 5, 8

34 Sometimes a warning, an admonition or a new insight can cause a feeling of "fear" because of a **lack of self knowledge** on your part. In that case "fear" [rooted in **"false evidence"**] is not the right word [or feeling] because *a person's positive response to this message* <u>does not</u> produce a negative result. The actual result could be knowledge enhancing, life affirming, attitude lifting, and produce new social mobility for you.

35 These life changing results would all be positive for the individual so it couldn't really be "fear" that brought about these changes it would be more like growing up, gaining a new consciousness and or an awareness of what was previously unknown or unseen. PL: 13; NS14: 39

36 Intercession, as we see, can produce **both** *positive* and *negative* results; both depend upon the nature, capacity and preparation of the potential receiver, NS4: 14b were they open to the new, willing to change, knowledgeable about the time we are living in, or were they closed

minded, in love with yesterday and or acting like know-it-alls in relation to the Devil's world. NS13: 2, 4

37 Blessed are those who hear this "word," reflect upon its meaning and internally grow to understand their own life. NS17: 8; PL: 5a; 1: 7b; 4: 2 a; 1: 23: b The over comers **_show_** by their action and or **_DEMONSTRATE_** by their behavior their "UNDERSTANDING" of the meaning of this Truth, this Wisdom of God and His Messengers by growing into a "God" over themselves NS15: 8 and sharing the process within their environment, or their world of activity.

CHAPTER TWELVE
Jesus: The Example of the Christ

The Object of Revelation:
The TRANSCONFIGURATION Mat. 17:1, 3-5-9, 11

"THE WAY, THE TRUTH *AND* THE LIGHT" For "The Dead"
***THROUGH* THE "NEW SONG"** R14: 3; OSHA81P3

1   "African Americans" and most people have a *distorted view* of the life of Jesus and have no realistic understanding of the concept, **"Christ."** They do not realize that their teacher is the very **"Lucifer (or Dajjal)** that *disappeared* and turned into an angel of light." Until now, we have been <u>unable to</u> *see out* of the <u>Arch Deceiver's</u> light. 19, 20 below Today we see <u>out of,</u> *into and* <u>through</u> his light. NS14:43, 47

   a   He is now the teacher and **temporary ruler NS8: 7** of **this, his** - *religious, academic, scientific, financial and political – world (as Gog, in <u>the East,</u> led by Russia and Magog, in <u>the West,</u> led by the U.S.).* "The truth of 'the dead', good or bad, *rising up in the Judgment* is now verified Ch 15. You are always **what** you are NS9: 2a and whatever you do *is written ahead of time by the Holy Ones."*

2   The people and nation that "stole a man:" T, p.92, 3ʳᵈ ᵖ *kidnapped, raped* and *murdered* the "Africans" **(The Seed of Abram** Gen15: 13, 14; Lk16: 23- 29, 31; Q2: 130, 131**)** and brought them to America, <u>starting in 1555</u>, are **the** *actual*

"anti-Christ," (opponents of God NS8:15, 18a) described in your Bible. These are the people who Mt15: 8 _**hide their real motives**_ NS8: 11 - "telling lies, stealing and how to master the original man"- _behind_ "Christianity" - or Bible based faith - which Jesus did not start _and_ never heard of _and their preaching_ of **"Jesus,"** which they do every day by all media. Q2:204, 205 The answer to the $64,000 question is what was done in the **64 years between** 1555 and 1619: Destroying of the original parents, the breaking of the original man, and the making of the first slaves. OSHA93P1, 4

   a   **But,** in their _policies_ and _social behavior_ they **are _opposite_ of - "anti"-** what **Jesus** taught or would do. NS8: 17, 18 This is historical and actual fact; they murder someone, somewhere, every day in the name of "_peace_" "_democracy,_" "_freedom,_" "_free trade,_""_justice_" _and/ or_ "_national security._" Q2:204; 205; Intro: 4, 6

3   Caucasians are **the arch-deceivers of scripture,** Jer.9: 8; Rev 12:9; Q3:71**,** this is the Truth from _your Lord._ However, most of our **"lost"** or **"spiritually dead"** NS12:66-73 people will find **this message** a mental and or an emotional **"vexation,"** Isa28:19, to accept _or_ believe. Q4:119, 121; 14:22 Of course, the devils don't like this truth being told either, but **they too, some of them, have a way out** NS5:15 M4. There are no means of knowing the true significance of prophecy before it is fulfilled. NS1: 4; 8: 30h Because of the TIME and The New Song we have been blessed to see The Supreme Being's Point of View, Ch 8 and 15 and we accept it, we hope that you consider well before you reject it. See 66a below

   a   All the while some of our people will **dismiss** or **forget** that these people were "good Christians" when they brought us here in chains and subsequently hung us from trees *while eating drinking and having a good time*; or shooting us down in the streets as they, and their "home grown slaves," do today. Need we discuss housing, employment, education, disrespect? You can add to this list.

4 Our *"dead"* people - raised and trained by Caucasians - will say to us **words of** *opposition to this "Song" in the devil's defense.* NS16: 7 To that God asks, **"Why do you talk so much when you know so little?"** God is saying, 'Whatever *you think you know* your mind **did not design** the idea, or the *aims,* the *goals* and or the *purpose* for it. You got and get *all* of your *ideas* and *desires* from and or through the devil.' Job 38:2; Q4:83; #8 below; NS16: 1, 2-7-9; 17: 18; Appendix, see 39a, below

5 However, The Seventh Angel *is at work* **removing** *"the mystery of God"* as it is written, and the scripture cannot be broken. Jn.10: 35 Scripture teaches us that Jesus and in fact all of the Prophets were *examples* to the people in their time among them. The question is thus raised in our minds, "What was He, or They, *Examples of?"* What did They symbolize? This question along with others will be discussed as we proceed in *unsealing* the Book(s). Q6:8; NS Ch 6, 7; 15

6 The *Wisdom* and *Guidance* presented here comes from the *Knowledge,* which became Scripture, Q5:112, *that the Prophets Taught in Their Own Words from the corner stone of knowledge given to Abu Ramu (Abraham), (without Satan's additions and subtractions),* **or** *God's Word to us directly. NS1: 31; 12: 27, 28; 14: 3-5, 8-14,*

20 Now, we may all **"choose"** to be Students of The Most High St.Jn.7: 16, *or* reject Him. Blessed are those who **"hear"** *these Words* and "understand."

7 Let me begin with a quote from one of the son's of Elijah, where he paraphrased the Honorable Elijah Muhammad's teaching. Mal.4: 5; Q32: 1, 3 If we would **reflect on it** and be **free enough in our minds or feel the vibration of truth and evaluate it**, we may go a long way in solving the various problems that confront us all, individually and as a complex society. NS17: 10

8 As we proceed, please keep in mind that the people who **resist the Truth** or are **deprived,** *by their own actions,* Q25:43; 4:64, 70; 6:70; intro: 4, 7 of Divine guidance are outside of the Divine Order of God Chapter 5 and are thus **shameless** in their personal life and **blood shedders** of those who are weak or those who stand in their way - *if they have the power,* or *authority,* to have their way. This is one of our **means of evaluating** who we are talking to, working with, watching, and so on. This includes watching and **"remembering"** ourselves. NS2: 20, 22; 13: 15, 20

9 Mr. Muhammad said: **"People are the product of words.** Mk7: 20, 23; NS4: 20. *A human being, a living soul, or a "conscience"* does not start to form in the Flesh Body until words (energetic vibrations) reach the ear or the eye or *affect the senses in some way* of a culturally automated being. TLOT: 3; 6: 12; Review Chapters 2, 4 and 5; OSHA123P3

    a The higher teaching is in the Divine Books, but the world is so far from *the real understanding of these books* that they have no more value to you than .50

cent pamphlets. They have no value to you because you are not able - because of **negative** *inner* *vibrations,* *words or concepts* - to innately **"understand"** the precious knowledge in them." Q6:122; NS14: 25 (**"Did you notice how difficult this idea is for you?"** See NS15: 6a)

10 Students of religion (meaning *self development*), or those of us who have sought Cosmic or *Divine Understanding,* have been taught that there are *three* **"stages," "levels,"** or **"wombs"** of human growth and development **beyond (inside)** the physical body. These **"wombs"** can be *categorized* as **the Carriage** (Flesh Body), **the Horse** (Emotional Body), **the Driver** (Mental/Rational Body), and **the Master** (Causal or Divine Body), which is the last and the hardest to develop – not that **we** are *in fact* developing It - **It has always Existed** (but *not actively* functioning in us *on a level that we can perceive* Its Work**).** NS2: 4-7; 3: 14; 5: 21

11 The '**Causal Body' is our Essence**, the **"**subatomic particles of energy (quanta), the **One Original Substance** out of which *all things* proceed. However, **we lost our way.** We must now 'learn' how to '**grow up' into our own upright 'self,'** **with our own Mind and have our own Voice." NS**13: 15, 20-23-26, 32 Reflect on Chapters 2 - 4, 5 - 9 –16, 17

a **We must develop our own capacity** within our own flesh and **reflect the Originator** in our actions by creating a body NS2: 5; 4: `14 to manifest our wishes and our desires. Reflect here: **We live in a**

Universally Conscious 'Yes' System. NS11: 17; 13: 15, 20-23-26, 32

12 What we ***are doing*** every day is learning to **'be'** by not being **'negative,'** or **identifying;'** and *learning* to focus our **'*intention*** - thereby making unity and internal harmony or 'balance' at *lower levels* of our being. These are the levels where – through our **identification** and or **negative emotion** - Satan is presently *dominant*; and where there can be **a connection made** NS8: 2, **oneness,** with our higher levels of *"Being"* through mental focus and our intent to escape. Intro: 7; 4: 1, 4; NS5: 15

13 ***Higher "Being"*** **must** **control** the *"Carriage"* or you will not be able to **attract** *and* **hold,** nor **accumulate,** *higher vibrations (energy)* and your potential for growth and *internal building* will be lost through dissipation and leaks. See 9a

14 At this point another question arises, **xx: 7, 11** **"*Why* is** the Divine Body the hardest to reach?" The Prophets have revealed the answer, but we have *not recognized it* because **we are dead** (spiritually) or *we have not accepted the fact* that we have been **"marked"** PL: 1; NS8: 10**, the** Prophets said, made **spiritually dead** by our captors up to this day. TLOT: 11 One of The Scientists said, "**By deceit Satan** brought about their fall." Q7:22; NS8: 8b -14; 17: 17, 18; see #4 above

15 Satan marked R19: 20 us by making us ***in his own mental,*** *emotional* and *spiritual image* NS17: 14 and *by naming us with his own names* LK15:1 5, and *through our ignorant* - **we didn't know any better at the time**

- practicing of their culture, education and religion, we became __as__ one of them. Q7: 22; NS8: 6b-8b-18; review PL: 6; 16: 1, 9

16 The Divine Body and two lower *but superior* <u>internal bodies</u> can be fully **"connected,"** to our Flesh Body. NS5: 15 We *can be* resurrected from spiritual death using the completed body of scripture known as Qur'an and referred to as the "Divine Mind" in print, **but** without the <u>proper guidance</u> we - as a people - <u>still</u> <u>won't know</u> **who __we are__** NS15: 6a, h we will act *other than* our own "self." **We are doing that now.** There is no Black Land, Black language, or Black culture. NS16: 1, 9

   a Africa is a continent with over 50 countries and more than 300 languages and cultures. <u>Our "new" identity</u> is *rooted with God* and the land He chooses.

17 According to the Prophets, our resurrection was designed to be accomplished using **the blended Light** of **the Bible,** described by Elijah, as our "graveyard" because of our "lack of self knowledge," **the Qur'an** (Divine Mind), and **"The Lessons"** designed to **shake up** the "dead" and make **this "Song"** possible, brought by our Savior, the Mahdhi; along with **Other knowledge "attracted"** *to this work* in the process of its accumulation. See 6, above (Q5: 112)

18 That describes *the Essence* of the **"New Song,"** <u>the purpose</u> of which is to provide the former slave with the <u>knowledge of the time</u>, provide <u>social and moral direction</u> and give <u>guidance into "self" knowledge</u>. Q5:112, 113; Rev.14: 3;TLOT: 11; OSHA184PI

129

a Yakub **saw us,** at the end of his time, **teaching other than what he taught** and saw thereby his people's end in that "the Lamb's Followers sung *as it were a* **New Song**" that *no one knew but them.* Yakub knew that *power flows from words* this is how he gained ascendancy in his beginning. Prologue; NS3: 2; 14: 19-42

19 Yakub told the Angels or Scientists, in his day, "I am going to *make* a **temporary ruler**, a **'Vicegerent'** (to supplant you) on Earth." NS8: 21, 23 They asked, "Are you going to *make one* who would cause mischief *and* shed blood?" *Why was that question asked?* "Surely," Yakub said, "*I know that which you know not.*" NS14: 4

20 **After** Yakub MFM3242 taught *his people,* he (metaphorically) confronted the Scientists, "Tell me *the nature of these* NS8: 18, if you are right (arrogantly meaning, "If you know so much!?"") Humbly, they said: "*We don't know.*"

a Arrogantly: Yakub told his *made ruler,* **"Tell the Angels *their natures!*"** *When* **the *made man*** *told the Angels,* Yakub said, "Did I not tell you that *I know* **the secrets** of the heavens and the earth and that *I know* what you reveal and what you conceal?" Q2:30, 33 After the "made man" was driven out of "the Garden" into the caves of West Asia, now called Europe, for 2000 years QCh18, Musa was sent to them with ONE Book of Yakub's wisdom to bring them out of the caves. Jn3: 14 Look at what they've built since then. Suppose he had been sent with more than **ONE** of Yakub's Books!

b Today the **"inheritor"** of the Earth arises from the conscious use of **The New Song.** NS8: 21, 23 We **recognize** and **see** through the 'veil' into **the nature of behavior,** in *both* "God" and the "Evil One" and his students. StMat12:25; see NS2: 4, 7; 4: 7a- 9; 11: 2; 14: 24-38a; Q7: 46; 45:13, 14; PL: 13- 1

21 "It is not our *external action* that makes things happen it is **our intent.** We should take no action *on anything* until we have **visualized our desire** and made it real enough *in our mind* that our next action or step, whatever it is, seems like the most logical and natural step to take. Intro: 5, 7; App VI: 18

a It is **not** *our role* to **supervise the creative process** *our role* is to **retain** <u>our vision</u> in our mind. <u>Stay focused</u> on <u>our purpose</u>; maintain our <u>faith, gratitude</u> *and* <u>awareness</u> of what has been **revealed to us,"** which puts us among **the 5%,** who are called the "poor righteous teachers," and or, the "Civilized People" of the Earth. L #2:16;

b The Scientists call these <u>new people</u> at the End: <u>The Watchers,</u> Who follow the Wisdom of **"The Supreme Being"** and <u>The Holy Ones</u>. NS15: 5, 6e-8

22 Actions *are* necessary but they are **the last** component of the creative process: First there is **"intention" or "Being," or "internally existing as..."** NS5:4, then *perceptual integration or Thought,* and last *Action* that produces, or maintains, '<u>balance</u>,' in that order. Anytime you are *struggling (not happy at what you are doing)* <u>that</u> is

not **your** essence responsibility you are **miss-creating** your future. **Your** essence is **joyful**, even though functioning through it may be difficult (doing something, or achieving results).

23 The creation of *anything* is through **our own vibration**. Everything vibrates, experiences, the creative process, it is by **our own vibration** that we **attract** and **harmonize** energy and things to ourselves, *or turn them away.* Ask yourself: How am I vibrating today? **How do I feel?** Your feelings will *show* your momentary vibration. How you **feel** determines what you have or will **attract.**

24 **Focus** only on what you want, **never** on what you don't want. All of this requires patience and *"right guidance."* This is all *"school work"* Matt. 7: 6, 8 -13, 21- 29; 13: 52 what, in fact, "religion" is supposed to be NS8: 2, **not** the deceit which is accepted by those who have "the mark – the mental and spiritual mind - of the beast," NS16: 7, 9 or those who "have not known *the depths* of Satan." R. 2: 24; 19: 20

25 **Many righteous men** have attempted to take the Book – completed and uncompleted scripture – out of the right hand of "He" Who sits on the Throne, but they were unable to loose **"the Seals"** Dan. 12: 4; Rev. 5: 1; NS6: 1 to **complete human development**, using the scripture, while remaining in a socio-political sphere of activity - around people rather than secluded or alone - and *in the wrong time.*

26 Now, 1400 years after Prophet Muhammad, "the son of a **Man**" having **the Seal of the Living God** has been

produced; R7:2 His name is Fard Muhammad Ibin Alfonso He is *The Mahdi* or **"The Self Guided One."** He has, through 42.5 years of preparation mastered the inner and outer requirements of raising the **spiritually dead** *captives* in the West and destroying the devil's world.

a He speaks, Mr. Muhammad said, 16 languages and writes ten of them fluently along with their dialects; He has studied with 24 of the world's greatest Original Scientists and also at seven of the world's greatest universities. He has retained a total of 150,000 years of Original history which He can discuss fluently. He has power over the forces of nature and as we can see **He is now "gradually reducing the land in their control..." as we watch.** Q21:44; NS1:31; 8:14, 20; MFMxxvii

b He is *The Ultimate Manifestation* of Divine Mind (Christ) in human form ("a body had to be prepared for Him" Heb.10: 5); His Father sent him *in the likeness* of **sinful** (Caucasian) **flesh.** Rom8: 3; Lk12: 49, *The Mahdi* is "the Son of Man (Alphonso Ibin Khaldun)" described by the Prophets as coming out of the East seeking to save the "Lost Sheep of the house of Israel" in the West. Lk15: 1, 6

27 As it was written: *"The Lord **Himself*** shall descend from Heaven..." Hab3:13; 1Thes.4: 16; Rev.21: 3 "As lightening strikes from out of the East and shines even unto the West so shall also the coming of the Son of Man be ("He came as a thief in the night," meaning *unobserved,* He has their flesh Rev.3: 3)." He said to us and the made man: "I will dwell in the midst of thee." Zec.2: 10; This is also

133

the story of Solomon *searching for the widow's son;* and He who *searched for the one "lost sheep."* See Chapter 17

a These verses all refer to a human being, **The Supreme Human Being, One Who is "prepared" or "formed"** NS14:16 **at the "Dawn" of His Time (He was born February 26, 1877) and at the end of the devil's time, which ended in 1914.** He spent several years of His youth traveling with His Father, MFM: 3824 and as a teen traveled in, out and around America before revealing Himself to us in Detroit, on July 4, 1930. We are now being **"sealed"** with His Knowledge Rev.7:3 on **"inner evolution"** and much more as we read, Q96: 1, The New Song. See Ch 17

28 He is the Founder of the teachings that produced the Nation of Islam in North America and many other groups and networks that are *not known to us.* Jn10: 14, 16 About His travels, it is stated that **"Burning coals went forth at his feet,"** a metaphor about the wars and disruption of all kinds that His travels produce. Hab. 3: 5 He has traveled throughout the world including the North and South Pole.

a He was Able to **"See"** – from a practical point of view and through the Wisdom of Those before Him – that *the rise of Developed Man or Mind* had to take place in the Western societies, even before their fall, or the beast like characteristics NS1: 31 which *materialism produces in man* would completely dominate and finally destroy **"man's"** moral capacity for development and thus bring total war and destruction to the entire world including His "lost sheep."

b The Savior's Presence produces conflicts **within** and **among** some **Caucasians** – those trying to get back, and those opposing them - because of *their nature* on the one hand and *Yakub's teaching*, which is _opposite to the Upright God's_, on the other NS14: 1, 2: **Their attempts and work in an effort to return produces conflict** because the most conscientious of them will be seen trying to _actually help_ original people. NS14: 41 _That is not Yakub's teaching_, reflect on #2 above!

c In like manner, **our presence among Caucasians** produces _conflicts in and among us_ because of our difference in nature from them on the one hand and many of us **loving them more than ourselves**, for various reasons (mostly rooted in ignorance), on the other. Then there is **added confusion** from seeing a few of them actually or seemingly trying to help original people, don't forget who we are dealing with here. NS14:7b

d John Hawkins, the English Admiral and slave trader *spent 20 years among us* and in 1555 promised our parents **"gold for their labor, more than they were earning in their own land."** They didn't receive gold. Review the Epilogue. Accept sincere help or support, but **"**_watch as well as pray._**"** NS9: 10, 11; OSHA92P5

e With all of this history is their _conflicting teaching_ – which has and still causes **conflict in our homes** - about God, which we had no way to refute (and many still accept today out of laziness, habit, tradition, ritual and 400 years of nothing else) until now. NS8: 14, 16-26 Being upright by nature, we embraced his religion since _they stripped us_ of all we had, giving us their names, language, ideas and behavior, until the Savior Appeared among us. As it was written before His birth, **He was born to save the "dead" in the West.** NS4:14a; Chapters 1-8 and 14; App I: 8, 10

29 Isaiah said, "The *heart of (automated) man* is <u>evil above all things</u> and <u>desperately wicked</u>, who can know it" Zec.2: 1, 2; Ps5:9 Our Savior Knows, "He" Who stood with *"a <u>measuring line</u> in His hand"* **- our Song -** to save and to destroy, Ps110:6 It is "He" who is measuring and weighing our reactions as we read and speak. NS5: 8-10B4a, f; App.VI: 4, 5

30 His teachings among the African Americans during the 1930's were of a **mystical intellectual order** owing to the psychological state of our people at that time. PL: 4; TLOT: 9 _He stayed three and a half years_. NS3:14 Those who believed in His teachings found <u>more order</u> in their lives and thus were able to <u>achieve some things</u> and know <u>a measure of happiness</u> that they did not previously enjoy. The essential result of His efforts was that the Flesh Body of those who believed in what He taught was *brought into submission* to Divine Principles, although they were not developed enough, at the time, to actually *understand* His teachings. Intro: 2; See Zec.3ʳᵈ Chapter. That work became *the basis* of what is possible for us today. Chapter 15

31 Out of the *Mahdi's* teachings, Rev.11:11, another mind was produced. **The Lamb**, Rev.14:4, **His Messenger, Elijah**. *The Master* is made to say through the mouth of the Prophet Isaiah, **"Who is blind, but My servant or deaf as My Messenger that I sent?"** 42:19

    a The Honorable Elijah Muhammad, the leader of the Nation of Islam, who, by *sincere effort*, was able to **develop himself** based upon what he was taught, to such a degree that the world of thought looked on in amazement as he accomplished things that prior to him seemed impossible among us, especially impossible for the **"blind, deaf and dumb"** uneducated son of former slaves.

32 Now, today, more than 32 years after him, we have come to *the third part* of the **"man"** that was to arise in the West, the individual NS15:8 who *puts on* the **"whole armor of God."** These are the children of the people who were the tail and are now rising up to be the *"inheritors;"* they of whom it is written, **"You are gods, children (today students) of the Most High God;"** and *you are the Apple of His Eye*. Zec.2:8; NS15:6f, g-12

33 Elijah taught us that "God is a product made by the actions of time. As long as we have no results <u>in time</u> (regarding *our efforts, our "self" work*) we have to sit down [or let others lead]." This *is* your time, *if you take it, if you use it!*

34 One cannot <u>revive</u> or <u>renew</u> "religion" (*our internal life*) without casting **new** and **brighter light** on it than was

previously available, Q57:28 this is going on today, right now, through this message.

a *The Mahdi* is made to say: ***"I will work a work in your days which you will not believe, though it be told to you."*** Hab.1: 15 This Light or Clear Truth represents the "Judgment" that every eye will be able to see once the clouds of *confusion* has dissipated from the 400 year **spiritually darkened minds** of the "lost" and now "found" "spiritually, mentally and morally dead" people of Abraham. NS1: 3; 8: 34a

35 It is written of those who believe, **"they shall see His face."** Should we not consider that even ancient history, or religion, teaches that "the dead" would arise in the ***Western lands***? That the tail would become the head? Does it not also say that the first shall be last and that the last shall be first?

a ***The choice is now yours, where do you want to be and with whom?*** NS12: 83

36 Remember what God told Abram (which is ***the basis*** of *our work* Q2:13): **"Know of a surety that thy seed** ("African" Americans) **shall be a stranger** in a land that is not theirs (America), and they shall serve them (Caucasians); they (Caucasians) shall afflict them ***four hundred years.*** *We lost* <u>*64 years*</u> *of time calculation, 1555 to 1619, by deceit. We didn't realize that the scripture was and is speaking about us.* NS8: 4-14-19 That nation - America - whom they shall serve, will I Judge: *afterward* they shall come out with great substance." Gen. 15: 13, 14; Ex. 21: 16; Matt. 24:27, 28; Joel 3:7

138

37 These verses are **not** talking about the Jews Q3:67 of any day or time. Notice their conversation with Jesus: "We be Abraham's seed, and were **never in bondage** to any man: how sayest thou, 'You shall be made free?'" Jesus answered them: "You do the deeds of *your father*." They said: "We were not **born of fornication** (why did they say that? NS14: 7a); we (both) have one father, God."

    a "If God were your father," **Jesus disagreed,** "you would love me: for I proceeded forth and <u>came from God</u>; neither came I of my-self, but **He sent me**.

38 Why do you not understand **my speech** #9a above is it because you cannot understand my (Spiritually discerned) **Word**? **You are of <u>your father</u> (Yakub) the devil** and the lusts of *your father* <u>you will do</u>. He was <u>*a murderer from the beginning*</u> and abode not in the truth, because *<u>there is no truth in him</u>*." #19 above

    a This conversation continues this is a **ROOT** conversation, *a key* that we need to understand for *<u>ourselves</u>*. St. Jn.8: 32, 51; see, R2:9; 3:9

39 Getting back to one of our questions, "Why is the Causal Body, which is called the Divine Body, last and hardest for us to reach?" Because **Satan educated our minds** NS17: 18 to believe in *materiality, selfish individualism* and *spooks* while **he controlled** <u>the spirit of our thoughts</u> with **his ideas** about <u>God</u> and faith… which **constantly clash with reality,** <u>fostering</u> our world of illusions. NSEL: 18g

    a **All we have are their ideas**, see #4 above; NS16: 7, 9 this has, <u>in effect</u>, made him **our father** <u>and</u> god *in*

the world he built. He has turned many people into **spiritual cannibals** by having them *"eat the flesh and drink the blood of Jesus"* in their "religious" rituals. NS8: 2 - 9; 16: 2

40 For us to really **access** the Causal Body <u>in us</u>, NS5: 2C, D we can't trust flesh and **its** forces **or** concrete things, which are external. Ibid: A, B In order for us to *realize* the Causal Body *within us* we must trust the **Unseen, The Original Substance** out of which *all things* proceed: The Eternal Cosmic Force that you cannot verify physically or rationally without *quantum physics or <u>inner evolution back to your upright nature</u>.* NS4: 12

41 To reach the Causal Body, you must <u>trust</u> **what you feel** from <u>your **highest nature**</u> and that *trust* or *vibration* will **transform** *your "spirit"* **into His Own,** NS1: 40 the subsequent energy will <u>create for you</u> what you **focus on.** NS14: 2 In time you will find yourself **doing without doing,** this action without effort will verify that your **internal development** is taking place and you've **aligned your energy with the Eternal Cosmic Force (God).** Consider NS4: 12

42 In our searching through the words of Jesus, we find him saying: **"I am the object** App V that receives **the action/work** of the prophets," in these words: NS6: 3

  a "I come to fulfill." He is saying, "I come as a *receiver* of guidance and prophecy from God and the Prophets before me, I've come <u>responding to It</u> evolving into *the internal moral form* that that Divine Word or Message was *intended to bring about for all Students of the Word."*

b *"The Word [Eternal Energy of God or Christ] was* **made (crystallized in) flesh."** Jn.1: 14 So he said: **"I am the Way, I am the Truth, and I am the Light."** Meaning, **"I am the thing - the "Being"** NS5: 4 **-** the previous prophets were trying to produce *within man (the human form),"* **I am, he is saying, an "example" of that work.** NS2: 5; 6: 3

43 "The kingdom of God <u>is</u> *within you"* (in the form of *primordial matter <u>responding</u> to Consciousness* that gives <u>*form*</u> to your **focused intent - *in time*)** Lk.17: 21 This is the manifestation of what we see in *The Mahdi,* Fard Muhammad, His Messenger and those who **accept this way of life** as we **evolve** *"in" and "through"The Word (energizing elements).* Intro: 5;TLOT: 15-18a; NS2: 4, 12; 9:19, 20; App 4, 5; Chapter 11

a "His name is called **The Word of God"** Rev.19: 13 **"I will write** on you My Own new Name," those who manifest a Divine Function Rev.3:12, **"you are the best."** Q3:10; See the Prologue and the Law of Three; NS8: 22;T, p. 176p.1

44 Mr. Muhammad has pointed out that "Prophets have been coming to complete an object, a *crystallized body* of <u>morally right knowledge</u> *in the mind* of man. The object is called *"Christ,"* and those prophets themselves had to be complete for that, their, time in order to complete the forming of the object." App V Christ means "man"

and *"man"* means an **Original, Developed or Divine Human Mind [The Crusher, In Which the Energy of God Is Actively Functioning].** NS14: 23a

45   Today, this is *The Mind* that has grown to the Third or Divine level – which the Qur'an describes as the "Mutma'inna" or *the Soul at rest* – which is not found in a Flesh Body moved by negative passions and impulses. Q25:43, 6:119, 7:179

46   **Christ** [in our time] is **a developed mind** that has gained *victory* over the *internal* and *external* forces of death *(mental, psychological and emotional* CH 15; NS5: 14*)*, those social forces, e.g., greed, envy, jealousy, hate, and so forth that **envelop the mind** that is not **focused** and **self-conscious** (and thereby the social circle or society these people belong to).

     a   This is a consequence of a person following *mental and emotional forces* that are "unchecked by a moral knowledge" or guidance from the **Inner Circle** of humanity (found in the New Song). NS8: 3; 5: 11, 16

47   As "man" *ascends* to God, or trusts in the Unseen Power within *the Word*, NS2:10, 12 a certainty comes over him, he **connects,** see16 above; NS13: 6 he becomes **One** with The Higher Consciousness PL: 8 that now works through *his* flesh and causes the automated forces of nature moving within his flesh to become His Servants and carry out His Will. NS2:5; Intro: 11; TLOT: 2; App VI: 4

48   In time that man's body, as **an object of Divine guidance**, will be in total submission to its Lord XIX: 2a; 14: 54b and will have fulfilled the Commandments given to,

and "through" all of the prophets. And, thereafter, the Message of God, in him as an Individual, will be complete he is ready for unsupervised service. Matt. 10:20; TLOT: 2; NS11: 7a

49 Consequently, He - the Rational Body or Intelligence - will be **"restored"** (to his *original* state) or **"resurrected"** (from the "mark of the beast:" mental and spiritual death caused by the *teaching and civilization* of Satan, Q5:94) ***back into the service*** of his Lord from Whom he had been separated by the *forces of darkness and desire* that had *masqueraded* as divine light (called Lucifer). #1 above

50 Adam (the last NS14: 33), or the human intelligence, had *no desire* to disobey his Lord, but in the search for knowledge – which can only come ***"through"*** the Flesh or <u>Sense body</u> – he found *desire* Q4:119; NS11: 5, 6 and got caught up in its fascinating world (now ruled by **The Prince of Darkness/ The Dragon/ Beelzebub/Lucifer/Satan/The Devil/ Dajjal/Gog and Magog and the Beast, all of these are <u>titles</u> and <u>functions</u> of *the made man*).**

    a <u>Not having</u> ***the power of a pruning moral eye*** NS5: 13 is what caused Adam to "slip" or "fall" to *<u>a lower level of activity</u>* than was divinely ordained for "him." Rev.2: 24; NS8: 13-30c; 14: 14, 16; see Ch 17

51 We cannot get to the Father, Jesus said, unless we come by him. There is no way that we can even deal with that statement unless we ask another question: "Who is Jesus?" and get a **meaningful,** not a spooky, ignorant,

or deceitful response (as we get from Satan and his students). Q19:21

52 *Jesus was a manifestation of Divine Word (Christ) in material (human) form.* Chapter 6 Regarding that the scripture reads: "When all things began, *The Word already was (unformed).* The Word dwelt with God, and **what God was, the Word was.**" St. Jn.1: 1 [**In total triple darkness:** NS5: 21 "Subatomic particles *of energy* (quanta), **The One Original Substance** out of which *all things* proceed" (take their shape).] See Chapter 2

53 With true *reflection* here we can "see" that Christ or "The Word" *in Jesus' mind* is the result, the **bringing together**, of a **cohesive Body of Knowledge** Q5:112, 113 whose roots are found in *the universal order of things requiring years of individual study* and *personal effort to crystallize* into the individual *"self" (flesh).* Study Ch 5

54 *All knowledge is material (all words are made of* "subatomic particles of energy which take on infinite forms"). Any person who develops their *"inner-self"* in this way becomes **a conscious-expression of "God" in their flesh** ("Moses called them gods unto whom *The Word of God* came"). NS2: 8, 12; 13: 16, 19

55 Those people who master their *desires* and their *emotional life* are able to do so because they *possess* and *manifest* focused morally right concepts and ideas whose *execution* produces - in time - *a permanent center of behavioral gravity within them*. They "feel" like they can succeed, and they do.

56 Their center of gravity, or crystallized personality backed by **essence** *[or, "subatomic particles of energy (quanta),* **The Original Substance** *out of which all-things proceed"]*, T, p.176p.1 constitutes a base from which these individuals are able to express the **Divine Will** in *the social order* without being **crushed by** or **"falling as a victim"** to the *forces of emotion and desire* (the devil's *intent* and *focus for us*) that are all around us and manifested in *"sport and play,"* money and materialism and all their offshoots, Rom.1: 20, presently controlled by the devil and designed to **distract our attention from what he is doing or planning.**

57 That body of Knowledge or Truth that Abraham, Moses, The Prophets, Q5: 112, 113, Jesus and Muhammad taught, **That Spirit of Truth**, is alive among us today, <u>can you feel it</u>? You are consuming it as you read. **Design <u>your</u> purpose, stay focused** and **watch your influence and happiness grow**. See NS 11:18a, b

58 **Our School** and community represent *the Resurrected Light* Q5:112 of Abraham, the Prophets, Moses, Jesus and the Lamb, Rev. 5:6, or Elijah. We are **refracting - the light** Q6:90 **blending and focusing the Prophets <u>together</u>** in *The Last Days* to resurrect the mentally and morally dead. Q5:112; NS14: 23a

   a This **"Song"** or **Light** NS14: 35 is **the Essence** of **all** of Their Teaching and backed by **The Source** of Their Teaching. This **Truth** is **Alive** within us today. <u>Hold fast</u> to this New Song so that no one <u>steals your crown</u>. R3:11; NS2: 4; 8:32a

59 *Our purpose* is to present **The Essence of Truth** as _an antidote_ to the "seduction" Q7:27 consumed by the spiritually dead former slaves, Abraham's Seed, and provide them with a **higher purpose** for their lives than what the devil "promises" Q14:22 them and *thereby help* resurrect the 144,000 Helpers to God's Purpose from among those who slept but are now awake. Rev.7: 1, 3 - 9, 17

60 If we **make our "self" an object** (*target* NS2: 16; PL:1) **of this "Good News"** then **"Christ"** (the power of *the Living* revealed 'Song' in us) will *destroy the power of bad habits, bad desires, false values, negative impulses*, and **their capacity to rule** *over* _our_ daily life. NS4:21; 7: 3F1 In due time, as with our own flesh, the entire social order will come under the Divine Will and follow Divine Guidance. Q7:34; 5: 94; NS2: 22

61 When the individual man (mind) comes under Divine Will and Guidance the animal (homo) part of him – the automated flesh form – can be *tamed* and allowed to perform its just role this frees the human spirit (sapient), or knowledge form, to honor "man" and not machines or lower level activity, love "truth" and not money, or things. Review Chapter 11; see NS5: 15, Causal Body

62 Only in the psychological state called the *"The Second Creation,"* or *"Resurrection"* will we find Men (meaning mind and _not gender_) who are *Able and Prepared* to spend their time, their money and their lives bringing true *freedom* (spiritual, mental and physical) to all of the "human" family following the lead of our Savior to _the true object of life_. Q3:185; 53:39-42, 47-55; 22:5; 31:28; Rev.20:6; Intro: 3; 8: 6

63 Let me repeat this idea: when the sky of man's *false personality* is rent asunder and listens to the Command TLOT2: a of its Lord (The upright nature), *then* "man" will be free from all of those inner forces (negative desires *provoked* by Satan's world) which are essentially *unchecked by right (moral) knowledge.* In time, society too will become free from the *chains of emotionalism* that foster hatred and other types of social diseases. See NS Ch 5; 12: 15-60; 14: 17-25, 26- 38

64 We should never lose sight of the fact that **society** (or your part of it) <u>ever</u> <u>mirrors the</u> *inner state* <u>of</u> "man." See #60 above When we see social decay, or *development*, it is just <u>an expression</u> of *conceptual decay, or growth,* as <u>manifested</u> *in* or *from* a <u>material form</u> or <u>social activity</u> **(or from me!)** NS7: F-K1

65 In conclusion, let me leave you with something else to reflect upon (smile). You *are* your *states of consciousness,* what you identify with NS2:9 and or your automated responses, these states are *manifested* <u>by your Flesh Body</u> **(no one can hide)**, which is, or should be, **your** servant, <u>*not*</u> Satan's. Intro: 5; Q7:20-22-27, 28; see # 2

66 **"Accept your own (mind) and be yourself,"** NS15:8 *The Mahdi* (The Self Guided One) told us. And warned: "Your *covenant with death* shall be disannulled, and your *agreement with hell* shall not stand." Isa.28: 18. Now, after 457 years, we fully *demonstrate* - **act like victims of** - what the devil calls the **"Stockholm syndrome."** Q5:107 You will be *"resurrected* from the spiritually dead, He told us, and called by a *new name."* Isa.62: 2; Rev.2: 17; Ep. 6:10, 14; Chapter 15

a We have been made the **"Foundation Stone"** for the New world. Isa.28:16; Ps118: 22 Daniel said we were "Cut out without hands, we were **"separated"** NS14: 8 with the "Words" (***values*** PL: 7; NS13: 11, 15: 6 ***vibrations*** NS4: 21, 22; 12: 9-13; 13: 17; App.VI: 6, 7) NS12:9 of Truth **not** the mysticism or ***methods*** of war and deceit. NS12:34-45

67 "I have ***formed*** this people ***for My-self*** (with *The New Song*)," Isa.43: 21, "They shall show forth My praise," as it was written. We will then have ***demonstrated*** that we were one of those **"lost in the West"** and now **"found"** there by *The **Mahdi**.* The focused scripture (**New Song**), in us, will *then* have been fulfilled as we form the basis for entering, reestablishing **'L Sh'b'zz**. NS15: 1

a ***The Holy One*** will then say to His Angels, "Bring everyone who is ***called by My Name*** to Me. **I have created them for My Glory.**" Isa.43:7; 34:11; Q20:41

b Oh, by the way, what did you say your name is?

68 I hope, with Allah's permission, that we sounded the proper frequencies - ***Truth Notes*** - *for your instrument (your body can be seen metaphorically as an instrument or a three-tiered building, a four room house, a tree, etc.) to* capture the essence of Truth. We understand, not every "lock" is the same nor is every door.

a For ***the seeker,*** we hope that our discussion format ***demonstrates* (through us)** the completion of

"The Second Resurrection" Q53:47; 31: 28 and gives a "Clear Vision," at least the substance, of what has been revealed through us. Chapter 17

69 We also hope, through this Message, <u>you see</u> the **manifestation** of the "Second Coming of Christ," (*"The Truth"* that has the power to crush **evil** or **negative** desire [the devil's ideas] <u>within any flesh</u> that **hears and submits to its Truth**), and *choose* "Him" to save yourself and your family. Intro: 3; NS1: 32; 2: 4; Ref: 7, 8; #26 above

70 **Our purpose, AGAIN,** is to help you *manifest right action* in and *from your "self"* by following **the guidance** of **"the New Song"** to <u>**the Path**</u> **that is straight.** We want to show you *how to think about your development* and help you to *accomplish* the Scriptural **mandate** - addressed to those who have recently *"awakened"* from 400 years of spiritual, mental, and emotional death - to *"overcome"* the power of the grave (mental and moral inertia following the Caucasians). NS Chapter 10; see APP: 6; Ps78: 65

71 **Learn**, *take off the grave cloths* and *"grow-up into Him,"* in your <u>made</u> "self," <u>***through school work***</u> and not just *read about "Him"* Ch 2; NS6: 3 in Scripture. This <u>*Way of Life (or submission to the Will of God), as embodied*</u> in the **New Song**<u>, is not to make believers following rituals</u>, but to **"make us like Himself,"** the Lamb said, "in order to **prove His Truth.** PL: 13

a If we did not **look like Him**, He could deny making us and we could deny being made by Him." God's Actions spring from an <u>upright nature.</u> **Let us take**

on Allah's essence and behavior, remember, Elijah said, **"After me is God,"** making him *the seal of the past* and *the Door to the Future.*

72 Finally, have we considered **the source** EL: 5, 7-12; Ch 16 of our present state of consciousness? #4 -15 above Have we evaluated the *quality* and *the nature* of our present activities in space (our or *your* social environment)?

   a To what degree are you attempting to acquire God's *"new"* **psychological constructs** NS14: 19 that will help you to climb the *evolutionary ladder of* "self" *consciousness* NS13: 16, 20 which is, of course, not done mechanically, or automatically. *You must actually apply yourself to it?* TLOT: 2; NS5: 6, 7 Did I hear someone say, "These ideas are not new." *They are new to you!* #34 above *You* are *not* living through them therefore the result or your life **is hell.** NS8: 10; 14: 25; PL: 1; EL: 5

73 How deeply have you looked into the **Stockholm syndrome** and related its principles to your own thought process and behavior? NS2: 4, 13 Do you really understand this syndrome and your relation to it? How far have you *identified* with our captors? Prov3: 31; NS8: 8; 13: 3 What is your present *intent* and *focus? Why?*

   a These are just a few constructs through which you may attempt to **unlock yourself from the Caucasian mind.** Review the principles in this message and consider your own unseen "Original" capacity. NS17: 3

b "The Son of Man" came to **restore** <u>our mind to its Original State</u>, and place us in a position of consequence in **His** new world. Q14:48

74 **"The Truth** has arrived and *falsehood* neither *creates anything new* nor *restores* anything (old)."Q34:49 "Announce the **Good News** to My Servants – those who listen to **the Word**, and **follow the best (meaning) in it:** Those are the ones whom God has *guided*, (in Person) and those are the ones endowed with understanding." Q39: 18

75 "He Q6:8, 9 who brings the Truth and he who confirms (and supports) it, such are the men who do right." Q39:33

76 "They shall have *all that they wish for*, in **The Presence** Q6:2 of their Lord: Such is the reward of those who do good." Q39: 34 **"They are <u>shown a Way</u> that is straight."** Q3:101; Intro: 4, 7

77 "Those who believe and **work** <u>deeds of righteousness</u>, and believe in the Revelation sent down to Muhammad – **It is the Truth from your Lord** – *He will remove from you your ills and improve your condition."* Q47: 2

78 Jesus, Q5:113; 19:21: The Example or "Sign" of **The Christ** (<u>*The Original Idea of Man*</u> -*THE HUMAN NATURE OR MIND manifested* - <u>*as*</u> *the Crusher of the power of evil* **[or conscienceless inner miscalculation** NS8: 18**]**), whom we serve as the Holy One or the Great Mahdi: Allah in Person. NS14: 6

a We have been **instructed** on <u>*how*</u> <u>*to*</u> **"Grow up** into <u>Him</u> *in all things*;" NS9: 12, 16b and shown how to "Return to our Source," **'L Sh'b'zz.** Q89:27; NS3: 7, a; AP: 6, 7; 8:17, 18, a; Chapter 15

79 Now the question: Have you **chosen** to be a Student, a target of this message? Will you learn this **"Song?"** Have you chosen to be **"born again?"** Jn.3: 3-5 If you have then your next assignment through Our School and beyond is to discuss and work through the **"Seals"** <u>on your own life</u> as we explore in more detail how to return to Our Source. NS6: 1

a We will learn and discover how to "grow up into Him" with *practical methods* and learn the final destination of "man." This is the journey, it will not be easy, but it is a glorious trip. Chapter 4

80 **Travel with your eyes open to the future** through *God's Presence and knowledge (through The New Song) in your mind,* NS2:2; 11: 6-8; Q3:8, Rev.3: 12, and with this **"New" Life (Consciousness) and Vocabulary,** NS4:21 *learn* how you can *work with the spiritually dead* and improve the world around you, while traveling *"the up-hill road."* One day you'll notice, *'I have wings.'* NS10:7A; PL: 13

81 You don't have to **know everything - ahead of time - before you act.** All you <u>need to do</u> is take the next *'natural step,'* if you can **see** 'the next natural step' or **70 feet in front of you,** NS5: 12a *__while driving at night__*. With a map (our "new song") and this method a trip of a thousand miles can be easily accomplished. PL: 10

82 Each Student's mind must have **ideas that are checked by conscience; and wide study in your area of**

interest; along with appropriate knowledge for your chosen task. P.xix: 3; TLOT: 3

a **Your** personal maturity level, stage or room is and will be **based upon your** "understanding" and fulfillment of **your essence responsibilities.** Q6:132; 7:46, 48; Prov.4: 7; NS14: 14-17-24; See NS Chaps 2 and 9

83 I say to you now as Moses said: "Choose life (be **mentally** and **spiritually born again**, through this New Song) so that you and your children may live." Jn.3: 3; Jn.10: 9-27; Deut 30: 19; Jer.21: 8; NS2:2

84 Let's discuss your reflections now keeping in mind that **our purpose** is developing inner balance *through* inner evolution *and* mental integration, or crystallization of perceptions that are **checked by an active conscience so that we may rejoin our Source: The Original Family of the Earth.** NS1: 4

CHAPTER THIRTEEN
An Intercession Model

1   Understanding **THE NEW SONG** as a tool to solve **personal** and **social problems**, e.g., emotional, family, criminal, abuse or <u>self esteem problems</u> - or **resurrecting the <u>mentally</u> and <u>spiritually</u> dead** – this is your basis for developing a "new mind" and *the* "new world" *through your own actions.* NS 12:9; Lk17: 20, 37; OSHA214P5, 6

   a   "By degrees will We teach you to **declare the Message** so that you won't forget. We will make it easy for you to follow <u>the simple Path</u>," [to the end]. Q87: 6-8; 43:23

2   **The primary factor** in all problems involving people is "IDENTIFICATION:" [a] '<u>how</u>' people see themselves; and [b] '<u>why</u>' people see themselves the way they do.

3   The **unseen** '<u>force</u>' behind a person's behavior is "attraction" App V (what a person is 'identified' with and why). <u>The 'power' of 'attraction'</u> is formed by the 'words' or 'ideas' (creating the unseen inner emotion or fuel) that shape or give form to the mind's choices or decisions and the bodies actions. NS4: 20, 21; Ch 2

4   'Identification' questions like, 'Who are you?' 'What are you?' and 'Why are you?' are all questions that are answered and or unmasked by unveiling **what** or **who** a person **identifies with** and **why**. For the former slave's <u>behavior</u> the **Stockholm syndrome** is a good study:

What is **the origin** of <u>identifying with</u> those who enslave rape, rob, deceive and murder you or your people? EL: 5, 8; Prov3: 31

5 **'Who' or 'What' made you...?** This question is the one that can get a person **willingly** involved in self-analysis, 'self-creating' or 'recreating' themselves. The role of the "intercessor" (or "Passenger") is to detect and support *their desire* for change, if they have such desire you can help them, if not, you cannot. Mat 7: 6, 8

6 To 'self create' or 'recreate' *requires* that <u>the person</u> **wants to make** *a new* **"CONNECTION"** with a 'force' - *body of words, ideas or knowledge* - outside of those that have created the present or current <u>form</u>, or 'personality,' in that person's flesh. NS2: 10, 11

   a **Self-analysis** - <u>using the foundation of our Original knowledge</u> - helps us readjust and redevelop our ideas consequently producing a **new life force** - **a *new* energy form** - within our flesh positively changing our behavior in space and time. NS2:7b, d

7 Our 'unique **– intercessional -** power' arises from **"The New Song."** Q:34:23 Scripture calls this work, the "quickening" or "resurrection" of "the dead" (**'the last Adam'**), 'a work that God said He would do **in Person** and that you would not believe although it would be told (and shown) to you.' Review 2nd Chapter

8 The people that you are working with must see themselves - **you must help them, bring them to a position mentally and emotionally, to see themselves**

- so they can **clearly** see others *opposite* to themselves and be <u>enabled</u> to make an informed and decisive choice about their own future rather than living the life *imposed* upon them as a child *or* by family, environment, circumstances, or ignorance. NS12: 15;TLOT: 11

9   Our intercessional model includes physical, emotional, mental, and spiritual components. When **employing** the model your intercession' includes any one or all components. Be clear on <u>your</u> *own* "self," when working with others. App V: 13, 18

10   <u>The most important</u> *single factor* <u>affecting an individual's behavior</u> - this of course includes groups – is their "self-concept," review 2 above. What a person does at every moment of his or her life is <u>a product</u> **- a result -** of how they see themselves *and* or the situations that they <u>find</u> *or* <u>put</u> themselves into each day. NS4: 13

11   Many people have literally thousands of ideas or concepts about themselves (or their group), i.e., what he is, what she stands for, what they do or do not do, where they live, how they live, why, and so on.

   a   People who are <u>spiritually</u> and <u>intellectually</u> **alive**, however, are generally not satisfied with descriptions and ideas alone. They are more interested in the **values** that a person has **inculcated** in their mind over the years: the ideas that <u>removed them from the world of automation</u> (thoughtlessness and or uncontrolled emotional behavior). NS 2:9; 11:6; Ch 5

12 The Wise People, NS10:7A, want to know <u>the qualities</u> that a person exemplifies *from* <u>their</u> "self-concept," that which was <u>not born</u> within their flesh by *automation* or *instilled by a negative culture* but what they **consciously created** within themselves, the "words," the "ideas," **the vocabulary** that <u>governs</u> their daily behavior. NS4: 20, 24; 12: 23; PL: 13, 1; TLOT: 2, 3-11; Appendix I; V

13 As an example, *if you are alive,* you don't just want to know that a person is a father, a mother, or a student. You want to know if he is a wise, a strong, a patient father or husband. You want to know if she is an honorable adoring and nurturing mother and wife; <u>function is the key to success:</u> **what you actually do**, *not what you say you believe or want.*

14 You want to know if the child, or <u>any</u> "student," is a real student, <u>**studious in fact**</u>, or is he or she generally a student <u>in name only</u> - showing <u>no evidence</u> of rising out of **natural** or **cultural automation**, or <u>out of an affinity</u> for the **life threatening force** of <u>negative emotion</u> or <u>attraction</u>. TLOT: 3 - 11; Intro: 5; NS5: 10B4b, d; 8: 8b

15 It is crucial to note here that a person's **beliefs** <u>affect</u> their potential interactions with others <u>through</u> their **decision making process.** The question is: Are their beliefs grounded in fact, feeling habit or illusion? EL: 5, 8 - 18a to i

16 The "self-concept" is not a thing as we generally understand physical "things." However, *it is* a spiritual **- energy -** "thing," "being," "presence" or "form" **crystallized** in the physical body by positive or negative **internal effort.**

17 We can call the **"Self"** an **"energy being"** developed from the concepts and emotions we've _attracted to_ _ourselves_ by our **essence vibrations** and then, in time, **_these vibrations_** (sub-atomic particles) become a crystallized body <u>within</u> our human flesh. Its **function** will then have **_a name_** _according to the "word's" "sounds"_ _and "images" that constitute its nature_ **+ (Positive)** or **–** **(Negative)**.PL: 2-8; 12:40, 45; EL: 11

18 The **"Self"** _is_ **an organization of <u>crystallized ideas</u>**; these ideas Constitute or become the "person" or **"Being,"** depending on the level of inner evolution, **+** **or -** _within the flesh_. Review the PL; Chapters 2-4, 5 and 12

19 The **"Self"** is that which you call **_"I"_** and others may see as your personality and or your power. Still others may see "God" _functioning_ _through_ your body. Intro: 5; NS1:40a; Review-The Prologue and Chapters 2 and 5, Study "His" Attributes.

20 The **"self"** is born from automation, auto-suggestion or self-<u>programming</u> and _education_. Consciousness enables **us to create** (or make) an _inner physical environment_, or _form_, _in_, _through_ and _from_ which **our "being"** **("existence as")** may function ("a body had to be **prepared** for Him"). NS2: 5, 6-19; 5: 19; 7: K1; 12:11a-53, 58

21 _The extension_ of the "self" is <u>observable</u> even more with respect to persons or groups, and is then referred to as **"identification:"** The feeling of _oneness_ that we have with these persons or groups who have come to have **special value** to us. For example, the "self" of a father is extended to his son, his daughter, his wife. When either is insulted he takes it as a personal insult. **If**

he has *power* or *influence* others are made to feel it.

22 *The group expression* can be described in these concepts, "my country," "my school," "my gang," "my brother," or "my sister."

23 Your "self-concept" serves as your **"glasses"** _or_ **the frame of reference** _through_ and _from_ which you make _all_ of your observations and reach _all_ of your conclusions. EL: 2; App V It is your own *personal reality* from which all other things are observed and 'comprehended' (rightly or wrongly, positively or negatively. Often we see an illusion as a fact). NS12: 29-55, 56

24 The physical self is also used as a yardstick for judgment, i.e., someone is taller, shorter, fatter, thinner, younger or older than **"I am."**

25 Through the psychological "self" we say that someone is smarter, more understanding, or conversely, dumber, and more caustic than **"I am"** - if you are smart you add - **"in my present state of development or evolution."**

26 Notice that ideas and experiences that are _consistent_ with your **existing** "self-concept" are accepted quite readily. They are _treated as though_ they are right, good or belong, even if accepting them may be painful, e.g., a failing grade for a person who feels he is a failure may not move or concern him because it supports what he _already believes_.

27 A person's "self-concept" produces a *selective effect* on his **perception** - if he is *not* **conscious** of his *actions* and or *the* **causes** *of his actions*. Notice, after reading this, *your perception will change.* NS12: 11a; 16: 1, 3

28 People tend to perceive what is **congruent** or who fits within their **already existing** *concept* of reality. New ideas, or "Truth," is hard for them to "see," "hear" or "accept" because 'the new' *requires change*, inner evolution, or work, which most people are generally to lazy or too deeply engrossed in Satan's negative attractions, to commit themselves to. See, 14:14-53b

29 "Selective perceptions" can have either a negative or a positive effect and suggests that the already existing belief about the "self" supports -- whether positive or negative -- those concepts that **maintain and reinforce** the status quo, or the "self-concept's" existence. Every "life" re produces after its own kind, positive or negative, notice the Devil's world.

30 The "self-concept" *is learned* as a consequence of experience gained on the **"highway to the self"**- your senses - through *interaction* with others, significant others and generalized others; this would include all modes of *communication*: reading, conversation, listening to mp3 and CD's, physical activity, T.V., video's and so forth.

   a **"Be fruitful and multiply"** is our command to. However, **we** cannot produce what **we** *are not* (either in essence or materially PL: 13-1; EL: 16). The results of our striving will soon be seen. Intro: 17; NS16: 5-11, 13

31 In defining a situation _notice_ that **if you define it** as true or good, you will tend to act as if it is true or good, and therefore, it may become true or good. Obviously then, if you perceive a situations as false or negative, _you will act out_ your own perception consequently, the event may turn out false or negative for you (and or others).

32 You should note that **every person is the Author of their own future** by the _decisions_ and _conclusions_ that _they reach_ in their _present_ or _current activities,_ See 8 above and EL: 18

33 The questions that **_each person_** [and those whom you are serving] **_must address_** are these:

   a "Have I **consciously** _and_ **willingly chosen** the concepts that have caused me to act in the manner that I am now acting: personally, professionally, socially, financially; and morally?" Am I right _now_ **_my best "Self"? Can I do better for and with my "Self"?_** See #'s 15, 20 above

   b "**What** was or **is my standard** for thought and my behavior?" **App II**

   c "**Would I be** a **_better_** human being _in my own eyes_ if I were to change my 'self-concept' to that taught in the New Song?" Review EL: 18: g

34 Your answers to the above questions could clearly **change** your entire life, _who can calculate_ **the ripple effect** of that decision.

35 A final question, **"**<u>Are you satisfied</u> with your present sense of what and who you are; and, how you are being treated in the world?**"**

36 **Remember:** Thinking and Reflecting through the New Song, YOU CAN HAVE THE POWER TO CHANGE YOUR LIFE AND POSITIVILY AFFECT THE LIVES OF OTHERS AROUND YOU AND THOSE YOU CAN REACH. **PL:** 2

CHAPTER FOURTEEN
Opening and Sharing "The Book" R5:2, 13
Loosening "The Seven Seals"

A- THE ORIGIN OF RELIGION: ABRAHAM, Gen 15; 13, 14; Ex 21:16; NS Chapter 8 THE TEACHINGS OF *THE LAMB* OF GOD: Lk16: 23 - 29, 31; Nahum, Habakkuk, Zephaniah, Zechariah, Malachi; MFM4144 Conclusion

B- "The Balance (of the former slaves) are poison and rusty and *will not take* this knowledge <u>on their own</u>. Psa110: 3 **The Son of Man,** desires that every one of you **Students** <u>help solve this problem</u>…" using the **"New Song" of Moses (the Beginning) and the Lamb (the End).** Rev.14: 3; 15: 3; 6: 16; Ps17: 8 Most of "the dead" will find this message "a vexation" or "a terror to understand," Isa.28: 19 however, **The Seventh Angel** <u>will</u> remove **"the mystery of God,"** as it is written, Rev.10: 7, and the scripture cannot be broken. Jn.10: 35; **He is a "<u>God of the living.</u>"** Mat. 22:32; Ecc9: 4, 5, 6-10

C- Our Discussion Outline or **School Work** starts with Matt. 3: 3; 7: 6, 8 -13, 21-24, 25 - 29; 13: 52; Lk12: 47, 52; Q5:112, 113; "He created you *all* from a single Person." Q 39: 6; 4:1

1   **"Elohim** (Called **"<u>God</u>"** NS12: 19-38a: *a Tribe of Original People* whose leader was named **Yakub**) said: **Let us** make man *in our image, after our likeness* and *<u>let them</u> have dominion…"* Gen 1: 26; Prov16:4; Hab1:12; R17:17; NS8: 18 "Male and female created He (Yakub) them; and blessed

them, and called **_their_ _name_ Adam** (pl. reddish), in the day when they were created." Gen. 5: 2 Yakub told them: "Be fruitful and multiply, fill the earth (with _your mind_ and _purpose_) and subdue it, (Along with) every living thing that moves upon the earth." Caucasians, _Yakub's made people_, have done exactly that in the last 6000+ years Gen.1: 28 [Discuss 2:21, 24] - These verses constitute their **"warrant"** for world domination, as they call it, their "Manifest destiny." See NS1: 40; 8; 4

2   **The Holy One's Promise:** "To him that **overcomes** _the devil in himself_ NS8: 19; Isa28: 19, Rev12:11 **(_after_ 6000+ yrs.** of made man rule) will I give to _eat of_ **the tree of life** ("peace of mind and emotional contentment")**,** which is in _the midst_ of the Paradise of God." Rev.2: 7 "I will take you from among the heathen, and gather you out of all countries, and will bring you into your own land. Lk15:4; Mt25: 32, 34 I will clean you of their filth, give you a new heart, and a new spirit, **_I will even put My Spirit within you_** and you will be My People - **'L Sh'b'zz -** and I will be your God!" Ez36:24, 28; NS4:3, a, b; Hab3:13, 1 4; Prov18:21; 19:20; Q10: 10:7, 8; 56:8. 10; NS3: 7.

    a   With **"This Book:** I have made **_you_** a fortified wall against evil." Jer15:20

3   Now, over 1300 years after Muhammad, The Original People have produced a Champion T, p184p4 - One to _"go forth for us"_ - the **"Man"** (**Mind**) called **_The Mahdi_** (**_The Self Guided One_** [He uses many other names or titles]). "Rising from the East**, having _the seal_ of the Living God"** He goes forth for the salvation of His people. R7: 2; NS12: 26 He is the manifestation of _The_

Divine Mind or "Christ" in human form, (or Possessor **of words** that function as the Crusher of the power of wicked ideas housed in the human mind NS1:25; 2: 112, 12). He is *The One* who says: **"*I will*** work a work in your days which you will not believe, though it be told - and shown - to you." Hab.1: 15; Ps. 68:30-34, 35

    a He will "Scatter the people who delight in war," **"His Strength is in the clouds,"** He gives Strength and Power to His people (to control themselves through **"a pure Language"** Zep.3: 9. For their <u>arrogance</u>, "We will **open a gate** leading to a severe Punishment: <u>then they will be plunged into despair."</u> Q6: 44; 22:77 "God carries out all that He Plans." Q22:14 "On **That Day** shall you be brought to Judgment: **Not an act of yours that you hide will remain hidden."** NS109: 2; Q69:18; 20:15 **"All the (Original) people, <u>as they</u> <u>awake</u>, shall spoil thee."** Hab.2: 5, 8; Isa5:16 **"<u>Suddenly</u> shall he be broken without remedy."** Prov6: 15; T, p183/4; see #40 below

4 "Elohim (Yakub, Gen.1: 26) Prov16:4 _came from Teman_," (Of whom it is written: "By man came death. In Adam (Yakub's made man) <u>all die</u>" NS12: 19; 1Cor.15: 20, 22 **Abram was told:** "Know of a surety that thy seed shall be **a stranger** in a land that is not theirs, and shall serve them; and <u>they</u> <u>shall</u> <u>afflict</u> <u>them</u> **four hundred years**. And also <u>that nation</u> whom they serve, **will I Judge**: and **afterward** shall they <u>come out</u> R18:4 with great substance." Gen15: 13, 14; Hab1: NS3: 12; 8: 19; # 2 above

    a Know this, **"He that stealth a man** and sells him, or **he be _found_ in his hand**, (as we have been "found" in America) *he shall surely be put to death.* Ex.21: 16; Mat.24: 27, 28; Ex.12: 40; 15: 11; Jn11; Ps35: 20; 37: 12; Neh.9:27; NS12: 2 **"For _this purpose_** the Son of God was manifested..." 1Jn3: 8; # 5 **otherwise** they could not escape Satan's power.

5   "The Holy One (The Mahdi) _came from Mt. Paran._" Hab.3: 3 -13, 14 It is He [*The Mahdi*] that **"the wind and the sea obey"** (today) Mat8: 27 and of whom it was written, **"I** will seek that which *was lost* (stolen slaves)," Mat.10: 6 *"I will make My-Self known among you,* ("the Lost Sheep")" Ez.34: 11-16; 35: 11 *when I judge them,* (in America, Ps 9:16) as **"I** send fire on the earth." Lk12:47, 49 **"The Holy God is righteous" unlike the devil's god who is wicked (look around you and _in_ your own life for proof).** Isa5:16; NS17:14

6   **"*In Christ* (*The Word or Truth of God* NS12: 78) shall all** (who hear) be made *spiritually alive"* 1Cor. 15: 22 *this New Song* is being "sown in corruption (the former slave); it is raised in incorruption (*their* **new Body** of **ideas, or "Christ")"** *They are* the last Adam, *which is a quickening spirit* for the resurrection of the mentally and spiritually dead. 1Cor.15: 42 – 45; Q15: 29; 70:4; Mat.9: 33 **"In** *that day* shall the deaf *hear* the words of *The Book,* and *the eyes of* the blind *shall see* out of obscurity, and *out of darkness."* Isa.29: 18; NS2: 20; 17: 18

a   *"I will direct your work in truth,"* Isa.61:8 *"*I will give you an *everlasting name* that shall not be cut off." Rev.2: 17; Isa.56: 5; St. Jn. Chap10 This represents mental and spiritual separation from former ideas, *consequently* former behavior. Intro: 15; See #28 below

7   The Ancient of Days, The Original Man, or The Mahdi, **the Founder** of the New World (of Consciousness), **"... came out of His Place** to punish the inhabitants of the earth for their iniquity." Isa.26: 21; Q14: 48; #5 above

     a   Yakub, <u>Elohim</u>, the god who came from Teman, is <u>the founder</u> of this *world of mysticism* that we now live in. "He raised you (Caucasians) up from **the seed of other (original) people."** Q6:134; NS8:8 "Caucasians are created **now** (6,698+ years ago) and **not** *from the beginning of creation* Prov8: 22, 36 ("We were not born of fornication." Why did they say that to Jesus? NS12:37)

     b   I (Yakub) knew that you would deal **very treacherously** - the Scientists NS12: 19 called you "a *transgressor from the womb,"* Isa.48: 6, 8; Q2: 30 - *and that you would be **"The deceiver** of the whole world (by the end of your time)."* Rev.12: 9; 16: 13, 16; Isa14:12, 17; NS15: 6f "<u>Evil will befall you</u> – scripturally, *"The eagles* (of America, Nah3: 4, 8)"*- in the <u>latter days</u>."* Duet.31: 29; Mat 24:27, 28; Rev20: 9; Lk17:37;

     c   The Devil's will have serious **internal division** *as their end nears.* St Mat12:26; StLk11:18; Q7: 34; see #55b7, below

8   "I [Mahdi] *will be* their (Lost Sheep) God and *they* <u>will be</u> My people." "I (will) plead with you face to face." Ez.20: 35 "In all-their affliction, **He (Fard) was afflicted"** Isa63: 9 "I will do <u>what you see as</u> a **strange work or act"** (separating you from the Caucasians *just when you think things are getting better*). Mat 25:30, 34; Isa.28: 21 *"I will bring*

this to pass."46:10, 11 **"I will purge** out from among you the rebels **(those who love this world)** and them that transgress against Me." Ez.20: 38 (remember the *wheat* and the *tares: they represent* separation Mt.25:32) Ps.51: 5 -10; NS4: 4; our people are Stiff Necked and rebellious and will not take this knowledge on their own Ex32: 9; Lk15: 15; NS1: 7; 12: 15-39a-74; 14: 48; EL: 6, 8; review #2 above

9 "Moses lifted up **the serpent** (Caucasians) in the wilderness (of Europe) StJn.3:14; Q Chapter 18, even so must the Son of The Original Man (the stolen one) be lifted up (in the spiritual wilderness of N. America)" through the teaching of The Lamb of God. Rev.15: 3; 17:14; 21: 27. **"Elijah truly must come first,** Jesus said, *to restore all things*" **[lost to the Original man for the last 50,000 years]** Mat.17: 11; NS14: 15 How: Through Allah's Spirit in this "New Song" *as we evolve and live this message.*

10 "I the Lord, your God (Yakub), am a **jealous God…**" Ex.20: 5; NS12: 38; *"I have made thee (Moses) a God to Pharaoh:* NS3: 12 and Aaron thy brother shall be thy prophet." Ex.7:1 Moses said: "Behold, the children of Israel have not hearkened unto me, *how* then shall Pharaoh hear me…" [This is a sign for us today] Ex. 6:12; Dut.31: 29; Pro 6: 34; NS3: 12 Note too that **"Jealousy"** *is not an attribute* **of the Upright Original Nature.** NS8: 30i; 14: 55a; 15: 12; Intro: 5; #5 above

11 "People who resist or are deprived of divine guidance are outside of the Divine Order NS2: 20 and are thus **shameless in their personal life** and **blood shedders of those who are weak or stand in their way."** "The unjust know no shame." Zep.3: 5 -12; Q7:28, Consider the religious, moral, social and financial *underpinnings* of the world we live in.

a   "O Lord, Thou hast **ordained them** (Caucasians) <u>for</u> <u>judgment</u>; and O Mighty God, Thou <u>established</u> <u>them</u> **for** <u>correction</u>." Hab1: 12; NS15: 6f; see 7b above

12 "You are of *your father*, **the devil** (Yakub), and the <u>lusts of</u> <u>your father</u> you will do (through education; and training in deceit). He was a <u>murderer</u> from **the beginning** (creating you from "the seed of other people." "Let us make man in our image..."NS1: 23a), and abode **not in the** **truth**, because there is <u>no truth in him</u>. When he tells a lie, *he speaks of his own*: for he is a liar, and the father of it."

13 Those that are of <u>the Holy</u> God (in the last Days #'s 2-5 above) "hear" ***God's Words*** (and **transform** their life following those *new* Words/Ideas) Intro: 16 **you**, therefore, *hear them not* because you are not of God (*The Upright Redeemer*)" Jn.8: 44 - 47 (Jer.15: 1; Deut.9: 24; 31: 29) Ps 49: 15; 19: 7 you follow ***your father*** in the "original sin." #4 above

14 "I (Mahdi) will <u>bring the blind</u> - former slaves - ***by a way*** ***that they know not*** NS1: 7-10; I will lead them in paths that they have **not known:** I will make darkness light before them and crooked things straight (*as evidenced* by this **"New Song,"** *in your hand*, **their God,** Yakub, spoke of it coming R14: 3). These things will I do for you, and not forsake you." Isa.42: 16; review The Promise, #2 above, **Think very carefully here!** NS5: 20

15 ***"I am the God of Beth-el"* [Mecca],** (Gen31: 13; 28: 19; # 168a MMA; 1Sam10: 3) <u>I put the *Original Man* to sleep</u> for *50 thousand years*, Q70: 4; Ps 3: 5; 17: 15 to <u>prepare the way</u> for the rule of the devil. Isa.29: 10, OSHA110P4 For the Original man, *thereafter*, everything divine was **"sealed,"** *thus*

his condition in our time. The basis of our work today is awakening the Sleeper, the Dead, whose work is ahead of him and within him.

16 Today however, **"I am giving** men for **you** and people for your life."** Isa.43: 4 **"You are My witnesses** and My Servant Whom I have chosen; <u>**before Me**</u> there was **no God formed,** neither will there be after Me (there will be no need)."** Mat 11: 19 (**The Son of Man came eating and drinking**) Ps74: 22; 82: 8 [Death Ps79: 3-9] **"I will make him (Elijah) My** <u>first born</u> (of My Ideas), **higher** than the kings of the earth,"** **after** I redeem or resurrect his Message. Ps.89: 27; Nahum 1: 13; **The End will not come until "We have** <u>sealed</u> **the** <u>servants</u> **of our God in their foreheads (minds, with new ideas)."** Rev7:3

17 **"You are a people** <u>robbed</u> (of **self knowledge** Ps106: 37) *and* <u>spoiled</u> (**corrupted**); you are all of you <u>snared</u> in holes (mental *and* emotional), and you are <u>hid</u> in prison houses: you are for **a prey** (of the influential, the powerful and the ignorant) and none delivers; for a spoil and none says **"restore"** (to **your original state**, *until now*, through The New Song)."** Nahum 3:1; Isa.42: 22; Mat 17: 11; #9

    a The former slaves have **not known** <u>the depths of Satan</u> Obad. 4:15; Nahum 3:1 **"Now I will break Satan's yoke from off of you...with the New Song"** NS15: 6f **"Jesus,** *the resurrected one*, **knows their thoughts."** St Lk11:13, 18-28, 36; 12: 47, 48

18 **"We** need a **new people and a new mind,"** the Honorable Elijah Muhammad taught us **"** *a new mind* will give to us **a base** for the building of something new."

OSHAI17PI; 123P3, 9 ("Don't put new wine in old wine skins" Mk2: 22)

a "To make all things new means to go to <u>the very root</u>, the Messenger said, *"<u>discover the foundation unto the neck</u>"* Hab3:13 of **everything** that exists." The disciples of Paul did not know exactly what **we** would look like - looking down the wheel of time - in the changed or new form that God would make us into, but they concluded; "<u>We</u> <u>will be</u> <u>like</u> <u>Him</u>." Ps110: 3; Allah Says to us: **"Consider your ways"** Hag.1:5, 7 "Be strong and work: I Am with you. **Fear not.**" 2: 4, 5 **Look through our lens [NS]**: *Can <u>you</u> see "Him"?*

b This "work," NS8: 25 establishing the **"seed"** of **'L Sh'b'zz** NS3:7a <u>through</u> The New Song, <u>is how</u> We, 'the Poor Righteous Teachers in this part of the world, have become part of **the 5%** Who do not believe in the teaching of the <u>10%</u>,' the rich, slave makers and *the blood suckers of the poor, <u>who teach the poor lies</u>.* The biggest lie being that the Almighty, True and The Living God is a Righteous and <u>Unseen</u> <u>Being</u> <u>Existing</u> everywhere, a spook that cannot be seen with the physical eye. Nay "He can be seen and heard every where He is The All Eye-Seeing (everything)." Intro: 3, 7; PL: 13-1; NS1: 7b – 8-28a, b; 8:21, 23a; Mat. 7: 24

c One Scientist said we will or have <u>become</u> *"All Wise"* - by working **through Allah's Spirit** NS2: 4, 7; 14: 2 - thereby making "a new mind and a new people" with our teaching as you find it here in The New Song. NS1: 28a; 2: 11; 4: 7; 4: 21; 14:14-26-29-45; #38a below

19 He, "Allah, *makes all things new."* How must the God of Righteousness begin? The first way to bring about something new is to **change the way of thinking** of the people.

    a When you have <u>removed</u> from the people <u>the old mind</u> (**Caucasians way of thinking**) and <u>the idea of *their world* and religion</u> <u>as upper most</u> along with <u>any 'mysticism'</u> only ***then*** can you <u>insert new ideas</u> into their minds. NS2:21; 15: 5, 9; Ch 16

    b This is <u>evidenced</u> by their **curiosity**, their <u>knocking</u>, <u>seeking</u>, or <u>asking</u>; their being ***"attracted"*** by a new set of teaching... *a new school* <u>of learning</u> to condition their minds to that thing that you are about to present to them that is ***altogether new*** and ***different*** from what they have been accustomed to." Mat 7:6, 8; NS5: 6; 12:9; see #14 above

20 "Behold, Allah said, I will proceed to do a marvelous work among this people." Isa.29: 14 Those who have listened - **heard** - 'view their righteousness, quietness and assurance,' 17 <u>those with Me</u> **"have the mind of Christ"** I Cor.2: 16 and *I have given them* **power to clean and heal and to cast out the devil** [negative-passion, envy, greed and deceit] see 6a above; Mat.10:1; 12:22; Mat. 9:32, 33; 12: 42, 48-53-60-78; 26 below

21 "We *(who have heard)* ought to lay down our lives for our brotherhood" I Jn. 3:16 **"As in ONE BODY**, we have many parts (members) so, we being many, are *one* body, group, community, **"Tribe,"** in **Christ (*the Word and Spirit of the New Song*)**, and every one members one of another." Rom.: 12: 4, 5; NS3: 7a

22 "The world (of Caucasians) knows us not because they knew Him (the Sign of us) not." IJn3: 1; Ps 21: 9, 11; Q19:21 "We shall be delivered" Micah 4:10, from America's (Babylon's) racial, moral, social and overall inequity.

23 "We are the **sons of God** and it does not yet appear what we shall be: but we know that when He shall appear, we shall be like Him: for *we shall see Him as He is.*" IJn. 3: 2; [see #'s 12 -15]; NS4: 20, 21; 8: 21, 23a

a *"Many Prophets* and *righteous men* have desired to see those things which *you now see*, and have not seen them; and to hear those things which *you hear* and have not heard them." IX: 4 "It pleases Me, *Allah said*, to make you My People." Mat. 13:17; Lk.22: 69; Ps 17: 15; 46: 10; ISam12:22; Hab3: 13; NS3: 7a; 15: 9, 10

24 "Enter into **life** (through **The New Song**) at the strait gate (right attitude): wide is the gate and broad is the way that leads to destruction; many go in that gate. Strait is the gate and narrow is **the Way** that leads to **Life**, and **few** there are that **find it**. Mat7: 13, 14; 6:33 "The Son of Man is manifested (in the flesh) to demonstrate **how** to destroy the works, rule *and* mysticism of the devil *in* and **over** the individual and thus *in time* the world. IJn. 3:8 [see # 12]; **He came eating and drinking, and stayed 3.5 years.**" He is our example. Mat. 11: 9; 12: 40; 7: 6, 8; Q4:31; EL; 15

25 "The god of this world (Satan) has **blinded the minds**" through mysticism IICor.4: 4 "He devises wicked devices to destroy the poor with **lying words.**" Isa.32: 7; NS4:20 He (Yakub) said, "My Lord, as Thou hast judged me *erring*, I

shall certainly make *(evil)* <u>fair seeming</u> to them **on earth**, and I shall cause them all to **deviate**, accept Thy Servants from among them, **the purified ones."** Q15:39; 40; 5: 94; Nahum 3: 4; EL: 16; NS5: 2c, d

26 **"If any man be *in*** (internally <u>exist as</u>) Christ (*The Spirit of Allah* in The New Song), he is *a new creature*: **old things** (negative thinking and action) *are passed away*, behold, all things are *become* new." #2 above This is **our standard of perfection** in and outside of **Our Circle (Al-Shabazz).** II Cor.5: 17; StJn10:21- 25; NS3: 7a; 5: 14

27 **"Make <u>in</u>** (your) self *of (the) two (chambered mind)*, **one new man [Mind or Consciousness]**, so making (inner) peace. Having **abolished in his flesh** the enmity (automation), *even the law of commandments* contained in ordinances..." Eph. 3:15; See: NS 11: 7 and 8

   a **For our Community**, "<u>The right way is clearly distinct from error.</u>" TLOT: 6

28 ***"Be renewed <u>in the spirit</u> of your mind***, put on the new man [Mind] NS 15: 6f *created* after God [The Mahdi] in righteousness and <u>true holiness</u>." Eph. 4: 23, 24

29 **"Wherever *the spirit* of** <u>the Lord</u> is there is liberty." IICor.3: 17; TLOT: 2

30 **"He that stops doing evil makes himself a prey (in Satan's world): and the Lord saw it and it displeased him that there was no (righteous) judgment."** Isa.59: 15

31 **"We called them gods** unto whom the Word of God Came."Jn10: 35; Rom. 8:14 (just as a doctor's [or anyone's] words and works will <u>reproduce</u> **them** in another).

32 **"How are the dead raised up,** with what body do they come? I Cor. 15:15 God gives a body as it pleases Him, *to every seed (idea) his own body (shape, form, appearance, personality or functionality)*.**" I** Cor. 15:38; See NS Chaps 4, 5, 9, 11; 15

33 Weakness, Power; Earth (materiality), Heaven (word/ spirit) I Cor. 15: 20, 58:

a Working with The Law of Three as "wombs" for inner evolution and development: NS2: 7a; 12: 10; 14: 7b; 15 6f Consider how **"EVE"** *or* "Eternal" "Vibration" NS2: 7c; 21, 22; 12: 7-9-13-23-41; 13:17; vi **produced** "Existence," the Crown of which is "Human Like" Consciousness and Thought PL: 7, 10; TLOT: 2-4-19a; NS2: 7

b Philosophical and Theoretical THOUGHT **produced** the Practical "AVA" **from** Cosmic-Consciousness, Perception **and** finally internal Conception NS14: 44, 45 **enabling our mind to interact with "AVA"** *or* "Awareness" and "Vibration" which **produced** "Able:" NS4: 7-14; 10: 2; 12: 13-55, 56-62 or our **"ability"** to **formulate** INTENT and FOCUS for any appropriate purpose or task NS5: 21; 13: 20; EL: 16, 18 our purpose is to **grow in** Power (Cosmically and Mentally).

Earth or Materiality	**Heaven or The Word**
Gen 2:7, 9-19	Jn1: 11, 14-17
1 Natural [Biological] Body	Spiritual [Energy] Body (Original Mind)

2 First Adam (culturally Living Soul)	Last Adam (Quickening Spirit) NS8: 30d
3 First Man (cultural pursuits)	Second "Man" (Cosmic Pursuits)
4 Mortal (cultural name)	Immortal (Has Original Attribute)
5 Corruptible (Unchecked Appetites)	Incorruptible – (Active Conscience)
6 Death (to self and others)	Victory (Inner Peace, Higher Mind/Life)
7 = Weakness (illusion of power)	= Power (Cosmic Mental)

34 <u>Be you</u> **angry** and sin not? <u>Let not</u> **the sun go down** upon your anger: <u>neither give place</u> to the devil (negative ideas in your mind) Eph. 4: 26, 27 (Learn to **Be** Self-Conscious, act on <u>balanced ideas</u>; remember your **'Self.'**) Review Chapter 5

35 "The <u>light</u> shined in darkness and the darkness comprehended it not" Jn1:5 How about you? **"Grow up into Him in all things."** Eph. 4:15 **"Whatsoever** makes things manifest (like **the New Song**) is **light."** Eph. 5:13

   a "I will behold **Thy Face** <u>in righteousness</u>: I shall be satisfied when I awake (*through, in* and *with*, **new ideas** and) with **Thy likeness."** Ps.17: 15; NS2:9

   b Through 'His Spirit,' in this message, "He teaches my hands to war..." through this message. Ps.18: 34; NS10: 4; #2 above

c The heavens are Q34:1, 3 telling the glory of God (unfolding cosmic secrets); and the firmament proclaims his handiwork (<u>if it is</u>, it had to be made or created)" Ps.19:1 The *Effects* or *Results* of Consciousness <u>working</u> <u>through</u> a form or a body, review the Prologue; The Law of Three. Q43:29; Prov8: 21, 33

36 "Let **the words of my mouth,** and the meditation of my heart, be acceptable in Thy sight O Lord my rock and my *Redeemer.*" Review Ps.21: 9, 10; 78: 39; 140:10; TLOT: 2 "The Lord will bless His people with **peace.**" Ps. 29:11 "I (Student) **humbled my soul with fasting** NSCh15 and <u>my prayer returned</u> into my own heart" Ps. 35: 13 "He that touches you touch the apple of His eye." Zec.2: 8; Rev12:11 **"Where your treasure is, there will your heart be also."** Mat.6:21

37 "God will redeem (make acceptable/pay the price for) my soul from **the power of the grave (mysticism).**" Ps 49:15; He gave power to heal, Mat.10:1; The Devil "was cast out." 9: 33 "We dwell in a rebellious house (country)." Ez.12: 2; Rev4: 7 **"like a flying eagle"** "Rebellious people eat <u>swine's flesh</u>... see themselves as holier..." Isa.64: 4

38 "The <u>misbeliever</u> is a helper (of evil) against his Lord!" XIX: 2a Q25:55 however, "I will bring forth a **seed** out of Jacob (America) an **inheritor** of My Mountain..." Isa.64: 9; Mark 12: 7, 10; NS9:14, 16

a "When I have **fashioned him** and <u>breathed into him of</u> **My Spirit**, fall down in obeisance to him." Q15: 29; Micah 7: 9-15, 20; Mat 24:27, 28; see 2 above

179

39 **"You are gods and all of you are *children* (Students) of The Most High."** Ps.82: 6; St. Jn.10: 35 <u>Remember</u>, **"*The Self Guided One* *cannot be tempted* with evil."** Jms.1: 13 The devil asked Jesus *what* He wanted. The Student *shows* the quality of his faith by his <u>works</u>, Psa62: 12, or <u>deeds</u>, Jms.2: 18, and **"engrafting"** or *learning* and *following* The Words or Ideas of The Most High, our Savior and Redeemer when **"He"** enters <u>the world of darkness</u> to redeem us from the devil's civilization. NS1:28a, b; Jms.1: 20

  a **"What is devil?"** "A grafted "man or mind" which is <u>made</u> weak and wicked" "<u>Or</u> any grafted *live germ* <u>from</u> the original is devil." see 1: 25a; 8: 17, 18a

40 "Can wicked rulers have fellowship with Thee [Mahdi] who make-*frame* **mischief** by laws and statutes?" Ps.94: 20 "Babylon (America) has <u>become</u> the home of devils" Rev18: 2, 9; Mal 3: 1, 2; 4: 1, 6 **"Suddenly** shall they be *wounded* they shall make **their own tongue** *(and written history)* to fall upon themselves..." Psa64: 7, 8; Rev 17:17; Nahum 3:13-16-19

41 "The stone (*stolen "lost" slaves, symbolized at Mecca*) which the builders (of the World) rejected has become the head stone of the corner (for the New World of God by *His Choice*)" Q35:39; Ps. 118.2; Dan. 2: 34-45; Mk12:10 Unknown to the Muslims of the world, **they are performing a pilgrimage every year** for the **"Lost and now Found" former slaves** who are represented by the **"stone" (cut out without hands)** they kiss at the <u>Sacred House</u>. Muslims then throw **metaphorical stones** at the devil (white pillars), <u>seven stones</u> **one for every thousand years**. Six thousand years for their rule and one thousand for their overall removal from power. <u>This ritual points to what is happening in the world today</u>. **The first 100 years** NS17: 2 **of the last 1000 (in the 7000th year) will end the made man's <u>political</u> and**

<u>financial</u> <u>dominance</u> of the world, those <u>among them</u> who help or support *the change* will be allowed to stay up to 900 more years. *They will have their dominion taken,* but their lives will be prolonged. Dan.7:1 2; 8:17; MFM: 3317; 4071; 4137

42 *Be not conformed to (the mysticism of) this world:* <u>**Be**</u> <u>**transformed**</u> *by the renewing of your mind* (through the **New Song**) NS8: 8b that you may <u>**prove**</u> what is the good and acceptable and perfect will of God." Rom. 12: 2 (If you would be one of His **<u>Regenerated</u>** "Students") Mat 19:28 *following the Spirit of Truth.*

43 "I will deliver *My* people out of *your hand,* I have said *The Word* and will perform it" Ez.12: 25 Ez13: 23. "I will put a *new spirit* within you." Ez36: 27 **"You (Students) are My Temple** *(where My Wisdom is displayed).*" I Cor. 3: 17 – 19; NS1: 40a; T, P27P3; #18a above

44 "Among the mature - *We do impart wisdom,* it is <u>not</u> <u>a wisdom of this age</u> *or of the rulers of this time,* **they won't be here,** *After the Judgment.* We impart <u>**secrete**</u> and ***hidden*** **wisdom of God** Q5:104, which God decreed *before* <u>the ages</u> for *our* glorification. *None of the rulers of today understand this,* if they had, they would not have crucified the Lord of glory (the Example or Sign of us)."

45 "But, as it is written, what no eye has seen, nor ear heard, nor the heart of man conceived, what God (*The Mahdi*), has prepared for those who love Him. God has <u>revealed to us</u> ***through*** the Spirit (of Truth). The Spirit <u>searches</u> ***everything, <u>even the depths of God</u>***." I Cor.2: 6, 16; Isa.46:10, 11; He is known by His <u>Judgments</u>, Ps.9: 16; Mt 4: 16; Jn11: 43, 44; Review NS3: 8 and Chapter 1

46 *"I - The Mahdi - will seek that which was lost (the stolen people of the East)."* Ez34: 11 - 16 **"He stood and measured the earth (and weighed the waters).** Hab.3: 6, 14 **The Lord Himself** shall descend (come among us, "like a thief in the night") from heaven" I Thes.4:16, **"for (our) salvation with His Anointed."** 2 above; NS 8: 23a

47 He came and has taught us **the Foundation of this world**, effectively <u>freeing our minds</u> to become like *His*. Hab.3: 13 His spirit shall not always strive with man for that *He also is flesh* Gen. 6: 3; Isa.40: 22 Of His own Will **He begot us** with the *Word of Truth* (that <u>transforms</u> *flesh, and behavior,* NS2: 20; 17: 21 through our <u>open</u> <u>acceptance</u> of His Truth)." We *are* **"doers of His Word,"** Jms.1:22, we <u>give shape or form</u> to the Body of Christ (Ideas in the New Song). We are "the First Fruits" (*results*) of His Teachings Jms.1: 18, raised up from the devil's **grave of ignorance**.

48 To **'the doubter,'** study The New Song VERY carefully <u>before</u> you enter into **open dispute**. Check your heart, your soul and your purpose. What is at the root of your doubt or dispute? <u>*Who shaped your present thoughts?*</u> Think it over reflect on Chapters 2, 4, 5 and App V.

49 Allah says: "If you are in doubt as to that which We have revealed to Our servant, (**The New Song** Ez4: 16) then y<u>ou</u> *produce a Chapter like it* (to benefit the spiritually dead in America), and call on your helpers besides God if you are truthful. But if you do it not, and **you can never do it**, than be on your guard against the fire whose fuel is men and stones and it is prepared for

the disbelievers." Q2: 23, 24 **"None** grasps the Message but men of **understanding**." Q2: 269; Pro21: 16

50 O man, **"Deliver thy-self"** Zec2: 7; Q5: 108 "Man can have nothing but what he **strives for** and the results of his striving will soon come in sight." Q53: 39; XIII: 17 "When this corruptible (stolen slave) shall have put on incorruption (the Divine Word in **The New Song**), and this mortal shall have put on immortality (*GOD'S NAME*, Isa.65:15), **then** shall be brought to pass the saying that is written, Death (mysticism) is swallowed up in victory **(behavioral "understanding"** Pro: 9, 10**)**. See Q94

51 "O grave - the **deceit** or **trick** fostered on Original people beginning in 325 at the Council of Nice, called the Bible - where is thy victory? O death - we who are mentally and spiritually _reborn_ after 400 years of living in hell - where is thy sting?" I Cor.15: 54, 55; **He taught as one having authority,** Mat.7: 29; Ch 2 "It shall come to pass that before they call, I will answer; and while they are still speaking, I will hear." Isa65: 24; NS1: 40a; 7: B

52 **"We have recounted** their and our _whole_ story with knowledge Q7:7; NS8: 8, for We have never been absent at any time or place," say the Scientists. NS17: 2 As for us, _our work_ NS1: 6 has **sealed the series** of the Prophets Q2:121 _bringing Them all together in the Judgment_ Q2:129 along with some **Worthy wise men** of our times whose turn of phrase and or nuance I was not able to frame in the manner that they did myself. Therefore these Worthy minds have provided helpful notes to this Song. NS: 1:5; EL: 18g

53 It should now be clear that **we (through our work) stand in the light** of those Worthy Ones of the past. *They* told us that *our fathers*, and therefore *we*, **were not warned** of today's conditions and circumstances. But, Allah chose us to warn today!

    a Our people today remain *heedless* of God's signs and His warning about <u>the Judgment</u> and <u>our place in it</u>. Q36: 6 Our people continue on following <u>the devil's illusions</u> about God and themselves, not seeing what is right before their eyes and all around them, *hoping for what the devil has as an equal.*

    b To this day, **98** years into the devil's last **100** to rule <u>unopposed,</u> and **82** years after the Savior came to us, our people still **tell us, in effect,** that they "found their parents eating, drinking and practicing whatever their faith or behavior is, or they've been doing whatever they are doing all of their lives, and they have <u>no "*intention*"</u> of changing their *pattern of life* because of what we say. Q7:28; 64:6; Intro: 7

    c In effect, they are saying, "Shall **mere human beings** <u>direct us?</u>" "<u>Who are you to tell me any different?</u> You have a handful of people with no strength among us." Q: 64:6; 11:40-91 Be careful don't charge us with falsehood. Q10:39 Allah has said: "If We had sent **an Angel** to you, <u>We would have sent Him</u> (too) **as a Man**" Q6: 9; NS1: 18; EL: 10 We have given you The New Song, a Message that you can touch with your hands. Q6:7 Its *Truth will turn darkness into light* see P.V and *weakness into strength* for those who are <u>seeking</u> a way to their Lord. Practice it and see for yourself.

54 I say, **We must grow up into Him** as outlined in this New Song and **find** _the way_ to **become** _the Essence_ *of* "**Guidance from Allah**" and be **Able** to say: "Surely there **has** come to you **guidance from Me**, then *whoever* follows My Guidance, no fear shall come upon them, nor shall they grieve." Isa.6: 8; Lk12: 47; Jn14: 16, 17; Q2: 38; 7: 61, 63; f; Prologue: 1

    a **Say:** "I seek refuge in **The Lord of the Dawn** from the evil of that which Yakub has created, and from the evil of the _intense darkness_ that we now live in, and from the evil of those who cast _evil suggestions_ in _firm resolutions_, and from the evil of _the envier_ when he envies. See, #1 above

    b Surely I fear if I disobey my Lord XIX: 2a _the chastisement_ of a grievous day. Isa.63:1, 3 He from whom it is averted, _on that day_, surely Allah has had Mercy on him and this is a **manifest achievement**." See, 46, 47 above; NS3: 4, 5

55 To the **"Over Comers,"** those who _overcame the mark of the beast_, those who are no longer **"affected"** by the power of this world _or_ automation: NS12:55, 56

    a Allah says: "_O soul that art at rest_ (with peace of mind and emotional contentment), **return** to thy Lord well pleased (with Him) and well pleasing (to Him). Enter among My Servants, enter into My Garden." Q89: 27

    b For the rest, know that the countdown has begun, consider the weapons Allah used in the past, **they are being used today.** "Hearts that Day will be in agitation." Q79:8 Allah gives Life and Death; and

when He Decides on an affair, He only says to it, "Be," and it is. Q40:68

1- **"We sent (plagues) [diseases of all kinds upon them]**: wholesale Death, Signs openly self-explained: but they were steeped in arrogance - a people given to (and blinded by) sin." Q7:133

2- What is the Sure Truth (Reality)? Thamud, They were destroyed by a **terrible storm of thunder and lightning**, and 'Ad, they were destroyed by a **furious and exceedingly violent Wind,** He made it rage against them for **seven nights and eight days in succession**, so that you could see the whole people lying prostrate in its path as if they had been roots of hollow palm trees tumbled down! Q69: 2-5-7

3- **"A terrible earthquake** came by night preceded by a mighty **volcanic eruption** which overtook them with Our Justice. We made them as the rubbish of dead leaves (floating on the stream of Time)! So, away with the people who do Wrong!" Q23: 41

4- "We sent against them the **devastating Wind** (see, NS14:5): It left nothing whatever that it came up against, it reduced everything to ruin and rottenness." Q51: 41, 42

5- "We - when the **water (of Noah's flood)** overflowed beyond its limits - did this so that We might send **a Message to you**, and that ears (that should hear the tail and) retain its memory should bear (its lessons) in remembrance." Q69: 11, 12

6- "We rained down upon them **a shower of molten stone and fire:** see then, what was the end of those who indulged in sin and crime!" Q7:84

7- "On you (spiritual leadership – **Jinn** – _and, or_ your social, political and financial followers -**men**-) will be sent a **flame of fire** (spiritual, social, political and financial folly along with crime; conflict; bloodshed; and war) and **a smoke** (_confused peer thinking, blind teachers_ and _visionless leadership_): **you will have no defense.**" Q55:35; NS8: 10; 14: 7b above

8- "Wait until We open on them a **gate leading to a severe punishment:** _then watch_, they will be plunged into despair." Q23:77

9- "I am no bringer of new-fangled doctrine among the apostles, nor do I know what will be done with me or (the final hour) with you. I follow that which is revealed to me by (the Prophets, the Honorable Elijah Muhammad and by) inspiration from Allah as found in The New Song; I am but an open Warner." Q46: 9

56 Allah is breaking the Caucasian's power on land, at sea and in the air to make you **re-think** your worshipping of them and their world. T, p72p1; NS8: 8b; 12: 15-39a; 14:3 -16

57 Match this, The New Song, with what you see in the world around you every day. NS8:20a; NS12:15; #3, 5-8 above.

   a "We are **gradually** reducing the land in their control (calculate your assessment from 1914 to now and keep on watching)." NS12: 26

      I By the _evidence_ of the **Time** _discussed in this Message,_ EL: 16

2 Surely **"automated"** <u>man</u> (mind) is *internally at loss* to *inner peace and emotional contentment,* Intro: 5; PL: 6; EL: 11a, e

3 Except those who **evolve** *Ch 2-4-5 and 15 and* do good *for themselves* and *others* thus **demonstrating** righteous <u>deeds</u> *from a Living Conscience* Intro: 4, 6; and those who **exhort** one another to **Truth** and exhort one another to **Patience.** Q103

58 Know that **with this "New Song,"** we are *following* and **fulfilling the message** that was given to and prophesied by Abram who became Abraham. See #4 above; NS8: 4-19, 20c; T, p76p3; Lk16: 22, 31; Q2:130, 131

59 Let us be clear: *Islam is not a religion in the sense of <u>something to believe in</u>.* Islam is an Arabic word intrinsically denoting **peace** and <u>something to **DO** or **BECOME**</u>; <u>a certain kind of **action,** or **behavior,**</u> along with the unique **nature** made by Allah in which He created the **"original man,"** whom He modeled after Himself; Q4: 1; 30: 30; NS1: 27, 29; 8: 30e **He, Allah, is "Self Created."** We are talking about **you** here, your <u>individual</u> intent, your purpose and your thinking. NS2: 2- 8, 12; 9: 2, 3-12; 11: 2, 3

60 *In the future there will be no <u>"religion of Islam,"</u> **as we have known it**.*

61 "Islam" has served the purpose of reestablishing the educational basis for Caucasian ruler ship after 2000 years in the caves giving them the opportunity to go "the right way," and setting the course for the devil's fall if they do not.

62 The "behavior" or the "way of life" that you see outlined in this New Song NS8: 16-30 constitutes the Doorway to your future. NS1: 40 OSHA176p3 Step through and live.

63 Allah has declared Abraham to be the leader of prayer in the Last Days. Take the "Uphill Road" while you can. NS10: 7A This is an admonition against a day coming that will turn children gray headed over night.

CHAPTER FIFTEEN
Allah Replicates Himself in
"The Tribe of Shabazz": 'L Sh'b'zz

1 The long awaited, world traveler, the **Christ** or the **Mahdi**, NS12: 26, 35 Who came among us in the Person of Fard Muhammad Ibin Alfonso, Who also holds the title of Allah, The Lord of The Worlds, The Lord of The Dawn and All of the other Titles relative to His Work in this **Time**, has given us His Guidance in re-establishing **The Ancient "God" Tribe of Shabazz as our "inheritance."**

a With a **Book Of His Wisdom** the Mahdi has established Elijah, His "Lamb," on the Throne of Authority *as the Ancient of Days.* We have extracted from that Wisdom *a root idea*: the "New Song" or how to make a **"new man"** for the coming world. PL: 13, 14; NS; 11: 8; 12: 9-20a; Prov.8: 17, 21; IIThes2: 9, 12; R5: 2, 13; OSHA Ch 18

2 He told us, *through Elijah* NS8:19b, 20-1, 21, 23-25, **"You will never be sick if you eat once every 72 hours. You'll be sick one day out of four or five years if you eat every 48 hours, and if you start your infants eating one meal a day, as soon as they are able to eat solid foods, it would enable them to live to an age of 240 years."**

3 He taught us that all foods contain poison and that eating well once a day (27 times a month, any three hour window) and fasting three days a month stops the

accumulation of poison <u>in our system</u> thus stopping sickness or disease from developing in our body.

a   After eating properly for several years (while living in Hell), cutting our caloric intake by eating once a day, our body will have no accumulated poisons and any offensive body odors will disappear. In time, fasting *can* stop following **this** life style. <u>*Know here that*</u> fasting supports **"Higher Being"** or **"The Causal Body;"** NS12: 11, 13 *and* that **"<u>fasting is for Allah</u>."** PL: 7, 8; NS2: 4, 7

4   All that is in the heavens and the earth is in our bodies, water, chemicals, stone, metals, vegetation, air and more. NS4: 1-6-21 The earth has no birth record (that is available for our review). It is *many trillions* of years old. The earth is what we are <u>made of</u>. When we are *active* as <u>**It**</u> is – exercising, eating well and being creative, we **<u>will renew ourselves</u>** and **<u>reverse the aging process</u>**, NS9:9, 10; 11: 3, 4, a; 14: 42; TLOT: 18, now we can't live **that** <u>long</u> (as the earth), but…

5   Clearly, using The Wisdom of The Ancients brought to us by The Supreme Human Being – which is and Who is **"<u>Opposite</u>"** *to what we know* - we can live **on, with** and **through** 'what we are made of' – and, be **very healthy** and **vigorous** - for more than the 40 to 80 years, on average, we get following the mental and the spiritual guidance, **the life style,** of the devil. NS8: 15-17, 18a; 14: 6a-14-19-26-44, 45; OSHA114:P5

a   Consuming their artificial *and* poison food, e.g., <u>GMO</u> and <u>aspartame</u>, poison ideas and their **morally** *blind* and <u>poisoned</u> <u>spirit</u> provides an ***artificially negative*** side to **our** *Emotional* <u>Center</u> which has been originally described as **"a fire free of smoke" (blue flame)** and later, **"Jinn"** NS12: 37a, 38 <u>*when its function is degraded*</u> (orange-red flame). NS1: 17- 39c-; 2: 10, 13; 8:9 a-14; 14:7b -25

b Metaphorically the ***artificially negative*** side of **our** *Emotional* <u>Center</u> *or the* **"Jinn"** produces **"three columns of smoke" or "Hell fire"** Review 8: 6b, c **when <u>its fuel</u>** <u>is changed</u> from Truth to falsehood. Q55:15, 11: 30; NS2: 10, 12; 4: 20, 21; 8: 23a.

c Words and ideas, if you ***identify with them***, <u>activate</u> "your innate power" TLOT: 2a or **"fuel"** your Emotional Center (your "horse" NS12: 10) - which has <u>no natural negative part in the Original Man</u> - to action. NS2: 7e, 12; 8: 18; 12: 9; 14: 2, 3 - 6; 15: 6f – review all of this very carefully.

6 Living a *longer* and *healthier* life <u>requires</u> *a change of values*: like upgrading our "nature" ***back*** to its "original or free of smoke" form – discussed throughout the preceding 14 Chapters of "The *New* - Song" - NS11:1, 2 just as *you* or *a farmer* would <u>turn</u> <u>over,</u> <u>sift</u> and <u>upgrade</u> *your* **poor quality soil,** <u>removing</u> that which does not belong there, <u>before</u> planting *your **new** seed or idea.*

a **"Ideas or Seeds"** like this example**: "Don't *expect* to *die* or *get* *sick! Follow* the *principles* *provided for you on these pages and live."* NOW: <u>Notice</u> how difficult that thought is for you? You can't even consider the thought let alone accept

that idea while believing in the devil's way of life. For some of us this won't work out perfectly, but for our *accepting* children (or new minds) this wisdom represents Paradise.

b Remove **the burden of mysticism** and **the boredom of mental stagnation** from your life. NS14: 25 Be creative, **start internally**. NS11:2 *Follow the developmental principles* in this ***"New Song"*** (and live) these principles will lead you to a whole *new dimension* of thoughts, feelings and happiness. NS11:8; 12: 66, a

c Even our former **slave master's children** can benefit from this message; as was the case with Nineveh, whom Jonah was sent to proclaim destruction from God in 40 days. T, p23p5 They **listened**, changed their course and *scripturally* became the people meant for destruction that were saved from it. NS8: 8; 14: 11a; notice **"e"** below

1 However, we see Jonah as *a place holder* for our time and that those forty days represent the **40 years** since Elijah's passing on February 25, 1975. Forty years of Lazarus searching in the wilderness, some looking for a way in, others for the right way out. Let's see what happens between now, 2014 and 2015. NS3: 12 Study the Epilogue

d The Original man NS1: 25; 8: 30g; 9: 1; Prov8: 17, 36 Allah Taught us, is the Asiatic Blackman, the Maker, the Owner, the Cream of the Planet Earth, Father of Civilization and **"God"** of the Universe. So that means we don't think in terms of sickness, suffering, death and want. We think about living a long joyous life *within our nature*, having great health and strength along with the capacity for supreme creativity. It is now time to build the **natural** verses an **artificial** civilization. NS12: 1a-19; #10 below

e Our people (who *have not* suspended their awareness to get hell's benefits) have felt and feel powerless in the face of our **dependence** on the slave masters children who **control all means of access**. Over 400 years now, we've silently thought, "Are **they** *willing to provide* **us** with 'peace of mind and emotional contentment –'heaven while we live'- rather than the 'pain, suffering and death'''- 'hell' – we've all experienced? NS8: 10; Review the Epilogue

f Allah answers our prayer saying, **"I will bless you with peace** (If you submit to Truth). *The Caucasians:* **I ordained them for judgment** in their beginning, **they were transgressors from the womb** and **I established them for correction."** NS14:7b, 8-11a; Chapter 8

g In this Message, **We have provided** for you a Straight Path. NS10: 7A, C; 13: 1; 14:23a, 24; EL: 5 Understand, however, your 'peace of mind and emotional contentment (heaven)' arises from **you** gaining mastery over **your own self, your own life.** Intro: 16; NS14: 50 This God Given Power, achieved through *your* *own* inner evolution, Ch 4 **cannot be** *taken* from you by any *negative* *external* *force*, since they did not - and *could not* - provide, *or give*, **this life** to you. NS10: 7A; 12:55, 56-74; 14: 36-55; Q34: 49

h "Accept your own mind!" This, **self (God) given authority,** is <u>The Source</u> NS9: 1, 2 of *<u>unending</u>* happiness *<u>and</u>* child like joy, while existing in the mental and emotional body and environment of an adult. PL: 6, 9-13-1; OSHA147P2

i <u>Our</u> **inner evolution** represents our **"unalike"** (the devil's) <u>nature</u> working to manifest <u>the wisdom</u> *and* <u>work</u> (of freeing minds bound by the consequences of bad habits), whose *<u>ripple effect</u>* - in time - will have a powerful and profound impact upon ***your*** and *<u>our</u>* environment. This ***crystallized*** "<u>Being</u>" the "<u>Living Word</u>" of Knowledge, Power and Joy will gain victory over the forces of 'deviation' which are all around you and us today. NS5: 4; 10: B; 12; 34; 13: 17, 20; 14: 2, 3

7 "Nurse [upgrade NS14:28] your life," Elijah said, "***<u>according to its nature</u>.***" NS8: 29c, 30c, d Allah said that your life, (because of its essence, NS7b, c) <u>can be</u> as long as that of the California Redwood tree. It is only our <u>ignorance</u> NS8: 13, 16; 9: 8 a, b, of **self** CH13; 14 and ***Allah*** NS2:1, 9; 12: 74, 77; Ch14 that <u>allows</u> <u>us</u> <u>to</u> <u>follow</u> <u>Satan</u> NS7: F; 8: 3, 16; 12:1, 6 -15-66 to a life of generally less than 100 years. NS8: 10; OSHA147P3

a **Wisdom** and **Water** *<u>have the same effect on life</u>*. As Water is **the source** of <u>all</u> <u>life</u>, plants and our own, *cultivate* <u>the soil</u> and *maintain the environment* **around a plant** and it will have an **unlimited life span.** Use this idea as a metaphor for your own life and health. MFM: 3693; NS9: 2; 16: 1, 2

8 <u>Our Own Wisdom</u>, found in The New Song, NS14: 44, 45-52 a, c *is* the Wisdom of Allah and the Ancients of our

people. *It is our own selves* that Allah brought and is giving to us. **Our Own Nature, Our Own Mind.** Now is the Time. Accept your own mind and live through your own <u>upright</u> <u>nature</u>: *Be yourself,* PL: 5, a <u>not a copy of the Caucasians</u>.

9 Our people are represented scripturally by **the Widows Son (Hiram Abif), Lazarus, Job, the Lost Sheep, the dead** and *through several* other scriptural figures in your Bible. All of them <u>represent</u> our history and <u>predict</u> <u>our</u> <u>future</u>. **Our identity** *was* **<u>unknown</u>** or **<u>forgotten</u>** *by our people.* OSHA 1170, 1575; NS14:15 The 'essence' NS9:2a of our lives has existed in these stories for thousands of years. It is Allah Who <u>revealed</u> **the fullness of these stories** *and* <u>our identity as His people</u> NS14: 2; CH 6; 7; EL whom He came to North America to "redeem" on His appearance among us July 4, 1930. NS14: 37; MFM1170, 1575

10 <u>Through His 'resurrected' and 'chosen' people</u>, **Allah** is recreating our Ancient Father's Nature. Those Giants Who originated the creation Prov8: 22, 30 and existed as the Original of Man for *a very long time* as compared to the last, nearly, 6698 years of the **"made" man's** temporary and <u>experimental rule</u> on earth as **the Devil, the Prince of Darkness** and as its **Evil Vicegerent.** NS1: 28a; 8: 16, 18a; 9: 21a, d; 12: 11, 13; 14: 1-4a, 7, a, b, 8, 9, 14-23a

11 We are now seeing a **"few"** NS1: 7b of the former **"home grown slaves"** accepting the Wisdom of "The Lamb of God" R7:17 *through* the New Song. NS14: 6a They have been "redeemed" by Allah's Truth, NS12: 74 and as predicted, "There is <u>none like them</u> on earth. They *are* <u>perfect</u> and <u>upright</u> in the face of Satan's *evil,*

corrosive and *hellish environment*; EI: 5, 6; R9: 20 they have become environment *shapers* and *creators* rather than environmental followers of the Caucasian's mentality.

a With you, "Allah's Word" has proven to be right and true. NS2: 10, 12; 11: 8-11; 12: 42b, 43a; 14: 2 You are the "over-comers" by the blood of the Lamb, R12:11 and have become members of **'L Sh'b'zz** (A Mighty and Glorious People), **or 'L Sh'b'llah** (The People of Allah [God] by His Permission) NS1: 38; 3: 7a; 14: 2; OSHA184P1

12 The Devil's Time is up; NS14: 4, a, *through* this Message, Allah is <u>resetting</u> the **Original Nature of Man,** NS5: 12-15 thus revealing the Essence of the Original; NS9:2a **that** is opening the Door to Paradise, NS1: 40 if you see the Way, step through and live. NS8: 8, 10 -16; 10: 5, 7; 14: 46, 47

CHAPTER SIXTEEN
Educating Our Children

1 Our problem today is we have or had <u>no</u> <u>conscious</u> *or* <u>active</u> <u>control</u> over **the environment** that <u>we grew</u> up *or* <u>developed in</u>. EL: 2-5; 14: 17 – 46; MFM: 3301

2 <u>Our</u> **lack of self knowledge** caused us to grow up with <u>*and*</u> pass on to our children, by osmosis, **"the mark of the beast."** PL: 1; NS12: 15 Only now, <u>through</u> *The New Song,* can we gain <u>personal control</u> over ourselves PL: 5 and *design* our own *internal environment* one that will in time spread its effects beyond our homes, and our personal life *without Satan's mark*. PL: 13-1; NS4: 13, 14-21; App V: 17, 18

3 Our new world will arise <u>from</u> our **living *through*** The New Song. Our children will grow naturally **because of** and **through** <u>the environment</u> **we design** and **"create"** or **make** for them NS12: 15; EL: 18e as we evolve *in our own <u>nature</u>.* NS4: 3

4 Today we have **"lost"** adults and **"lost"** children, <u>*they have no knowledge*</u> of themselves as **"**Original people**"** or anyone else. <u>It is</u> **our role** to change that. NSTLOT: 7; 12: 65, 67; 14: B - 17, 19 Focus, creating, happiness and love are **within our grasp if we would but reach for it.**

5 The **result** of our <u>*overall ignorance*</u> **is seen** Intro: 5 <u>*in the behavior*</u> of our children who are <u>*growing up wild*</u> in this **"**spiritual wilderness**"** of North America**: "As a tree is bent so shall it grow;"** Intro: 17 many of

our neighborhoods, the prisons, the hospitals and the graveyard attest to this truth. EL: 18g, h

6   Most of those who think (or who we think) have escaped our reality really haven't. Although "educated" and some have high positions, they too have "the mark of the beast" and *their behavior* demonstrates it. EL: 6; NS12: 15 - 39; 17: 18

7   Most of our *"educated"* people *think as a devil would think* NS12: 4-15 and they don't even realize it. They see their thinking as the "normal" or the "right" way to think. When making decisions, **they do what a devil would do, if not the devil couldn't trust them.** NS12: 4 They too are without the knowledge of **'self'** as an "Original NS8: 30i mind," with all the *implications of that thought* in this *"New Song."*

8   Our people's position with the devil is **too weak** for them *to have a thought other than one of the devil's thoughts* even if they are at the top position. EL: 5

9   If you don't think like a devil would think, they won't **let you** into their political, professional or social order to **rule them** and all that they have made or conquered. Why should they? Think about it! How could they do otherwise, they were instructed by their 'God' to subdue everything **even our thoughts** NS14: 1 the devil is the ruler, the teacher and the guide in **his own world?** NS8: 7; 12: 19, 20 - 37a

10   **To disagree with the devil** *is to become* a rebel, radical, nationalist, terrorist, or whatever name he designs for you and *his system* is then arrayed against you.

11 **We can** *leverage* *our* *children's* *intelligence* and their *behavior* by **creating** *student based education*. **Talk to them - watch them -** *find out what is important to them*. Be creative: ***build educational models*** in reading, writing and mathematics **around what interests them**; around ***what captures their imagination*** while at the same time guiding them to our world's social needs and values and the moral good: including **our** means and methods of achievement, NS4: 1, 3; EL: 18 a, I; App V outlined in this Message.

12 With **this method** they *become empowered* by finding their own voices NS12: 11a and connecting to the adult world with a level of maturity that we don't, today, realize they have. Unleashing our *natural potential* for achievement NS11:18a, c *increases our* inner happiness and **consequent capacity** for love of "self" as an "Original." **"Creativity and Achievement"** through an upright nature is *the soil* from which springs our "Being" and our total happiness as a people. Chapters 5 -11-15

13 Let the children, starting at 12 to 15 years of age, begin to teach the seven year olds **and up,** *what they have learned from our teachers* thereby **building on their self esteem and a sense of responsibility and connection to the world _we are building for them_**. Not providing *"space"* EL: 16 for their growth will deprive them of (1) the motivation that leads to achievement; and (2) internal happiness which evolves into external love. Without ***THIS* "created space"** our children (and adults) will be *attracted* to ***distractions*** (an enemy's space NS14:25) which will lead to callousness and external

difficulties for all of us as they grow and or interact in Satan's world. Consider Chapters 2-8-11-13

14 <u>As the children are shaped</u> to interact with their own worlds by responsibly **"doing,"** they **create** or **recreate** <u>themselves</u> App.V: 16, 18 and we end up with a new world of powerful thinkers, with new ideas guided by <u>our teachers</u> in an environment of love, trust, knowledge and power with the <u>demonstrated</u> wisdom to guide us into tomorrow.

15 **To recapture our children's minds** we must <u>live through</u> The New Song, <u>speak through</u> The New Song and **in these times** teach our children **through** <u>what they experience</u> guided by The New Song. Only then will we **get and hold their attention**.

16 Again, teach our children what they have to learn, what our society needs tomorrow, through their own experiences, then *they will want to learn, they will come back for more* or ask you (or their teacher) not to leave, or ask, **"Can I stay?"** or **"Can you stay?"** You will have to send them away or leave to get home. (But this is a very rewarding dilemma, Smile)

17 <u>The atmosphere, the environment</u> that **we create, that we live by and through,** should foster for our children, **no, it must actually say to our children** <u>what we think</u> about <u>their future</u> and the world we want for them and ourselves.

18 *Don't let your life be* **a living** *or an* **actual** <u>contradiction</u> of what you say to our children. App I: 9, 10; II: 1

a **REMEMBER:** The greatest human struggle is that for the conquest of "self." NS13: 15, 20

19 The Human – *Original* – Process of Evolution, or "HOPE," is found in the principles of this "New Song." NS4: 7; 5: 20, 23; 8: 23-30

20 **Consume** NS2: 16, 19 this message for yourself, your family and your associates. Become an example of "hope" in your own environment. NS8: 8b -26; 12: 15; EL: 4; R10: 9

21 Share this message of peace with *whoever will accept its principles* and secure, thereby, your own "new life" in the new world "here-after" as the world of materialism we have known crumbles to dust before our eyes NS1: 7-25; 8: 29b; 9:19

22 **Remember**, falsehood like truth is composed of energy NS2: 7 and manifests characteristics and behavior that flow through and from the human form NS2: 10, 12; 4: 14b thus the "unseen" becomes "seen" or *apparent* in and through human behavior as knowledge, capacity, functionality, character, strength, power and of course, so does there exact opposites.

23 Without *words* **(energy)** there would be no Wisdom for life, as without *water* there would be no Chemistry for life. Use *your life* to consume the Fountain of Wisdom found in this "New Song." PL: 13; TLOT: 2; NS1: 39; 4: 3-17; 9: 19; 11: 8; 12: 66; 13: 1; 16: 3; 17: 3; R5: 9; 14: 3; 15: 3

CHAPTER SEVENTEEN
The Original Man And
The Made Man

1   Why did God make a man called The Devil? NS8: 17a, 18a
He made a "man" NS14: 1 to demonstrate His Power
through; a man **to demonstrate** that He is All Wise and
Righteous. NS2:5-10, 11 And that He could make a Devil (a
man) and *let them* have Dominion T, p204p4; NS12: 17, 20; 14:
1 over the entire Earth for **"6 days,"** or 6000 years.

2   He also *let them* rule the Earth with **unrighteousness**
and **war**, *letting them* convert as many of us as possible
to *their way of thinking*; T, p.200p1 and finally, to *return* and
destroy His **made Devil** in one day (scripturally, the 7th
Day, NS14: 41 or **during the first 100 years** *of the 7000*th
year NS14:41) without falling *as a victim* to the Devil's
civilization, or way of life. Otherwise, to show and prove
that Allah *is* God, always has been and always will be.
NS14: 52, 53

3   The making of the man-devil was to **show us** (and the
world) how much Wisdom and Capacity was locked
up inside the Original Man. The mental, emotional
and psychological environment, the atmosphere and
conditions (of Hell) in which the Original Man was
taken to live for 400 years **never existed before**
the **making** of the Caucasian race. NS14: 4a; MFM: 3179,
3227 Read the Bible's *place holder stories* **about us**
below.

a Allah has never had a **natural innate enemy** before Caucasians. NS8: 17, 18; OSHA120PI Consequently ***the full range*** of Wisdom in the Original Man has never been made clear, or manifested before now. NS15: 6c; 11: 3

b Today it is our honor and opportunity as the Original of Man who was "lost" in the West to get up from the shallow grave w**e were put into** at the call of Allah; take off the grave clothing and evolve up into our own "Godlike" character and manifest this truth of the Original Man as "God" and servant of <u>the Most High</u> God, Allah, unleashing a worldwide moral and intellectual reform. NS1: 6; 8: 30L; 15: 6d; Chapter 2

4 Stop thinking of what happened in the past. Allah has forgiven you for that which you did in IGNORANCE. OSHA85P2 Now is the time to accept your own people and be yourself, as an Original among the Originals of the Earth. T, p198p2; MFM: 3283, 3297

5 <u>That is why</u> ***we are here in America***, <u>to demonstrate</u> what **The Original Man** ***is made of*** and ***that*** <u>is the basis</u> of the Job story, the Lost Sheep story, the Lazarus story, the Donkey story, the Prodigal Son story T, 233/2; Q56:35; Jn3:2 and many more stories in your scripture. NS 15: 8, 9 Many of the Lost Founds attributes manifested under duress are, in <u>Essence</u>, Divine. Chapter 2; NS9: 2a

6 Time and ***the manifestation*** of the made man's defects of thinking and behavior has now <u>affected</u> the Original Man and His Home, **the Earth**, to the degree that ***removing him from power*** <u>has become a necessity</u>. The

made man has poisoned the Original Man with food, water, medicine and ideas. R11: 18

7 He has produced a race of orphans and **"Half Originals" out of us, a people who he made in his own image** without self knowledge NS12: 15 and *yet we survive* and *expand* **in his filth.** He thought we would be destroyed by now, he miscalculated. What could we accomplish under *true freedom?* It is now time, Allah says, for the evil world to be removed, destroyed from the Earth. T, p205; R9: 20

8 Our Savior *Has* Arrived. MFM3682; NS1: 8 We are over 98 years into the Seventh Day and the devil's time is up. The Supreme Being is now teaching us, *through The New Song,* how to rid the Earth of the "man" devil and reproduce the "Original Man." Compare it with what you learn elsewhere. Ch 2-4, 6 We are the ones to become the "Angels who are told where to go and how to stand [on the square of life]." MFM3789; NS14: 2

    a However, **_we must be clear_** on the Theology of the devil's **6000** years of time or we will <u>not</u> understand ourselves, that is, **_our role_** in this story for the last **400** years and more. NS14: 15; 5 above

9 We have not known the knowledge of the Caucasians, which is really the *science of tricknology.* NS14: 17a **This is why** many of our people cannot understand what we are saying in this New Song. *The 'Lost Found' think like a devil and have the devils values without knowing it* T, p198p4; NS12: 39; 16: 7 they cannot **recognize themselves** in scripture

– **"Self"** has been <u>hidden</u> for over 400 years. T, p 204p3; NS8: 16; Chapters 6, 7- 16

10 *Our body has become an* <u>*unbalanced instrument,*</u> *it is unable to harmonize the Truth Note, having been raised and taught* <u>*unreality*</u> *and* <u>*illusions*</u> *by the devil since we were babies.* Come let's show the world how intelligence looks <u>from the actions</u> of those who have **arisen from** <u>mental</u> and <u>emotional</u> **death.** T, p. 203p1; NS12: 68; 14: 43; EL: 5, 6

11 We are teaching The Theology**, in plain language, of** <u>**secret things**</u> said in a theological way by the Caucasians. These are things, ideas and concepts, we have not been studying. In many instances things we have never thought or heard of before now. NS11: 9; 12: 7; Chapters 6 and 7

12 We have never known **the theological side** of things, **who would have taught us.** NS8:8, 16 The Devil and his students!? No, that knowledge was sealed until our time and the coming of "the Son of Man." NS6: 1; 7: A, B; 14: 15 We are discussing history, concepts and ideas; and some things which are primarily taught in Caucasian *private* or *secret schools* and or *organizations* through signs, symbolic language and rituals. Many of them don't understand what they have. 184, p4; 185; NS1: 20, 21; see References Today, Allah has brought us the plain Truth in common language easily understandable once you are made aware of it. EL: 18g

13 If we evolve (and ***"come out of her ... sins"*** R18: 4); if we go through The New Song's inner evolutionary process, we will, ***in time***, be able to hear the thoughts of people

when we need to, and if we evolve to a high enough level we will be able to communicate with people without using material instruments of any kind. T, p.187p2 Allah has given us Power wherever we *focus our attention*. T, p224p1; NS4: 12; App VI; OSHAP26, Chap. 10

14 Satan has made us *in his own moral and intellectual image*, NS12: 15 **he has taught us other than Righteous Behavior.** T, p189p3; NS12: 15 He has taught us to murder ourselves and he helps us to do that. Living *through Conscience*, developed to 70% or more NS5: 12; and eating the right foods at the right time will re-*produce* and *prolong* our lives. NS15: 5, 6

15 When we have no sickness in our body, we call that happiness. OSHA114: 4 When we love ourselves emotionally as *demonstrated* by eliminating anger, envy and jealousy from our character, we will enjoy peace of mind and emotional contentment. T, p190; NS14:10; 15: 6d, e

  a Let us make our homes *a teaching environment* and an example for this Message. Invite those you care for to come and discuss its principles and practices with you, your family, your neighbors and your associates. Relate the text to **yourself**, back to the text, the world, people, conditions, issues *and* things.

  b Learn to read this Book from the *inside out*, **not** the *outside in*. This requires a *change* of mind and attitude. PVII: P4 Go there, be there, **feel it.** Make it a part of your "self."

16 Understand, **we do not have a set time to die**; and, know that _sickness is not normal._ We make ourselves sick _and_ we make ourselves die **by what we think and how we live.** T, p190p1; Ch 15; MFM3685

17 When you **understand** that _you can_ **see** "God" Num12: 8 **and** the "Devil" **and** live – have your "life preserved" Gen 32: 30 - _then_ you can clearly understand what I'm saying here _and_ **how** the Devil has been hiding as the Angel of Light for the last 6000 years. Intro: 5, 6; NS7: B; 12:1- 4

18 When you see "God," through _His Spirit in this New Song Ex33: 13,_ **you will die** as the "home born slave" NS14: 28-38; EL: 18g of the Devil _and_ be **resurrected** or **reborn**, as an "Original Man of God." Now you are able to understand how and why the Devil was able to **_hide his identity_** and thus he was able to _function as_ an agent of light in the world he built and sit in the seat of God as **the source** of all _your_ knowledge from Pre-K to PHD, + PL: 13-1; NS4: 20; 12: 4-39; 14: 25 _and_ your consequent behavior. NS8: 9; 16: 7 See, #4 above

19 The devil has made everything in the spiritual world _he built_ NS8: 5a _(through_ "_Christianity_") immaterial; ghostly. The New Song puts _flesh_ and _some materiality_ back from where the devil removed it: **both worlds are now visible to the eye.** Intro: 5 **The "veil"** Q7: 46 that separates Heaven from hell is **Righteousness (Conscience).** Dying the death of the righteous means you are not supposed to suffer when you die. **Peace in life** and **death** is the lot of the righteous **when God has no opponent** to His righteousness in your life. T, 193; NS14: 55a; Num23: 10; MFM3667

20 The Supreme Being has come among us to teach us how to get back to our own, NS1:31-12: 25, 28; Ch 14 and how to sit on the **Throne of Self**, as a flesh, bone and blood God among the Gods, while *in submission* to The Supreme One (Present or Absent), The Supreme Human Being, Allah, The Most High "God." NS5: 18, 23; 8: 21, 23; PL13: c; Chapter 2; MFM3682; OSHA184P1

21 *After* NS7: E, H our inner evolution (developmentally, One through 100 NS5: 23 in degree) NS8: 23 the *Will of Allah* can be carried out **through us** T, p 203 (as with a *caterpillar*, who after inner evolution *can fly* as a **butterfly**: notice, they live in different realities or **dimensions,** *in* this [our] world). Consider well what I'm saying here and move through *the veil* while you can. T, 194; NS10: 7; 11: 10; 14: 47

22 Elijah said: "I am *designed by Allah* to help push you into hell if you reject this Message." NS4: 12

Note: Hell's destruction looks like this in the Bible: "At the noise of the taking of Babylon (America) the earth is moved, and the cry is heard among the nations." Jer50: 46 "The Day of The Lord will come as a thief in the night; in which the heavens shall pass away with a great noise and the elements shall melt with fervent heat, the earth also, and the works that are therein shall be burned up." IIPet3: 10; NS8: 8, 10

EPILOGUE
The Psychology of Human Development
THE BREAKOUT & THE SEPARATION

---

1   **The Divine Mind** presented on these pages provides readers, Students and Members with a **"new mental and emotional world"** through **a New Vocabulary of Life. NS4: 20, 24**; MFM 3315, 3511

2   **The New Song** (NARRATION NS6: 10) is *a framework* NS13: 23 for **personal** and **spiritual** "freedom" outside of the "crib," the "box," the "bottle" or the **"geocentric"** world that we have known. The world in which *we were raised* by <u>our adversaries</u> NS14: 17 whom most of the former slaves in America don't want to acknowledge, or *consciously admit,* we have. This behavior arises **out of fear of one kind or another,** fear that is rationalized away (on the surface) in order to fit in through education or profession, personal need or identification. PL: 1, 18g, h below

3   Within the **"new world"** there are no "higher authorities" to *impede* our mental and our spiritual progress, our creativity, or our emotional freedom. **"The right way is clearly distinct from error** (when we enter the heavenly internal state Chapter 4 with peace of mind and emotional contentment)." NS3: 7a; 5: 12, 14; 8:25; 14:55a

4   Is that kind of **"freedom"** P. v, viii *Scary* for you to contemplate! Yes, I would say so for many, but not for

all. NS11: 8, 17 <u>Assess this message of hope and justice</u>, it is **"the"** *real* **"Truth"** that Jesus brought and said we would be *freed by it,* if we were of those "blessed to hear and understand it." PXI: 10; XIII: 16; NS1: 3, 10

5   Living over **"400 years"** of our lives *in* and *under* seen and <u>unseen</u> **Restraints** we were *taught, told* and *pressured* into what to *think* and **what to believe**, with no qualifiers, and no means of evaluation or verification. We were also taught, or pressured into, **our behavior**, *how to act;* what was acceptable to Caucasians. This provided our "masters" with **effective control** <u>over our minds</u> and consequently our lives **enforced by fear of loss:** audits, employment, housing, travel, beatings, imprisonment and death. You can add to this list. *Even now* this environment NS16: 1 **produces** *various levels of trauma* in the former slaves and their children. The New Song is God's **Treatment** for <u>all</u> of our maladies. Reflect on Chapter 7; NS15: 11a; T, p. 71

6   Today, most of our people still live in and out of *fear, anger and confusion,* <u>unaware of the 'cause.'</u> NS8:10 Many people are **"vexed"** to hear *this Message* because of their "education," "training" and their expectation or desire to have what they see others with, or what has been held out to, or back from, them. For others how to even act if they wanted to be different is a problem. Review #'s 2 and 5 above, again.

   a   **Allah's message provides <u>a basis</u> for new thought and "different," upright, actions** NS12:16, a-39, a-59; Ch15 instead of *serving idols* and *sacrificing our children* to the Devil. Ps.106: 36, 37; NS4: 7, 10

7   If you ask the former slave today if this is true, most
     would deny it. They **don't "see"** their adversary to actually
     be their adversary (some may want to make me the
     adversary for teaching what the Prophets taught and "the
     Son of Man brought" NS14: 2 out of ignorance of "self").
     Some will make excuses for Caucasians because of their
     <u>underlying fear</u>**: Stockholm syndrome.** Prologue: I

8   God said these people are the **blind**, **deaf** and the
     dumb, with *no metaphoric reasoning capacity.* **They reject
     the God of Truth** (Consciousness and Mathematical
     Analysis) NS2: 8, 16 and follow their own **passion** *and*
     impulse, *their illusions (about what the devil told them* Q14:
     22), <u>*as their god*</u> Q.2:7-18; 8:22-55; # 5 above

9   The **"self conscious life"** will be a totally "new *internal*
     life" in "the New World" ("peace of mind and emotional
     contentment") while physically remaining where you are in
     this world for a time. You'll be *"In their world but not of it"* as
     Jesus described it. In the beginning it won't be easy because
     you won't find many people in the world we are building
     (including our families), but you'll be just fine. NS 12:19-42

10   "The Spirit of Truth," we are told, would come to us *in
     the time of Satan's Fall.* Notice how he was received: *"He
     came to His own and His own received Him not."* NS14: 35
     "Don't let this be a description of me." The truth is actually
     plain enough for a 'blind *man*' to see' it however, **fear
     and identification blocks our vision.** NS14: 53a, b, c; Ch 10;
     see #5 above

11   Let's *focus* or *re-focus* our **minds** and our **vision** so that
     we do not become or **"fall as a victim"** to, or of, any of

215

the **negative forces** outlined in our discussions, being ever mindful of the fact that *"the human soul, <u>without a developed conscience,</u> is prone to evil.* Q12:53; PL: 5; NS5: 10B4; 8: 9 -13; 11: 7d; App II

   a - The *identifying mark* of "consciousness" (social heaven) is *self-control* - seeing the past, living freely and balanced in the present and creating the future.

   b - Heaven (Conscience) is *marked by* honesty, integrated thinking and love.

   c - Spiritual death or flawed consciousness (Hell) is marked by being under *external influence or control; and or having uncontrolled passion and impulses* Q25:43; not seeing the past, not living freely or being balanced in the present and not creating the future. NS8: 10; #5 above

   d - Hell (spiritual death and its ramification) is *marked by* dishonesty, accepting illusion as fact, short sightedness and or perverse love. Q55:41; NS8: 9, 11

   e - <u>Neither</u> "Heaven" nor "Hell" is a geographical place, Ch15, both are - like everything else - **internal states of "being"** Q3:185 that <u>**can be materialized**</u> by the possessor of the **"internal state"** according to their idea(s), knowledge, power or *capacity* **to materialize** their thoughts, hopes, dreams and desires. NS2:7f; 12: 21, 22; 13:17, 18

12 After so many years of being *shaped* and *taught* [in church] that there are these **"higher powers"** and **people - Caucasians sitting in the seat of "God"** - that are so

much wiser and more powerful than we are, their proof being **our servitude** on one level or another **to them - to this very day and hour** we serve at their pleasure - and the incapacity of the 'original man' to secure himself and his woman, we [our mothers] made an **"agreement with hell (Caucasians)"** just to keep their sons alive (review the Stockholm syndrome here). NS 8:7; 14: 40

13 But now **"the Son of a Man"** has brought us **"the Truth"** NS14: 2; XI: 10, as promised, **"Truth"** to *set ourselves* "free." zec.2:7; PL: I The **Spiritual** *and* **mental freedom** are *the first freedoms given, to* enable us *to change our internal state* **if we chose to.** *This Message of "Truth"* **must be used** in our own life in order for us to "grow up into Him." If not, His knowledge, His wisdom and His power will have no value to us. Unlike the followers of Moses, we are not being asked to fight others. Just ourselves, our beliefs, habits and the daily rituals that keep us nailed to the present time and the Caucasian mind. Intro: 8-15, 16; Ch 15

14 Scary, maybe. And, **"Yes!" for some,** but this is a very fulfilling life, with unlimited Universal potential. After you learn to practice your **"essence"** freedom - having instead of a tribal, national, cultural, or 'geocentric world view' - **you evolve into a cosmically-centered Consciousness and a new world view.** This is the **"breakout"** to your psychological freedom and the **"regeneration"** of your mental and spiritual power. This is your **"separation** and **"resurrection"** from "spiritual death" and from the "agreement" you made with "hell" in your spiritually dead - automated - state. NS8: 30; Mat Ch 13

15 **"Right** attitude thought and actions are upper most in the mind of the **"conscious person."** Courage, without a sense of "right" makes rebels of the great (upper or privileged class) and thieves of the poor (those without money, education, or insight)," So said another of our Wise men. NS14:24

16 **WHY DO WE NEED THE NEW SONG?** See #11 above and Chapter 17 This Message, or **"SONG,"** is the "repairer" of "the breach" NS8: 2 between slavery and the "Here-After." The New Song, constitutes the bridge over which life has meaning *on the other side of our present life style* NS8: 8, 10 which has been called "Hell" by the Prophets to describe our current "roller-coaster life" of glitter, joy, sorrow and torment. NS17: 8

　　a **THE NEW SONG PRODUCES:** *Space, Time, and Opportunity; a New Vision, New (Re) Formation, New Functionality and finally a New World (from the working of your own new mind created from your new vocabulary of ideas)* NS 4:21

　　　　　　Space, mental and inner space - peace of mind, thus removing tension and internal stress;

　　　　　　Time - spiritual and practical - for reassessing your life your values your beliefs and how you have shaped your life to date. Your energy will increase here as you evolve;

Opportunity to reflect upon the color of your personal essence and assess what is possible for you in your life; see **Time** above, NS8:21, 23; 12:33

New visions of the future, your future, see and determine for yourself what is or will be;

A new formation or **a recreation** of your mind to perform the role you've envisioned for yourself. NS1: 28a, b

The Functionality that you see for yourself, NS5: 7, 8: gather <u>knowledge</u>, <u>people</u>, <u>systems</u>, and or <u>things</u> to materialize your vision;

The new world of your own choosing - by design - with the power to bring about functional and /or operational change where needed.

17 Ponder over the words here and know this, when the **mark of the beast,** PL: 1; NS12: 15 **mysticism,** PL: 4 and **negative identification** NS12: 12; 13:3 **are absent,** <u>you do have power</u> to see and the ability to *hear* and make *decisions* for yourself.

    a "The right way is clearly distinct from error." **The choice is yours.**

18 **DECISIONS** and **JUDGMENTS** determine/shape **CAUSES** and **EFFECTS**

a The decisions you make today, <u>now</u>, will affect your life and the lives of others now and in the future depending upon your role, function or station in life.

b The shape of your life now - the track, path or style of your present life is the result of decisions made by others before and since you were born. We do have choices, however many decisions that we saw as our own were decided upon long before we were born.

c On the other hand, <u>we do have an opportunity to choose</u> the "role" we will play out in the paths, styles and or professions created or decided upon by those people who shaped the world we live in and the roles of life that we were born into.

e Now we have a chance - [after evaluating *what they did* <u>through</u> the principles in the New Song] - to **choose** or **decide** for ourselves – [*make a conscious decision*, <u>knowing</u> <u>the past</u> *and* <u>the present</u>] - what part we want to, or will play in <u>the decisions others made</u> before us that shaped our lives and <u>then</u> affect, or **shape the future by our own actions, our own words and deeds.** NS2: 11

f The New Song provides you with a look at the decision making process, some of <u>the results</u> of other's decision making; and ***how*** the world got to be the way it is. NS8: 8

g The "TRUTH" of **the New Song** is a far better *narrative,* NS17: 18 it is - *mentally* and *emotionally* - far more satisfying *to* and *for* us than the **illusion producing** story our captives gave to us. NS8: 13, 14; 14: 25 Clearly, This "TRUTH" *agrees with* – rather than clash with - *the reality* that we can see with our own eyes; *study* the history of with our own minds; and *feel* everyday through our own bodies as we live our daily lives in America. NS8: 8; 14: 52 Never think that Allah would fail in His promise: Allah is Exalted in Power, The Lord of Retribution. Q14:47; NS14: 4

h What can be *the basis* of your argument, or a disagreement here? *Your* **experience** NS16: 1, *their history* and the **Scripture** agree with The New Song. To focus on this idea go to the **Concept Index** and study **"Judgments, the three levels of," "Your," "God's" and "Devil's."** You'll find it very interesting. Of course, there are many other ideas to track or review through the **Concept Index.** Go through **The References** and the **Appendix** they too will be helpful in expanding and focusing your thoughts.

i **The "Judgment" is now in your hands!** You decide, "Choose!" *Where* do you want to be and with *whom?* In either case, you might want to consider **why** you've decided as you have? NS11: 12, 13

19 "O People of the Book! Believe in what We have revealed, **confirming what is with you** (your Bible, your Qur'an and/or your N.O.I. Lessons and your life's experience)…" This is your time to reflect Q4:47 and *act in your own best interest.* NS8: 8-19

REFERENCES IN "THE NEW SONG"

1 The references that I use through-out **"The New Song"** either,

    (1) Show directly as a quote what was said and where it came from, or

    (2) Show experiences other receivers of Messages have had similar to ours, or

    (3) Where the same idea is discussed in different words, and maybe in a different way, or

    (4) Show the opposite idea or result of what has just been expressed, or

    (5) Show or outline results from the last 6000 year history or our own experience.

2 As an example, if I saw something as good in a verse, etc., a reference to it may refer to something that is bad from history, experience or a metaphor, to round out the concept or idea and build awareness.

3 We must understand that most of the scriptures were written to *hide* Q20:15 or *shield* it's Truth <u>from us</u> as we, nor the world, other than the wise, were supposed to know or learn of its Truth until the devil's time was up.

    a The Books were **"sealed:"** as it is written in Revelations, 'the conscious devil knows that his time is short (<u>now</u>) and he is very angry' (you can see their anger or feel it in their behavior). He realizes that his rule is over because he has been unmasked to **the former slave** and the world by the Lamb of God, Who, **through His people**, 'sits at the right Hand of God as He makes his enemies his footstool (again, as it is written).

4   In the Devil's secret schools and organizations, they teach a meaning of scripture but even then it is taught under signs, symbols and rituals. These then must be further **interpreted** by their elders for higher level students as they rise up into their system. All of their students (devils) must swear to **"keep the secret,"** keep their knowledge away from those who might hear it or read it by accident or by stealth.

5   Most of the devils, including the students, don't know the **real meanings** of what they have been taught, **_nor who "they" are_**. They are happy to just be a part of the school, system, association and conquering race for the inherent benefits. Of course they are also the "tools" or throw away parts when they become necessary for the leaders to gain or maintain power and control.

6   And since so much time has elapsed - "they" forgot the time NS6: 6 - many of their leaders have forgotten **the real purpose** of their schools, fraternity or system. Most even believe their-own "dazzling speech" and that of their leaders, not recognizing the **inherent conflicts** and **contradictions.** NS9: 8a, b, 9; Q58:7, 10

7   Funny thing, with all their knowledge, most of them don't see what they are facing. But, <u>even the devils</u>, like the former slaves **have an out in this Message** however

the Prophets said, **'There will be few that <u>take it</u>'.** Q5: 54; 7: 72-95; Isa5:20

8   A reflection for the wise: Nineveh was saved by 'submission to The Truth,' she wasn't too proud. Will America do the same? Allah says, **"Live: Wash <u>your</u> robe in the blood of the Lamb"** before Jonah's *"40 days to destruction"* Jon3: 4 message is carried out here before your own eyes and **<u>include you</u>** NS8: 8b; 14: 42 *among* **a guilty people.** NS1: 31; 12: 2; 15: 6f

9   **We** are now *Forty years* <u>after </u>the passing of "Elijah" (1975) NS1: 19-23; 14: 9 and approximately 100 years after 1914, when the Caucasian's 6000 years of *unopposed* rule ended. NS14: 1-7b, 8-11a; 15: 6f; Q32: 3 Now, *The Christ* is due to <u>return</u> NS1: 31 with the "sword" of *justice* and *destruction*. Mat10: 34; NS3: 1, 5; 12: 26b; 14: 3-5; 15: 1

10 Of course, no one knows the Day or the Hour of The Final Judgment. However, in 2014 Caucasians will have had 100 years of grace from Allah. *We can see and evaluate how they used that time.* From Feb. 25, 1975 to Feb. 25, 2015 they will have witnessed 40 years of our traveling in their spiritual and emotional wilderness *seeking a way out* of our troubles after the passing of Elijah. These 40 years served as a *test* and a *trail* for Elijah's followers. Many are in dire need of "Ar-Rahim" (The Merciful) or they too will perish. NS14: 54b

11 If we calculate from Dec. 2014 to Feb. 2015 we have an ***approximate time frame*** that could cover both calculations.

12 In any case, we would do well to start **"washing our 'robe'** (our mind and spirit which is our ***true covering*)"** before our time runs out. NS3: 5; 10: 7A; EL: 18g

APPENDIX I

1 Should you accept our "invitation," your focus, time and energy should be spent on Chapters 2 - 4 - 5 - 8 - 9 – 11- 12 and 15 *for your __personal development__ and __inner evolution__.* Of course, all Chapters say something about _inner evolution_ whether using or not using that term. You'll find at the same time that we are discussing history, physics, chemistry, psychology, sociology, religion, astronomy, language, mathematics and more.

2 The idea is to prepare the ground, body, format, or **however you want to describe it**, the foundation for your own **new** inner life or world. Actually, **Chapter 14 is** "**_The Beginning_**" **- exposing the secrets of this world -** the rest of the Book expands on or explains the details. However, any place is a good place to start just keep reading, watching and living **the life described**. The meaning will all become very clear over time.

3 The "judgments" **you make** today will determine, give shape and form, to **your life tomorrow.** EL: 18

4 The New Song was designed to be studied in relatively small groups since the concepts are new and need discussion and explanation. If you **work on yourself** the inner growth will come, even if you work (on yourself) alone. It will, however, take more time.

5 Every day that you **study** and **practice** the principles, the words will take on more and more meaning as you

observe yourself and participate in the world around you. NS 2:11, 12; 8: 33; 13: 1

6 Purpose/Focus, time and energy - **within an open mind** - are the keys to our success. You will see or notice your own power, *ability to do,* enhanced over time as you practice "*self-remembering*" through the New Song. NS 12:70

7 This New Song Intro: 4, 5 is an *Upright Behavior System, a "Straight Path",* a _mind expander_, leading the formerly "dead slave" back to our **Source** - 'L **Sh'b'zz, or The Ancient God Tribe of Shabazz -** rather than to a *division causing* self righteous ideology and or an *unchanging belief system* **rooted in our 400+ years of living with an open enemy.** PL: 4: NS8: 16; 17: 18; EL: 18g

8 "Religion", *as it has been taught to us,* has caused us to argue about whose beliefs or "thoughts" are right about "X" NS1: 34 or multiple other kinds of things without any knowledge other than the former slave master's. NS14: 17, a; 15: 8 We have no mental or emotional discrimination (How could we? Based on what? Review NS4: 1-6-15 and Chapter 8 in detail).

9 As a people, we have not considered *inner development* as taught here. No, each religious person thinks, "Our/ My belief is right and anything else is wrong," that is a recipe for recrimination and finally war not purposeful unity among us. NS3: 7, a; 8: 29c; Q35: 5, 7; Ecc.7: 29

10 What is needed is *upright behavior* rather than hiding behind rituals and or an _external_ _show_ of *"faith." "Upright*

behavior," **THAT** is the most important thing for us today. *The New Song shows you how to achieve it.* NS14:14a-39; 15:8; Ecc7:20

11 Bring an *active* consciousness into your life. NS12: 55, 56 Demonstrate an *active conscience* and *"human" values* NS11: 7d over *unfeeling methods* and or *mysticism [mechanical, habitual and/or automated behavior]* NS14:40 *in all aspects* of your life. "Peace" will arrive for you when the **causes of division** within you are removed. NS17: 14

12 Mental and emotional balance, real **"Hope"** NS13: 1, has now arrived among the lost and now found dead in America in the *form* of this "New Song!" NS14:3 *consume it as you would food* and add years to your life and peace to your soul.

NOTE: Consume the Book,
Embody its message, and
Share it in your environment. NS16: 19; 17: 20, 21

We are a *product* or a *result* of what we eat (mentally, emotionally, and physically)! NS2: 8, 12

Enjoy!

II - A GENERAL COMMUNICATION PRIMER TO HELP US IN RAISING OUR DEAD

THE FOLLOWING DISCUSSION POINTS SERVE TO DIG UP AND TURN OVER THE SOIL OF OUR LIVES ENABLEING US TO REMOVE THE ROCKS, DEAD ROOTS AND OTHER IMPEDERMENTS TO OUR RISING FROM OUR GRAVE OF IGNORANCE. WE HAVE 400 YEARS OF ROT MIXED IN WITH OUR CURRENT GROWTH, THIS ROT MUST BE REMOVED. FOR THIS REASON WE ASK YOU TO JOIN US IN THIS CONVERSATION, BEING AS OPEN MINDED AND NON DEFENSIVE AS POSSIBLE. MOST OF US HAVE NEVER THOUGHT OF THESE QUESTIONS, PRIMARILY BECAUSE WE WERE "LOST", WE DID NOT KNOW WHO WE ARE. THE NEW SONG WILL HELP "REDEEM" OUR LIVES, IF WE PERMIT IT TO DO SO. APP I: 7

1   What is **your basis** for living your daily life? Intro I: 7
    ➤ Do you have _a standard_ for your behavior?
    ➤ _Why_ and or _how_ did you arrive at **your basis** for living your daily life? NS12: 4

2   What is **your standard** for judgment, and or decision making, e.g., is it
    ➤ **Your belief:** what you were taught growing up (as a tree is bent so shall it grow),
    ➤ **Your study:** _research_ and _testing_ for **validity** and **reliability** (palm tree concept).

3   _How did - or will - you determine_ what is Right; what is Truth; and what, or who, is God?

4   What is your thinking **built upon**?

5   What are your **resources** for developing "self" awareness (after 400 years of spiritual, moral and mental death)? Review EL

6   **How** *do you think?*
>   *What is* **your method?**
>   *What* or who *is* **your existing or living example**?
   Intro: I I, I2

7   **To what** or **to whom do** you **submit** or give allegiance: God, Truth, Right, or …? NS14: 38a

8   What **authority** has the final say in and or over your daily affairs?

9   **Honestly contemplate** these questions you will certainly feel differently when you have answered them (most likely before you complete them, if you honestly reflect. Have you read Willie Lynch?).

10 **The key questions for your development are** who is God, who is the devil and who are you. Those answers may be found throughout the New Song. Ch 2-4-5-8-9-12-14

11 Know that it is by Caucasian "deceit", NS12:I, 3 a-28d that we are in our present condition. Don't let this mental or emotional condition NSI:17, 19; EL: 5, 8, remain because of **pride, arrogance** *or* **ignorance.** Intro: 7

12 How long shall we shut our eyes against the *hard facts* NS5:I presented in The New Song and keep on expecting a **mystery**

God and a **mystery Devil** to appear which ***exists nowhere*** but in our own imagination TLOT: 16; <u>*both ideas*</u> were put in our minds EL: 5, 8 by our open adversaries. NS8: 13, 14-26a; 14: 25; see 1:28-b and Chapters 7 and 16; OSHA94P4, 6

III - PARTNERSHIP RELATIONS:

To what or to whom do <u>you</u> submit or give allegiance: God, Truth, Right, or …? Explain?

<u>Why</u> and or <u>how</u> did you arrive at <u>your standard</u> for living your daily life? Explain?

Do you think your standards (AND VALUES) are right? Intro: 4, 7 Explain?

What is your thinking **built upon**, what is/are your **resource(s)?** Explain?

Is your standard for judgment the same as your partner? How about values? Explain?

Is your partner's standard or values wrong? If yes, based upon what evidence? Explain?

How much study or effort (resources) did you apply in reaching your conclusion(s)? Explain?

Are you willing to study, research, and or follow where truth, good judgment or experience leads; testing for validity and reliability as you go? TLOT: 2

What did you each bring to the relationship? Match what you've each brought to the relationship tangible and intangible, can what you both brought be reconciled in your minds?

Are you equals in **mental** and *emotional* **maturity?** If the answer is "yes", then discuss the points below:

1 Embrace who your partner is (very difficult without sharing the same standards/values)
2 Be your partner's best friend, the friend you would like to have
3 What are your needs discuss them openly and come to a balanced agreement
    If you must argue make sure it is on the issues, not the person
5 Find, or make sure you have, some common Interests
6 Contribute something to your relationship every day
7 If you must argue, get undressed before you begin, if you can't …
8 Actively, mentally, emotionally commit to your relationship above everything else
9 "Nothing will make me leave you" (non of this can happen without #1 above)

Teach our children to discuss and negotiate their relationship *before* getting intimate:

1 Values
2 Clothes
3 Food
4 Home
5 Money
6 Power/Authority
7 Who do we talk with or bring our troubles to

Make sure they study The New Song, all the standards required for success are available to you.

IV - IT TAKES THREE FORCES, WORKING IN HARMONY, TO PRODUCE ANY ONE THING

There are three inseparable forces within our **human spirit** understanding and shaping them will enable us to make **a new body** and **a new world** (or a new future for ourselves). Review TLOT The New Song is our *hope* and our *guide* for tomorrow.

1 **"Self"** Remembering *as an* **"Original"**, not a slave, African American, or a Blackman, etc. [Ch 9] NS1: 6a-8

2 Consciousness of your **made** "Self" [NS12:9-39a, 40; 14: 14, 18c] and your Cosmic [TLOT: 15, Ch 5] Self

3 Desire: Purpose, Motivation [NS2: 7e-12; 9: 3-7c, 9; 13: 6-16, 20]

'L Sh'b'zz represents our Personal Development and Group Functionality, TLOT: 4a, b; NS3: 7a

Our Measuring Standard: MOMENTUM - MASS/VELOCITY – GRAVITY, Where

E = MC sq = G: (E) Energy = (M) Mass (C) Speed of light squared = (G) Gravity

MOMENTUM: THRUST, **ENERGY**, FORCE, DRIVE **[Our Movement, Inner Work or Essence]**

MASS: OURSELVES, COLLECTION, GROUP, ORGANIZATION, ACCUMULATION **[Out of or from which *Things* Appear]**

VELOCITY: **SPEED**, RATE, RAPIDITY, SWIFTNESS, PACE, QUICKNESS **[Our Activity along a Specific Path or Direction]**

GRAVITY: SERIOUSNESS, IMPORTANCE, SIGNIFICANCE, MAGNITUDE; SEVERITY **[The Effect or Affect of "E" or Our Work and Commitment]**

(**E** or <u>The New Song</u> *in us*, the Source of our) Momentum/Force or Motivation, Inner Drive **=**

(**M** or <u>the Seed</u> of **'L Sh'b'zz** is our) Group/Tribe (How it is accepted or known) **multiplied by**

(**C or** <u>Inner Evolution</u>) Work/Velocity/Pace **multiplied by** Work/Velocity/Pace **(of our work) =**

(**G** or <u>New World</u>/<u>Future</u>) Seriousness/Importance/Significance (How we see or how we are seen and or accepted because of *our personal effort*)

REFLECTIONS:

E= MC sq = G can be used as *a metaphor* which enables us and others to <u>measure</u> - get a *verbal picture* of – the '*seriousness*' and the '*importance*' with which *we* and *they* take our <u>Words</u> and <u>Deeds</u>.

Our Energy, Force or Momentum is *equal to* our Personal and or Group Effort, *multiplied by* the Pace and Quickness of our inner effort and Self Replication, *multiplied by* those in whom we have Replicated and multiplied ourselves.

If *our inner effort* has <u>significance</u> and <u>gravity</u> *then* the magnitude of our personal and our collective work will become *clear, visible and apparent to all who see.* Intro: 5-17; NS14: 55a

As an example: Our individual growth and the growth of 'L Sh'b'zz through our replication activities.

<u>If we are working</u>, The Significance, Gravity and Magnitude of **<u>Our Work</u>** will soon become apparent. Intro: 17, 18

V - HUMAN MOTIVATION

1   The key NS2: I to our success is *"going to the root"* NS1: 1-4-7a, b of <u>our</u> *"self"* NS1: 1; 16: 2, that is the purpose NS9: 3 behind this writing: *bridging the gap* for some people with regard to Spiritual, NS11: 8, 9; EL: 11c psychological and sociological concepts and behavior.

2   The best in psychology and the best in sociology manifest the principles of "True" EL: 18g Religion NS8: 2 with its Source, or "God" NS1: 21; 2: 2, 5; 8: 23a; 14: 39; 15: 6, *taken out of it.*

3   All we need for peace of mind and success in our life is to <u>put back</u> NS15: 6 into ourselves – *back into our nature* or *behavior* - the <u>true basis</u> of ***all knowledge,*** the <u>Unseen</u> <u>Principle</u>, <u>Factor</u> or "God". NS2: 3, 4; 8: 22, 23a; 9:2a; PL: 7, 10

4   Don't focus your life on the *'seen'* material facts, forms, or forces of the world around you – *if they are devoid of any Divine Source or origin* – this would leave you growing <u>without a conscience</u> (the inner power applied to water App VI). Intro: 5; PL: 9; NS5: 13; 8:15

5   In developing <u>our premise</u> for **The Nature of Human Motivation**, we will show that "Human Motivation" can be *seen to develop* from what has been called "<u>Symbolic Interaction</u>".

6   What is "**Symbolic Interaction**"? It is a term which *describes* people who are acting in a manner *consistent with what they believe*, although not necessarily with what is actually true.

7   In other words, "Symbolic Interaction" **describes** people acting, or behaving, on **the basis** of the meaning that *their world of objects* have for them. Review Chapter 13

8   What do we mean by the "Word" NS1: 21; 2: 9, 12, "*Object*"? There are several kinds of "objects" NS7d-10; T, p.184, 2nd p

   [1] There are physical objects: chairs, books, trees, houses, and the like.
   [2] There are social objects: friends, enemies, relatives, priests, and so forth.
   [3] Finally, there are abstract objects: beliefs, ideas, values and attitudes.

The foregoing are just some of the concepts, feelings or physical realities housed in these "objects".

9   What is the origin of *the meaning* that each person attaches to his actions? The origin of each person's actions is to be found in the social (environmental) interaction NS16: 1; EL: 5, 6 that they had from the time they were babies. NS13: 23, 30

10 A mind has to *interpret meaning* in order to construct its actions, NS13: 31, 32 from this perspective we see that a person develops and attitude about himself - about what he is, by interpreting the actions of others towards him. Human behavior, or motivation, is nothing more than a person constructing his actions -- or basing his behavior -- on his interpretation of the meaning that *his world of objects* have for him, positive, negative or neutral. Intro: 7

11 In another way of putting it, "man" NS2: 9, 12-20 is not merely a neutral link, or a reflexive mechanism NS11: 1-- *an animal -*

that responds without *first* thinking about the various *stimuli* which he receives from his world of "objects", which we can generalize as family, neighborhood, training, and his social and working environment, unless – of course - he has no knowledge of himself and or he is morally dead, then **he is** a reflexive mechanism fueled by **external stimuli.** NS2: 12; 5: 1; 11: 5, 6

12 How is meaning learned through social interaction? This Learning requires a process which we call "the self," which is better seen as the mind (the Bible teaches, "As a man thinks -- *in his heart* (**his Moral or Conscience "body,"** if he has <u>made one</u>) -- so is he."

13 "The Self" NS13: 16, 20 is a process of consciously talking to one's "Self" and also listening to one's "Self" as if one were two separate people.

14 "The Self" is an *internal process* not a structure. "The Self" is a process of ingesting ideas and, *in time,* their **internal crystallization.**

15 "The Self" is the process whereby (unseen) minds function through or think in words about how other (unseen) minds define "objects" and *requires the use of language*, and all languages are abstract, in time their concepts become internally and maybe externally concrete. PL13-1; NS12: 55

16 The concepts that we have thus far discussed point out that man has the ability to be creative, that is - transmit abstract knowledge and think in abstract terms.

17 Among the living, only "man" Ch 2 possesses a "Self," *as we know it,* "**he" is self-created.** The transmission of abstract

knowledge through the "Self" can be called culture or civilization and is the blood of a social order. However, if the blood is weak can the Body it nourishes be strong? NS8: 18

18 It should be noted here that *human behavior* is not inherited, *it is learned TLOT: 2* **either by social-automation or conscious personal effort.** NS12: 60; Intro: 15 <u>Behavior is an expression</u> NS11:14 of an individual's, or a groups,' or a societies' general perception of their needs and or values and is consequently *expressive* of their <u>internalized</u> "unseen objects or beliefs." This is *how* <u>we see</u> the "unseen." Intro: 5; NS8: 23a, 13: 8

19 This writing should therefore be helpful to anyone desiring a *simplified view* of human psychology, especially if he majors in himself. Intro: 18

VI - COSMIC COMMUNICATION IS ACHEIVED THROUGH WATER

All of the numbers below are designed to make the point, or **amplify the title** of Appendix. VI, to various minds that will approach and understanding of *"Inner Evolution"* as taught here. Clearly some metaphorical insights and or basic physics would be helpful in extrapolating the essence and significance of what we are discussing. But, it is not absolutely necessary.

1   "Among Allah's Signs is the creation of the **heavens** and **earth**, and <u>the living creatures</u> that He has scattered through them: and He has power to gather them together when He wills. Don't let this present life *[of materialism]* deceive you." Q42:29 "Don't let the Chief Deceiver deceive you about God."Q35: 5; Chapter 8 and 14; T, p.1; p.69p3, 4

2   "Allah's Throne is always on water" Q11:7; **"He is the Lord of Sirius."** Q 53:49 The harmonic *sound of the sun* structures and restructure's water into its highest vibration and form.

3   *Water is alive* at its highest vibrations it can promote communication instantly over any distance. "We made from water every living thing." T, p169p3; Q21:30 The speed of thought is 24 billion miles per second; the speed of light is 186,355 miles per second; our galaxy (the Milky Way) is about 100,000 light years in diameter; and the distance to the most distant object seen in the universe is about 18 billion light years.

4   Water, *hydrogen* and *oxygen*, <u>is in</u> the sun. *At its highest vibration*, <u>water</u> enables human faculties to function in the realm of the miraculous. Reflect on 2 above

5   The Universe has harmonics and vibrations that an **opposite consciousness** cannot receive - this is the purpose of **our inner evolution**; we want **our spirit** to become One with the Universal Order. NS8: 13, 19b

6   **Consciousness**, e.g., intentions and prayer, focused on water **provides Spirit** to water which restructures it to **form the life** <u>or</u> **structure** of that conscious thought or prayer. T, p.69p.2

7   **Water is conscious** <u>and</u> **has memory** an example of this is seen with plastic, which is artificial, and its memory or, e.g., the information laden DVD.

8   Sound, Consciousness, intentions, music and thought waves, **all of these forces**, <u>and</u> **more**, structure and restructure water for good or for ill, e.g., RNA and DNA. NS4: 20, 24

9   **Water can be structured or restructured** with thought, vibrations, and sound.

10 **Water is everywhere in the universe. "The earth came out of water and was made from water"** 2Pet3: 5; T, p188p1

CONCEPT INDEX

This **CONCEPT INDEX** is not exhaustive but it may help you with some of the essential ideas presented in *The New Song* pulling them together for mental, emotional and practical cohesion. The purpose here is to **invoke** *or* **provoke** *individual development*. Chapter, verse, number and letter are designed for ease of study.

20278338R00152

Made in the USA
Charleston, SC
03 July 2013